Stefan Gabányi

WHISK(E)Y

Illustrated by Günter Mattei

ABBEVILLE PRESS   PUBLISHERS
New York   London   Paris

English-language edition
EDITOR: OWEN DUGAN
DESIGNER: LAURA LINDGREN
MANUSCRIPT EDITOR: CAROL M. HEALY
PRODUCTION MANAGER: STACY ROCKWOOD

Translated from the German by Russell Stockman

German-language edition
EDITOR: RIA LOTTERMOSER
DESIGNER: GÜNTER MATTEI

First published in the United States of America in 1997 by Abbeville Press,
22 Cortlandt Street, New York, N.Y. 10007. First published in Germany in 1996 by
Wilhelm Heyne Verlag GmbH & Co., KG, Munich.

First edition
4   6   8   10   9   7   5   3

Library of Congress Cataloging-in-Publication Data
Gabányi, Stefan.
    [Schumann's whisk(e)y Lexikon. English]
    Whisk(e)y / Stefan Gabányi : illustrated by
Günter Mattei.
        p.   cm.
    ISBN 0-7892-0383-9
    Includes bibliographical references and index.
    1. Whiskey-Encyclopedias. I. Title.
    TP605.G3313   1997
    641.2'52'03—dc21   97-3339

FOREWORD

NOT SO LONG AGO BARS WERE SOMEWHAT PERFUNCTORY IN THEIR TREATMENT of whisk(e)ys. A well-stocked bar might display the better-known brands of Scotch and bourbon, to be sure, but Irish whiskey lovers, not to mention malt addicts, were generally out of luck.

We would eagerly welcome the few connoisseurs of whisk(e)y—most of them foreigners—fascinated to hear what they had to say. They surely didn't need advice from us; they knew a lot more than we did. Then malt whisky became popular virtually overnight, and suddenly it was a race to see who could stock the widest variety of brands. But still there was almost no one to turn to for advice.

A couple of years ago, when asked if I would like to write a whisk(e)y lexicon, I felt that I wasn't the right person. I mentioned the offer to my longtime colleague, the whisk(e)y lover Stefan Gabányi, recognizing that if anyone was qualified to write it, he was. For two years he tramped around doing his research, studying the relevant literature, and sampling, becoming increasingly devoted to whisk(e)y and eager to make new discoveries.

I am certain that this book will not only complement my cocktail book, *American Bar,* but will become an indispensable guide for all whisk(e)y lovers.

We are indebted for much of our success to Günter Mattei, who designed and illustrated both books with such great enthusiasm. Without him the decision to produce *Whisk(e)y* would not have been so easy for us or for the publisher.

I hope that this is not my collaborators' last book.

CHARLES SCHUMANN

INTRODUCTION

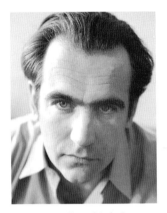

Over the course of its history—from its legend-enshrouded origins in the early Middle Ages to its ubiquitous presence in our own century—whisk(e)y has acquired a stature unmatched by that of any other spirit in the world. This has less to do with its actual popularity—people worldwide drink far more vodka or spirits made from rice or sugarcane—than with the myths that have come to be associated with it. Just as absinthe was the favorite drug of artists at the turn of the century, whisk(e)y was the inspiration for many of the young century's writers. In countless books and films it was presented as the ultimate masculine drink. It was never far out of reach of gangsters, whores, secret agents, bankers, and lonely men-about-town. Ladies and other decent folk stuck to gin, the second most popular spirit in the English-speaking world.

It cannot be determined whether the Irish or the Scots were the first to distill *uisge beatha* ("water of life"). But we do know that the English were responsible for transforming the Gaelic word *uisge* into *whisk(e)y*. The different spellings used by the Scots, the Canadians, the Irish, and the Americans were adopted only in our own century. (*Whisky* is used by Scots, Canadians, and Japanese; *whiskey* is used for all others, including generic references.) The English also gave the drink its worldwide prominence. On the one hand, their subjugation of Ireland and Scotland led to mass emigration and thus to the rise of independent whisk(e)y cultures in the United States and Canada, and even in Australia and New Zealand. On the other, they opened up world markets for the Irish and the Scots in which whisk(e)y could compete with gin.

Today whisk(e)y is drunk around the world, and more and more countries are producing it themselves. Japan was the first, then came European countries like Spain and Germany. At the moment it is mainly the emerging markets—Brazil, India, Korea—that are getting into the business in a big way, constantly introducing new brands.

Decreased sales in the traditional markets of Europe and America and the increasing concentration of the whisk(e)y industry in the hands of a few huge concerns have at the same time tended to reduce the number of available brands to those of the few world leaders: Johnnie Walker, Jim Beam, Canadian Club, Jameson. Under the shadow of such mass production there suddenly developed a small, elite market concerned with quality. Scottish single malts, especially limited single-barrel bottlings, are now rightly considered the noblest of spirits, and increasingly the finer American brands, small-batch and single-barrel bourbons, are providing stiff competition.

The market is always in motion, making it virtually impossible to provide an overview that is accurate for very long. Especially short-lived are the various versions of particular brands; not only do many firms constantly present new special bottlings, but the independent bottlers of malt whiskies seem determined to add to the confusion. Year after year, many of them keep putting the same labels on bottlings of new versions whose alcohol content alone can vary widely.

The present survey was accurate at press time, in the spring of 1997, when the Scottish whisky industry was again in turmoil, indicating that the ownership of any number of brands may soon change.

DRINKING RITUALS

THE POPULARITY OF THE VARIOUS TYPES OF WHISK(E)Y IS JUST AS SUBJECT TO changes in fashion as is the way they are consumed. For a long time blended Scotch was considered the supreme stimulant, drunk either over ice from the heaviest possible tumbler or with soda in a tall glass. Now, however, Scottish malts are attracting increasing numbers of devotees who prefer to sip them from "nosing glasses," slender flutes resembling the Spanish *copitas,* which allow one to appreciate their diverse aromas. They disdain ice cubes but will accept a few drops of water, which often help to reveal the malt's complexity, especially that of the heavier malts. For this reason it has become customary to offer a patron bottled spring water from Scotland. All other additives are forbidden, and anyone who orders a whisky sour made with malt is sent packing.

By contrast, bourbons and Tennessee whiskeys are great for mixing. Only their most venerable versions should be drunk straight, preferably from nosing glasses and not, as one occasionally sees people doing in the United States, from cognac snifters, which prevent one from appreciating their aroma. The plainer bottlings are stronger and not as complex, so a few ice cubes do no harm—on the contrary, the ice makes them more palatable.

All of these customs can be justified, but one must not forget that whisk(e)y is meant to be enjoyed, and no one should allow his pleasure to be diminished by arbitrary rules.

Love makes the world go round?
Not at all. Whisky makes it go round twice as fast.

Compton Mackenzie,
Whisky Galore

ABBOT'S CHOICE

Blended Scotch from John McEwan & Co., a subsidiary of UD.

An old-fashioned, rather strong blend that was already very popular in the last century and is now very difficult to obtain; the base malt is probably LINKWOOD.

ABERFELDY

Scottish single malt (Southern Highlands) from UD.

A typical Highland malt, well-balanced, gentle, and full-bodied. It is currently available in the following versions:

Original bottling: 15 years old, 86 proof.

Gordon & MacPhail: 1970, 1974 and 1977, each 80 proof.

Cadenhead: 17 years old (distilled 1978), 115.8 proof.

The distillery was built in 1898 by John Dewar & Sons (see DEWAR'S); it was their first distillery, and the famous firm owns the license for Aberfeldy to this day, obtaining from it most of the base malts for its Dewar's blends.

Aberfeldy has 4 stills and gets its water from the Pitilie Burn.

(Tel. 1887 82 03 30)

ABERFOYLE

Scottish vatted malt, 8 years old, from ROBERTSON & BAXTER.

ABERLOUR

Scottish single malt (Speyside, Glenlivet) from CAMPBELL DISTILLERS, a subsidiary of the French spirit giant PERNOD RICARD.

A digestif malt and the ideal whisky for curious cognac drinkers who want to experiment. In terms of sales, Aberlour has been among the top international brands since the late 1980s. It is currently available in the following versions:

Original bottling: 10 years old, 80 proof; 12 years old, 86 proof; 21 years old (distilled 1970), 86 proof; also as Aberlour 100, without age designation, 114.2 proof; and as Aberlour Antique, without age designation, 86 proof. In Italy there is also a 5-year-old at 80 proof.

Signatory: 21 years old (distilled 1974), 111 proof.

Dun Eideann: 20 years old (distilled 1970), 92 proof.

The distillery was built in 1826 in Aberlour, a small village in the heart of Speyside. Since 1945 it has belonged to the

Campbell firm. It has 4 stills; the water comes from Ben Rinnes, a mountain famous for the purity of its water. Aging begins in sherry casks and is then continued in bourbon casks. These are sealed with corks rather than the customary wooden plugs, as the cork allows the cruder aromatic substances to evaporate, producing a mellower whisky.

(Tel. 1340 87 12 04)

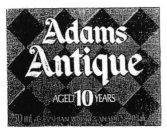

ADAMS
Canadian blend from SEAGRAM.

A brand sold mainly in Canada in the following versions: Adams Antique, 10 years old; Adams Double Distilled; and Adams Private Stock, all 80 proof. Private Stock is also exported to Taiwan.

ADELPHI DISTILLERY LTD.
Scottish independent bottling firm founded in Edinburgh in 1993 by James Walker. Walker is the grandson of one of the owners of Adelphi, a Lowland distillery that operated from 1880 to 1960.

The firm offers mostly malts in SINGLE-BARREL BOTTLINGS but also has various blends in its program, including Adelphi Private Stock (de luxe, 80 proof) and Breath of Angels.

The whiskies are intended almost exclusively for export.

(3 Gloucester Lane, Edinburgh EH3 6ED, Tel. 131 226 66 70, Fax 226 66 72)

AFFINITY
A Scotch MANHATTAN with orange bitters instead of Angostura.

AGE
The minimum age prescribed by law for Scotch, Irish, and Canadian whisk(e)y is 3 years; for U.S. whiskey, 2 years. Any age designation on the label always refers to the youngest distillate in the blend.

According to U.S. law, if a whiskey is less than 4 years old its age must be indicated on the label. Therefore, if there is no age designation one can assume that the whiskey is at least 4 years old; it is often as old as 6. Ages are normally given only for whiskeys aged for more than 6 years.

Age does not necessarily translate into quality, although a product's advertising may imply that it does.

Many malts, for example, are at their peak when they are between 8 and 12 years old; some, only at 15, 17, or even 21 years. Only a very few can age longer without damage. The complexity of aromas increases with age, to be sure, but a whisk(e)y can also become woody or simply "tired"— even though it is certain to be more expensive.

Here, too, it is one's personal taste that matters. Whereas the Italians are mad for the fruitier and livelier 5- to 7-year-old whisk(e)ys, in other countries connoisseurs will do anything to sample older, rarer ones, despite the occasional disappointment—that, too, can be a singular experience.

AGE OF SAIL
A blended Scotch from Lombard Scotch Whisky Ltd. (see LOMBARD's).

A. H. HIRSCH RESERVE
Straight bourbon, 16 and 20 years old, both vintage 1974 and 91.6 proof, from Cork 'n' Bottle.

A splendid whiskey: luxurious, complex, and perfectly balanced, but unfortunately very scarce.

A. H. Hirsch is the only American whiskey still produced by the POT STILL method. It was produced by Michter's Distillery in Schaefferstown, Pennsylvania, until that operation shut down in the late 1980s. Michter's was founded in 1753, and before it closed it was thought to be the oldest

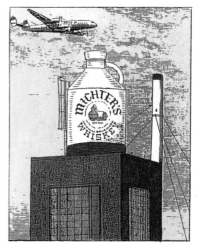

continuously operating still in the United States. It advertised its product as "the whiskey that warmed the American Revolution."

Until the 1940s, the distillery produced exclusively RYE WHISKEY. Then a new distiller from the famous Beam family began experimenting with other techniques, and soon it was also producing a bourbon with a considerable portion of rye, which was distilled a second time in a pot still. This was marketed, beginning in 1956, as Michter's, but it was only a minor sideline; the main emphasis continued to be on rye whiskey, which the distillery supplied to WILD TURKEY and OLD OVERHOLT, among others, until 1984. Some time later the business was closed, and the major part of its stores were acquired by Adolf Hirsch, after whom the brand is now named. In 1990 the trading firm Cork 'n' Bottle took over the whiskey, contracting Van Winkle (see OLD RIP VAN WINKLE) to bottle it.

The distillery itself was placed under landmark protection, even though roughly 5,000 barrels of whiskey were still in its warehouses. After more than 1,200 barrels had been stolen, a local judge ruled that to prevent vandalism and fire the remainder should be burned. Talk about vandalism!

AINSLIE & HEILBRON

Scottish producers with headquarters in Glasgow. Founded in 1868, the firm was originally called James Ainslie & Co. and for a time owned the CLYNELISH distillery (see BRORA). It merged in 1921 with David Heilbron & Son. It now belongs to UD, for which it produces the following blends: Ainslie's, Ainslie's De Luxe, and Ainslie's King's Legend.

Ainslie's Royal Edinburgh, at one time the best-known of the Ainslie & Heilbron brands, especially popular in Australia and Belgium, is no longer produced.

ALBERTA

Canadian brand and distillery belonging to JIM BEAM Brands (AMERICAN BRANDS).

In this Calgary distillery the U.S. firm Jim Beam Brands produces its Canadian blends Alberta, Alberta Premium, and Alberta Springs. The packaging of the latter two is very similar to that of JACK DANIEL's, although the words "charcoal mellowing" on the label have nothing to do with the filtration method used for Tennessee whiskeys; here they refer to the normal filtering through charcoal dust, which is also practiced in Kentucky (see FILTRATION).

The Alberta distillery, which Beam acquired in 1987, also produces the following brands: AUTUMN GOLD, CANADA HOUSE, LORD CALVERT, and the WINDSOR whiskies.

ALBION'S FINEST OLD

Blended Scotch from Scottish Albion Blending Co., a subsidiary of KINROSS WHISKY CO.

ALCOHOL CONTENT

The minimum alcohol content prescribed by law in most countries for whisk(e)y is 40 percent by volume, or 80 proof. Only in Canada and in certain exotic markets is it permissible to sell weaker spirits as whisk(e)y.

After distillation, the fresh distillate has an alcohol content of up to 80 percent by volume, or 160 proof. To promote the aging process, it is reduced by the addition of water to roughly 63 percent by volume, or 126 proof, before being placed in casks.

Scotch usually loses alcohol during aging. In the United States, however, owing to lower warehouse humidity, the alcohol content tends to rise. Before it is bottled, the whisk(e)y is again diluted to bring the alcohol content down to drinking strength, which for Scotch is 80 proof; for some export Scotches, 86 proof. Diluting is mainly a financial consideration; lower alcohol content means lower taxes. There is always a loss of flavor, to be sure, and accordingly there has been a trend in recent years toward barrel-strength bottling (see Single-Barrel Bottling), especially of malt whiskies.

In the United States the standard is also 80 proof, but there are bottlings of 90 and 100 proof (see Bottled in Bond). Barrel-strength bottling

of bourbon is also on the rise (see Single-Barrel Bourbons).

ALEXANDER DUNN & CO.

This British blender specializes in gift editions; a purchaser can have the name of the recipient printed on the label (see Slaintheva). Buyers can also choose among several different ages and strengths of Alexander Dunn Scotch: in addition to a 3-, 5-, or 12-year-old blend, there is also a 12-year-old vatted malt. The concept was developed in the 1980s for a French supermarket chain. Meanwhile Dunn's whiskies have gained a certain popularity in Japan, under their own label.

ALLAN'S

Blended Scotch from Eaglesome, a subsidiary of J. A. Mitchell.

ALLIED DISTILLERS

Scottish producer, a subsidiary of the British firm Allied Domecq. Within the larger firm Allied Distillers is

responsible for the production of Scotch whisky, and thus for the following distilleries and brands:

Malt: ARDMORE, GLENBURGIE, GLENCADAM, The GLENDRONACH, GLENTAUCHERS, IMPERIAL, INVERLEVEN, LAPHROAIG, LOMOND, MILTONDUFF, SCAPA, and TORMORE.

Grain: DUMBARTON and STRATHCLYDE.

Blended Scotch: AMBASSADOR, BALLANTINE'S, DOCTOR'S SPECIAL, LONG JOHN, OLD SMUGGLER, STEWART'S CREAM OF THE BARLEY, and TEACHER'S.

ALLIED DOMECQ

The second-largest spirit producer in the world has its headquarters in Bristol, England, and controls, through various subsidiaries, the most diverse whisk(e)y brands: ALLIED DISTILLERS (Scotch), CANTRELL & COCHRANE (Irish), CORBY (Canadian), DYC (Spanish), HIRAM WALKER & SONS (Canadian), and MAKER'S MARK (bourbon).

The concern's history begins with Allied Breweries, one of the 3 largest beer producers in Great Britain. With its takeover of the famous whisky firms Stewart & Sons (1969), Wm TEACHER (1976), and HIRAM WALKER & SONS (1986–88), it evolved into the concern known as Allied-Lyons. In the mid-1980s it failed in its attempt to take over the DCL, but with its purchase in 1990 of the spirit interests of the British brewer Whitbread (GLENUGIE, KINCLAITH, LAPHROAIG, LONG JOHN, TORMORE), Allied has continued to be a market power. Since its merger with the Spanish wine and brandy producers Pedro Domecq in 1990, the firm has operated under the name Allied Domecq.

It is now concentrating on new growth markets in Latin America and Asia, where it has set up joint ventures with firms in China, Vietnam, and India. It is also affiliated with the Japanese whisky giant SUNTORY.

Allied Domecq also operates the British pub chain John Bull, and owns additional world brands, including Beefeater gin, Courvoisier cognac, Harvey and La Ina sherries, Cockburn port, Lamb's rum, and Carlos and Fundador brandies.

ALL MALT

Japanese vatted malt from NIKKA.

A light whisky created from 2 different malts.

A

ALLT-Á-BHAINNE
[Gaelic for "whitewater brook"]

Scottish single malt (SPEYSIDE, DUFFTOWN) from the SEAGRAM subsidiary CHIVAS & GLENLIVET GROUP.

A rather sweet malt with a medium body, now obtainable only from independent bottlers:

Cadenhead: 15 years old (distilled 1979), 118.2 proof.

Signatory: Vintages 1981, 114.2 proof, and 1979, 110.4 proof.

James MacArthur: 12 years old, 86 proof.

The Castle Collection: Vintage 1979, 86 proof.

The distillery was built by Chivas in 1975, and has a capacity of 5 million liters (more than 21 million gallons) a year. After BRAES OF GLENLIVET, it was the second and last in Seagram's plan to add "five distilleries in five years," which was then scrapped on account of the oil crisis. Allt-á-Bhainne is outfitted with all of the most modern technology, and even the architecture departs from tradition. Recently, 4 small pagoda-style roofs were erected above the main building. They serve only a decorative function.

The distillery has 2 stills and gets its water from a spring on Ben Rinnes. Most of what it produces goes into the Chivas blends.

AMBASSADOR
Blended Scotch, de luxe, from HIRAM WALKER & SONS (ALLIED DOMECQ).

Once a famous brand, whose slogan, "Scotch at its lightest," made it especially popular in the United States. Today Ambassador is hard to find; it was bottled at 8, 12, and 15 years old. Originally, it came from the house of Taylor & Ferguson, founded in Glasgow in 1820 and taken over by Hiram Walker in the 1930s. Taylor & Ferguson now operates the SCAPA distillery for that concern.

AMBER GLOW
Scottish whisky herb liqueur from HALLGARTEN.

AMERICAN BIKER
Kentucky straight bourbon from TWELVE STONE FLAGONS.

A motorcycle rider adorns the label of this brand, first produced in 1996. He is supposed to symbolize the independent American spirit and thereby appeal mainly to U.S. bikers, a target group said to consume a great deal of beer and JACK DANIEL'S OLD NO. 7.

The firm Twelve Stone Flagons, which made its name with the blended Scotch USQUAEBACH, buys its bourbon from HEAVEN HILL DISTILLERS.

AMERICAN BRANDS
A mixed U.S. concern involved in the whiskey business through its subsidiaries JIM BEAM Brands and WHYTE & MACKAY. Among the giant's other holdings are the cigarette brand Lucky Strike and the legendary Pinkerton detective agency.

AMERICAN CREAM
U.S. whiskey cream liqueur from IDV/ Grand Metropolitan.

One of the countless BAILEYS ORIGINAL IRISH CREAM imitations that have flooded the market since the late 1970s. The liqueur is produced by the IDV subsidiary HEUBLEIN INC.

ANCIENT AGE
Kentucky straight bourbon from SAZERAC's LEESTOWN DISTILLING COMPANY.

A somewhat sweet whiskey that is very well suited for MANHATTAN cocktails. It is available in a number of different bottlings. The standard version comes in 80, 90, or 100 proof (BOTTLED IN BOND); the Ancient Ancient Age (also called Triple A or 10 Star) is 90 proof or, in the 10-year-old export version, 96 proof; the most recent bottling, also 10 years old, is called Barrel 107, and is sold at 107 proof.

In addition, there is a blend by the name of Ancient Age Preferred

(80 proof), as well as a mint julep pre-mix (70 proof).

The brand first appeared in 1936. At that time, however, it was still produced in Canada as a "bourbon-style" whiskey, for after the end of Prohibition the distillery did not have enough stock in its own warehouses. Ancient Age has been a true Kentucky straight bourbon only since 1946.

ANCIENT PRIVILEGE
Blended Scotch, 5 years old, from W. BROWN & SONS.

AN CNOC
Scottish single malt (Speyside, Banffshire) from INVER HOUSE DISTILLER'S KNOCKDHU distillery.

A mild, medium-heavy malt, currently sold in 2 versions.

Original bottling: 12 years old, 86 proof, on the market only since 1993. Before that time the malt was available only from the independents, under the distillery's name, Knockdhu. When Inver House decided to bottle the malt itself, they chose the Gaelic name An Cnoc, to avoid confusion with KNOCKANDO.

Inver House has owned Knockdhu only since 1988; previously it belonged to DCL, which had built it in 1893–94. Until it was closed in 1983 the distillery produced the base malts for the HAIG & Co. whiskies. It was reopened in 1989 and has 2 stills. The water comes from Knock Hill.

(Tel. 1466 77 12 23)

ANGEL'S SHARE
Blended Scotch, produced for the U.S. market by the firm Robert Denton (see BUSH PILOT'S PRIVATE RESERVE).

The "angel's share" is the portion of the whisk(e)y that evaporates while it ages in the barrel (see ALCOHOL CONTENT).

ANGUS DUNDEE

Scottish vatted malt from Angus Dundee

Ltd., a firm established in London in 1950 that also produces a vatted malt called AUCHTERAR and various blends: CASTLE PRIDE, Clan Ben, THE DUNDEE, FORFARS, HIGHLAND LEGEND, PARKER'S, PIPER'S CLAN, and SCOTTISH ROYAL.

ANKARA

Turkish blended whiskey, 86 proof, produced since 1961 by the state-owned Tekel firm in the Ankara Brewery in Istanbul.

THE ANTIQUARY

Blended Scotch, 12 years old, 80 proof, from UD.

A brand named after a novel by Sir Walter Scott, and one that has probably finally reached its peak. The Antiquary is an elegant, de luxe blend and, like its base malt, BENROMACH, is very difficult to get and also rather expensive.

The license situation is somewhat complicated. Originally, The Antiquary came from the house of J. & W. Hardie, a firm established in Edinburgh in 1861. In 1917 the brand belonged to the firm of J. & G. Stewart (see STEWART'S FINEST OLD), which in that same

year joined the DCL. Hardie, in turn, was taken over by Wm SANDERSON & SON, and when this firm finally joined the DCL as well, the license again reverted to Hardie, but production was del-

egated to BUCHANAN. Since UD has owned the group, The Antiquary has been bottled only rarely, with Hardie identified as the owner.

ARDBEG

Scottish single malt (Islay, Port Ellen) from ALLIED DISTILLERS (ALLIED DOMECQ).

Ardbeg has a small but enthusiastic following of connoisseurs—little wonder, for the whisky has everything one would want from an inside tip. In terms of familiarity, it has always stood in the shadow of its neighbors LAGAVULIN and LAPHROAIG. With its overwhelming complexity and strength, it appeals mainly to the specialist. If you can find it, it will be in the following versions:

Original bottling: 10 years old, 80 proof; it is unlikely that there will be any more from Islay—these are now available only at collectors' prices.

Gordon & MacPhail: Vintages 1974 (bottled 1991), 80 proof, and

1963 (bottled 1994), 80 proof; another 1974 version, also at 80 proof, is being bottled by the Gordon & MacPhail subsidiary Speymalt Whisky.

Cadenhead: Most recently the firm offered it at 19 years old (distilled 1975), 116.2 proof, and 20 years old (distilled 1974), 102.4 proof.

Signatory: 18 years old (distilled 1975), 86 proof; 21 years old (distilled 1974), 86 proof; and 28 years old (distilled 1967), 106.4 and 107.4 proof. This last vintage is from either light or dark oloroso casks. Comparison of the 2 versions reveals how important the influence of the barrel can be on a whisky's development. For 1997, Signatory plans a 30-year-old bottling.

Adelphi: 19 years old (distilled 1976), 104 proof.

Ardbeg is one of those malts that do not suffer even from very long aging. The 31-year-old from Gordon & MacPhail, for example, is no less dazzling in its way than the 10-year-old original bottling.

The distillery was established in 1815 in a picturesque spot on the south coast of Islay, where a band of bootleggers and smugglers had camped earlier. Beginning in 1817 Ardbeg belonged to the McDougall family. In 1977 the distillery was taken over by HIRAM WALKER & SONS, and it was closed 4 years later. Since 1989 it has again been in operation, but in a different way. Ardbeg was formerly known for its traditional production methods—the British whisky expert Michael Jackson described it as "old-fashioned

in the best sense of the word"—and its intense peat flavor can be traced not only to the large quantity of peat employed but also to the fact that the pagoda-style roofs over the malt houses had no ventilators. The malt was thus subjected to more smoke than usual. These malt houses have now been closed; future Ardbeg bottlings will therefore taste somewhat different. The distillery was bought by GLENMORANGIE in 1997.

ARDMORE
Scottish single malt (Speyside) from ALLIED DISTILLERS (ALLIED DOMECQ).

A medium-heavy whisky on the malty side, and a good digestif. It is sold only by independent bottlers.

Gordon & MacPhail: 14 years old (distilled 1977), 80 proof; 1981, 80 proof.

Cadenhead: 17 years old (distilled 1977), 119.2 proof; 13 years old (distilled 1980), 122.2 proof.

James MacArthur: 18 years old, 102.8 proof.

The Ardmore distillery was built in 1898–99 by the Wm TEACHER firm, which has been a part of Allied since 1976 and uses the malt mainly for its Teacher's blends.

Originally furnished with 2 stills, the distillery now has 8 of them and is one of the largest malt distilleries in Scotland. The stills are still fired with coal, and the water comes from Knockandy Hill.

(Tel. 1464 83 12 13)

ARGYLL
Scotch whisky from Beinn Bhuidhe Holdings.

Since the late 1970s, various whiskies have been bottled for the Duke of Argyll, head of the powerful Campbell clan. These are sold only at his Inverary Castle, in the county of Argyll.

There are 12-, 15-, and 17-year-old Argyll malts. The first 2 most likely come from the TAMNAVULIN distillery; the oldest, from TULLIBARDINE.

An Argyll blend is also available.

ARRAN See ISLE OF ARRAN DISTILLERS.
ASAMA
Japanese blend from SANRAKU OCEAN.

AS WE GET IT
A mysterious Scottish malt whisky that is bottled by J. G. THOMSON and is said to come from the MACALLAN

21

distillery. There, however, they turn up their noses, mutter something about inferior quality, and decline to say how the stuff got out of the plant. Nevertheless, in the few Scottish pubs where the bartender suddenly produces a bottle of it, As We Get It is recognized as something very special, and that it is. For one thing, it is bottled at cask strength (roughly 120 proof), and for another, the content varies from bottling to bottling. This is probably because it is bottled from occasional leftover barrels passed on by Macallan on the quiet.

At one time As We Get It was also available from the firm Bruce Macfarlane & Co., Inverness, and in fact not only from the Macallan distillery but also from BALVENIE.

AUCHENTOSHAN
Scottish single malt (Lowlands, Glasgow) from MORRISON BOWMORE DISTILLERS (SUNTORY).

Of the two remaining Lowlands distilleries—the other is called GLENKINCHIE—Auchentoshan is doubtless the better known, and its product is often described as a "classic" Lowlands malt. Distilled 3 times, it is light-bodied and rather dry.

Original bottling: Without age designation, 80 proof; 10 years old, 80 proof; and 21 years old (distilled 1972), 86 proof; occasionally one also finds older bottlings at 5, 8, 12, and 18 years old.

Cadenhead: The firm has had Auchentoshan in its program since April 1996.

Signatory: Vintage 1981, 86 proof.

The distillery was established in about 1800 and has frequently changed hands. Since 1984 it has belonged to the Morrison group, which is in turn a part of Suntory. Auchentoshan has 3 stills. The water comes from the Kilpatrick Hills or from the Highlands, even though the distillery is in the Lowlands. Some of the distillates are aged in sherry casks; others, in bourbon barrels.

(Tel. 1389 87 85 61)

AUCHROISK See THE SINGLETON OF AUCHROISK.

AUCHTERAR

Scottish vatted malt from ANGUS DUNDEE.

AULD ACQUAINTANCE

Scottish single malt, 10 years old, 86 proof, from MACARTHUR.

This is not an original bottling from one distillery, but a so-called brand bottling, which is to say that the bottler buys the whisky from an unnamed distillery and bottles it under its own label (see INDEPENDENT BOTTLERS). (There was once a blend sold under the same name by McCallum.)

AULD SANDY

Blended Scotch from Balls Bros.

The Balls brothers got their start in London in 1854 as wine and spirit dealers; for a time they also had a parallel Irish brand in their program by the name of Ould Paddy. You can get Auld Sandy only in the 8 Balls wine bars in London or from their warehouse.

(Tel. 171 739 64 66)

AULTMORE

Scottish single malt (Speyside, Keith) from UD.

Although whisky expert Michael Jackson gives it the highest rating, this malt continues to find little demand. Yet it is well-balanced and suitable for both beginning Scotch drinkers and connoisseurs.

Original bottling: 12 years old, 86 proof, from the "Flora & Fauna" series; sometimes one can also find the bottling by J. & R. HARVEY (12 years old, 80 proof), an old blending house that owned the distillery license until 1992.

Signatory: 15 years old (bottled 1978), 86 proof.

Aultmore was built in 1895 and belonged for a time to John Dewar & Sons (see DEWAR's), in whose blends its malt probably still plays a role. The distillery has 4 stills. The water comes from Auchinderran Burn.

(Tel. 1542 88 27 62)

AUSTIN NICHOLS DISTILLING COMPANY

U.S. producer that has belonged to the PERNOD RICARD empire since 1980.

Austin Nichols began in 1855 as a grocery, wine, and spirit business. Shortly after Prohibition it created the brand WILD TURKEY, which it has produced itself ever since it acquired its own distillery in 1971.

In addition to the various Wild Turkey bottlings, there is a SINGLE-BARREL BOTTLING called KENTUCKY SPIRIT and a blend based on Wild Turkey called NICHOLS.

AUSTRALIAN WHISKEY

When Australia, a member of the Commonwealth, thinks of whisk(e)y it naturally thinks of Scotch, and in fact the country was the most important export market for Scotch whiskies up until World War II. Scotch is the highest-selling spirit in Australia even today, followed closely by bourbon, which is becoming increasingly preferred, especially by the younger generation.

At first the country's own whiskey production (initiated with the erection of the Myers distillery in Ballarat, Victoria, in 1866) hadn't a chance against imports from Scotland. It was only in the 1920s, when the Australian government raised the import duty on spirits, that whiskey production became competitive and, with

the blend Old Court, Australia had the first successful brand of its own.

The Scottish distilling concern DCL was quick to notice, and in 1927 it joined with 4 local producers to build a modern distillery in Corio, Victoria. The group United Distilleries (not to be confused with United Distillers) was formed out of this collaboration in 1931, and until a few years ago it produced 2 of Australia's most successful whiskeys: CORIO and Four Seasons. Another important brand, BOND 7, was also created by a British firm, namely the IDV subsidiary GILBEY.

Despite a temporary high in the 1950s and 1960s, domestic production has never been able to prevail over competition from Scotland. In the 1980s demand fell to the point that all producers have ceased operation, most recently United Distilleries, which redistilled its large inventories into gin before shutting down in 1995. (Rumor has

it that in the spring of 1996 a new distillery began operation in Tasmania.)

Production: All the important distilleries were in the southeastern part of the country, in the region around Melbourne and in Adelaide. Not only did that area appeal to the first European settlers on account of its climate, but it also produces the best grain in Australia and has abundant water. Australian whiskey, almost always in the form of blends, is made from barley, corn, and millet. Its malt whiskey can be distilled only from barley malt and must be aged at least 2 years. Blended whiskey must be aged for the same length of time and contain at least 25 percent malt.

AUTUMN GOLD
Canadian blend, 70 proof, from JIM BEAM BRANDS (AMERICAN BRANDS).

A smaller label for the U.S. market.

AVERY'S OF BRISTOL LTD.
This prestigious wine dealer (established in Bristol in 1793) now has 3 blends in its program: BRISTOL VAT, HIGHLAND BLEND, and QUEEN ELIZABETH.

AVOCA
Blended Irish whiskey, standard, 80 proof, from COOLEY DISTILLERY.

This simple supermarket whiskey is available only in Ireland and was named after a river south of Dublin.

AVONSIDE
Blended Scotch from Avonside Whisky Ltd., a subsidiary of GORDON & MACPHAIL that also markets the malts GLEN AVON and STRATHAVON.

This above-average blend is sold at 8 years old at 80 and 114 proof.

AWARD
Blended Scotch from Wm LUNDIE & Co.

B

Gimme a visky—ginger ale on the side—
and don't be stingy, baby!

Greta Garbo's first spoken words on screen

BAGPIPER

Indian blend, 85.6 proof, from Herbertsons Ltd., a subsidiary of the UB group.

The standard version of this brand is the best-selling whiskey in India. There is also a Bagpiper Gold.

Bagpiper's popularity is based in no small part on its connection with the Indian film industry. Major film stars allow themselves to be used for promotional purposes, and there is also a weekly Bagpiper television show that reports on the doings of actors—only males, of course, for in India whisk(e)y is considered especially macho.

BAILEYS ORIGINAL IRISH CREAM

Irish whiskey cream liqueur, 34 proof (with cacao added) from GILBEY (IDV/Grand Metropolitan).

Baileys' rapid climb to best-selling liqueur brand in the world began only in 1974. Up until then there had only been whisk(e)y liqueurs made with herbs or citrus flavors, and the new mixture of cream, cacao, and Irish whiskey obviously appealed to the taste of the time. Today there are a number of more or less successful imitations, and in the United States one can also buy Baileys in a "light" version.

BAILIE NICOL JARVIE, B.N.J.

Blended Scotch from Nicol Anderson & Co., a subsidiary of MACDONALD MARTIN DISTILLERS.

An elegant de luxe blend based on GLEN MORAY. The name comes from that of a character in Sir Walter Scott's famous novel *Rob Roy*.

BAIRD-TAYLOR'S SELECTED

Blended Scotch from Baird Taylor Ltd., a firm of wine merchants founded in Glasgow in 1838. It now belongs to UD.

BAKER'S

Kentucky straight bourbon from JIM BEAM Brands (AMERICAN BRANDS).

A 7-year-old SMALL-BATCH BOURBON that is amazingly mild, given that it is 106 proof. The whiskey takes its name from Baker Beam, a grand-nephew of the famous Jim.

BAKER STREET
Blended Scotch marketed in the United States by CONSOLIDATED, produced by INVER-GORDON DISTILLERS.

BALBLAIR
Scottish single malt (Northern Highlands) from INVER HOUSE DISTILLERS.

A light, dry malt that is rarely seen on the market. The greater part of it disappears into the BALLANTINE blends.

Original bottling: 10 years old, 80 proof; in Italy you can also find a 5-year-old version.

Gordon & MacPhail: Vintages 1964 and 1973, 80 proof; 10 years old, 80 proof.

Cadenhead: 26 years old (distilled 1965, sherry cask), 88.8 proof.

The first Balblair distillery was built in 1790 or earlier, but it did not meet the demands of later owners, who in 1872 opened the present distillery a few yards away. The exterior has changed very little since that time, and it is a lovely example of traditional 19th-century distillery architecture.

In 1970 it was taken over by HIRAM WALKER & SONS, but since 1996 it is part of INVER HOUSE; it is managed by George Ballantine & Son. Balblair has 3 stills, and the water comes from a stream called the Allt Dearg.

(Tel. 1862 82 12 73)

BALLANTINE'S
Blended Scotch from George Ballantine & Son, a subsidiary of ALLIED DISTILLERS (ALLIED DOMECQ).

One of the most successful liquor brands in the world, currently available in the following bottlings: Ballantine's Finest, premium, 80 proof; Founder's Reserve de Luxe, Gold Seal, 12 years old, 86 proof (until a few years ago called The 12); 17 Years Old, 86 proof; and Very Old, 30 years old, 86 proof, one of the most expensive blended Scotches on the market. Ballantine's blends are based mainly on malts from MILTONDUFF, BALBLAIR, GLENBURGIE, and OLD PULTENEY. They are relatively light-bodied and—with the exception of the older versions—intended for the mass market.

The rise of the house of Ballantine began in 1827, when George Ballantine opened a small shop in Edinburgh and soon made a name for himself as a whisky dealer as well. His son became increasingly active in the export business, and by the time he sold the firm to 2 businessmen in 1919 he had managed to build up an important distribution network (see James & George STODART). The new owners focused special attention on the United States; their first representative there—not a very good one, apparently—was David Niven, who was later considerably more successful as an actor. In 1936 the Canadian firm HIRAM WALKER & SONS, which had developed a nose

Ballantine's
FINEST

ESTABLISHED 1827

BLENDED
SCOTCH WHISKY

Blended & Bottled by
George Ballantine & Son Limited
Distillers—Dumbarton, Scotland
PRODUCT OF SCOTLAND

G. Ballantine

1 LITRE
40% ALC./VOL.

IMPORTED BY
HIRAM WALKER
& SONS, INC.
FARMINGTON
HILLS, MI

for profit during Prohibition, entered the Scotch business in a powerful way. It took over Ballantine & Son and in 1938 built DUMBARTON, at that time the largest and most modern production center in Europe and today still run by Ballantine & Son. With its impressive capacity, it then set out to conquer the U.S. market —and succeeded. It accomplished the same feat in Europe in the 1960s and in the former Eastern Bloc in the 1970s. Today Ballantine's Finest is the largest-selling Scotch in Europe and one of the 25 highest-selling liquors in the world.

BALMENACH

Scottish single malt (Speyside, Cromdale) from UD.

A highly individual malt, full of character, formerly available chiefly from independent bottlers. Since 1992 it has also been bottled by the producer.

Original bottling: 12 years old, 86 proof.

Gordon & MacPhail: Vintages 1970, 1971, 1972, 1973, 1974, all 80 proof.

Cadenhead: 12 years old (distilled 1981), 125.2 proof, and 13 years old (distilled 1981), 125.8 proof.

James MacArthur: 10 years old, 86 proof.

Adelphi: 15 years old (distilled 1980), 124.2 proof.

In 1824, when this distillery was built, the area was still teeming with bootleggers. A fine description of conditions at the time is presented in the book *Scotch* by Sir Bruce Lockhart, a great-grandson of the founder.

The distillery has 4 stills; the water comes from the Cromdale Burn. The malt serves as the base for the blends from John Crabbie & Co. (see CRABBIE's), the former licensee. The firm was closed down in 1993.

THE BALVENIE

Scottish single malt (Speyside, Dufftown) from William GRANT & SONS.

Balvenie malts are excellent representatives of the milder school of whiskies, in which the malt flavor thrusts the peaty tones into the background without loss of strength or sweetness.

Original bottling: Founder's Reserve, 10 years old, 80 proof; Double Wood, 12 years old, 80 proof (aged first in bourbon casks, then in sherry casks); single barrel, 15 years old, 100.8 proof (a limited edition from selected casks).

Before Balvenie appeared on the market with these 3 de luxe bottlings in 1993, there was only Founder's Reserve (for a long time without any designation of age, then as a 10-year-old) and a Classic, roughly corresponding to the present-day Double Wood. If you happen to turn up what is left of the latter, don't be put off by the somewhat unconventional look of the bottles.

Cadenhead: 15 years old (distilled 1979), 115.6 proof.

Dun Eideann: 16 years old (distilled 1974), 114.2 proof.

The distillery was built by W. & J. Grant in 1892–93, and is now owned by the 5th generation of the family. Balvenie is a fine example of the uniqueness of Scotland's distillers: it

SINGLE MALT ESTᵈ 1892
Distilled at
THE BALVENIE
Distillery, Banffshire
SCOTLAND

SINGLE BARREL
MALT SCOTCH WHISKY
from a single barrel

AGED **15** YEARS

BOTTLED BY HAND

| *Bottling Date* | | *Cask No* | |
| *Int cask Date* | | *Bottle No* | |

CERTIFIED BY THE BALVENIE DISTILLERY

shares not only water and malt with the neighboring GLENFIDDICH distillery (also owned by the Grants), but also the stillman, and yet the 2 brands are totally different in character. One of the reasons for this is that the stills of the 2 distilleries are different in shape. Balvenie has a total of 8 stills, the first 4 of which were bought secondhand from LAGAVULIN and GLEN ALBYN. Balvenie still produces some of its malt on its own malting floors; the water comes from the spring Robbie Dhu.

(Tel. 1340 82 03 73)

BANFF

Scottish single malt (Eastern Highlands) from UD.

An earthy, smoky malt, which is now almost impossible to get, but if you do, it is, as MILROY says, "a good bite."

Gordon & MacPhail: Vintage 1974, 80 proof.

Cadenhead: 17 years old (distilled 1976), 121 proof.

Banff was built in 1863. It was badly damaged by German bombing raids in 1941 and finally shut down in 1983. Before then the distillery had been run by Slater, Rodger & Co., which used its malts for their RODGER'S OLD SCOTS BRAND blends.

BANKER'S CLUB

Blended American from KASSER LAIRD.

BARCLAY'S

Kentucky straight bourbon, 80 proof, from BARTON DISTILLERY (Canandaigua). A sweet, everyday, light-bodied whiskey.

BARREL

Aging in barrels is of extreme importance for a whisk(e)y. One obvious effect is the color it provides, for all distillates are essentially as clear as water; only in the wood do they take on the range of colors that makes them visually appealing.

In addition, a whole series of physical and chemical changes occurs in the barrel that affects the flavor of a whisk(e)y more than almost any other process in its production. It used to be that particular stress was placed on the influence of the water and the shape of the still, but in recent years more and more attention has been paid to the effect of the barrel on a distillate.

Up until the 19th century, long aging was considered a pure luxury. If people bothered to take the time at all, they used whatever barrels were at hand, and since new barrels were expensive, they bought used ones—bordeaux casks, sherry casks, liquor barrels. Even barrels that had been used for foodstuffs such as butter would do once all traces of the previous contents had been burned out. This gave rise to a technique that is still crucial today. Before being used, every new barrel is charred on the inside. In the United States, producers of STRAIGHT WHISKEYS are even required by law to use charred barrels. The resulting layer of charcoal not only gives the contents a stronger color, but it also contains important aromatic components such as wood sap and oils that are absorbed by the whisk(e)y as it ages. This is where bourbon takes on its typical flavors of vanilla and caramel.

Bourbon barrels can be used only once; they are then exported, mainly to Scotland and Ireland. There distillers use various combinations of bourbon barrels, new barrels, and sherry casks.

Sherry barrels were already highly sought after in the 19th century, for they significantly help to round out the flavor. Malt whiskies aged in them are extremely popular today, especially with lovers of mild malts (see THE MACALLAN). But not every whisk(e)y

can take long aging in sherry casks without losing something of its individuality. For this reason producers have begun aging malts in different barrels, using sherry casks only for the "finish," the final rounding off.

More imaginative producers have even begun experimenting with aging for various lengths of time in port, rum, and brandy casks. These change a whisk(e)y dramatically; even brief aging in such barrels results in a product very different from that produced by bourbon barrels (see GLENMORANGIE).

It is important to recognize that the aging process is different in every barrel; two different barrels never produce an identical end product. This is why single-barrel bottlings are rare; it is much more common to blend a large number of different whiskies so as to guarantee a consistent product over the years.

The newest development has come from the United States, and has been introduced in the Asian market, where the use of oak barrels is not prescribed by law. Stainless steel barrels with oak lids help to lower costs, since they can be reused repeatedly and are easier to clean than wooden barrels. They also prevent evaporation, the loss of the "angels' share," as it is called. In standard bourbon casks this can amount to roughly 10 percent per year. To ensure the desired flavor, additional pieces of charred wood are simply placed inside the container. (See also BOTTLING, KELT "TOUR DU MONDE," SINGLE-BARREL BOURBONS, SINGLE-BARREL BOTTLING.)

BARRISTER
Blended Scotch produced for the U.S. market by KASSER LAIRD.

BARRISTER'S
Blended Scotch produced for the U.S. market by the firm Gaetano (see JIM GRANT).

BARTON DISTILLING
U.S. producer and distillery in Bardstown, Kentucky, owned by Canandaigua.

The distillery was established in 1889 by TOM MOORE. It was closed down during Prohibition and then reopened under its present name. Beginning in 1944 it belonged to Oscar Getz, who is admired by countless bourbon lovers today for the unique whiskey museum he founded in Bardstown. In the 1970s the distillery became part of the Barton Brands concern, which for a time became involved in the Scotch whisky business by taking over the LITTLEMILL and LOCH LOMOND distilleries. In 1982 the British group ADP took over Bar-

34

ton Brands, producing the somewhat obscure firm Gibson International, which recently disappeared from the scene without a trace. The Scottish holdings went to GLEN CATRINE, and Barton has since become a possession of the Canandaigua Wine Company.

Canandaigua was founded in New York in 1945 and made its name as a producer of inexpensive wines—not especially good ones (there was talk, for example, of Château Screwcap). But the firm was not to be ignored, and today it is one of the 3 largest wine producers in the United States. The Barton whiskeys are similar; none of them has real class, but for everyday use they'll do, and they keep their place on the market by their sheer number. In the Barton plant, with its modest-looking exterior, a whole range of brands and varieties are produced.

Bourbon: The most important are TEN HIGH and VERY OLD BARTON; in addition, there are the smaller names BARCLAY'S, CLEMENTINE'S, COLONEL LEE, TOM MOORE, KENTUCKY GENTLEMAN, and KENTUCKY TAVERN. These are distilled from a grain mixture consisting of 75 percent corn, 10 percent barley malt, and 15 percent rye, so they are rather dry. The sour mash component is 20 percent; the yeast culture dates back to the 1940s.

Blends: Barton's Premium (80 proof), Barton's Reserve (80 and 90 proof), CORBY'S, FLEISCHMANN'S PREFERRED, IMPERIAL, KENTUCKY GENTLEMAN, and OLD THOMPSON.

Corn: CABIN HOLLOW, CORN CRIB, GOLDEN GRAIN, and OLD DISPENSARY.

Lights: Barton's QT and COLONEL LEE.

Canadian (imported and bottled exclusively for the U.S. market): Barton's Canadian, CANADIAN HOST, CANADIAN SUPREME, and NORTHERN LIGHT.

Barton took over the GLENMORE and MEDLEY distilleries in 1995. Although the latter is used only as a bottling plant, Glenmore is supposed to begin production again soon. Barton also owns other distilleries in Georgia and California that produce gin, vodka, rum, tequila, liqueurs, etc.

(Tel. 502 348-3991)

BASIL HAYDEN'S
Kentucky straight bourbon from JIM BEAM Brands (AMERICAN BRANDS).

An 8-year-old SMALL-BATCH BOURBON on the market since 1992, 80 proof, with a relatively high rye content. It is thus rather dry for a bourbon and is served as an alternative to Scotch or Canadian. Basil Hayden was a historical figure for whom another bourbon was named as well: OLD GRAND-DAD.

WHEN BASIL HAYDEN, SR. began distilling his smooth BOURBON here in 1796, KENTUCKY was but four years old and GEORGE WASHINGTON was PRESIDENT.

Today, we make BASIL HAYDEN'S Kentucky Straight

BAXTER'S BARLEY BREE
Blended Scotch from UD.

BREE actually means "brew," "sauce," or "liquid," and was once used in Scotland as a synonym for whisky.

This old brand was originally produced by James Watson & Co. and is now sold mainly in South Africa, Surinam, and Lebanon. For the British Augustus Barnett chain there is a special 5-year-old bottling.

James Watson & Co., founded in Dundee in 1815, was an important producer until the beginning of this century and owned, among others,

the Ord and Pulteney distilleries (see GLEN ORD, OLD PULTENEY).

BEER
Inasmuch as whisk(e)y is essentially just distilled beer, it is no wonder that the fermented grain mash from which it is made is often referred to as "beer" or "distiller's beer."

In Great Britain especially, breweries are also involved in the whisky business. Many of them own a chain of pubs that they supply with their own brand of whiskey, and many of them are distillery owners themselves. A prime example is the huge Irish brewer Guinness, owner of the liquor giant UD (see also ALLIED DOMECQ, COCKBURN & CAMPBELL, ELDRIDGE & POPE, FINE OLD SPECIAL, GAIRLOCH, GALE'S, GOLDEN CAP, HEDGES & BUTLER, NIKKA, and SCOTTISH & NEWCASTLE BREWERIES; for the custom of mixing beer and whisk(e)y, see also BOILER MAKER and A HALF AND A NIP).

BELLOW'S CLUB
Kentucky straight bourbon from JIM BEAM Brands (AMERICAN BRANDS).

At one time there were various blends for sale under the name Bellow's, but now the only one is Bellow's Partner's Choice.

BELL'S
Blended Scotch from Arthur Bell & Sons, a subsidiary of UD.

An old and very successful brand, especially in Scotland and England. It is the 7th best-selling Scotch in the world.

The standard bottling, Extra Special, 80 proof, is a solid, everyday whisky and was the market leader in Scotland until 1980. It has now been pushed aside by the 8-year-old version of the same brand, which was launched on the British market some years ago with a gigantic advertising campaign aimed at luring the younger market to Scotch. In addition, there are a pleasant, old-fashioned 12-year-old De Luxe, 86 proof; a 21-year-old Royal Reserve; and Bell's Islander, 86 proof, which came on the market in the late 1980s and contains a high percentage of island malts.

For years Bell's has been issuing bell-shaped ceramic decanters to commemorate the British royal fam-

ily's various jubilees and weddings. These decanters enjoy great popularity among collectors.

Arthur Bell (died 1900) was one of the pioneers of the Scottish whisky industry. He began as a young employee in the wine and spirit business of the Sandeman family (famous for their port and sherry), then set up his own business in Perth in 1851. He saw the potential for blended whiskies and began experimenting in that direction at an early date. Bell showed great skill in the marketing of his products: he was the first to open a branch office in London, and he was influential in introducing standard bottle sizes. By 1895 he had built up a worldwide merchandizing network. His sons, entering into the business of distilling themselves, first introduced a brand under their own name in 1904. In 1932 they acquired the BLAIR ATHOL and DUFFTOWN distilleries, and in 1936 they added INCHGOWER to their holdings. In 1974 the firm built the PITTYVAICH distillery; in 1983 it bought BLADNOCH.

Arthur Bell & Sons was one of the last of the old firms to maintain its independence, but in 1985 it was swallowed up by Guinness and in 1987 incorporated into UD. It still owns the licenses for Blair Athol and Inchgower, which would suggest that important components of the Bell's blends come from these distilleries.

BEN AIGEN
Blended Scotch from Strathnairn Whisky Ltd., a subsidiary of GORDON & MACPHAIL.

BEN ALDER
Blended Scotch from GORDON & MACPHAIL. The brand has been on the market since 1920 and was formerly called Dew of Ben Alder.

BENCHMARK
Kentucky straight bourbon from SAZERAC'S LEESTOWN DISTILLING COMPANY.

A full-bodied whiskey that can also be drunk straight.

The brand was first placed on the market by SEAGRAM as a premium bourbon in 1967 and was sold to Sazerac in 1989. The new owner offers it as Benchmark Premium, 80 proof, and since 1995 as Benchmark XO, 94 proof. The latter is a SINGLE-BARREL BOURBON and is almost exclusively exported to the Far East.

BENEAGLES
Blended Scotch from SCOTTISH & NEWCASTLE BREWERIES.

The ownership of this brand, once very popular in Scotland, is somewhat complicated. Peter Thomson, a relatively small family business in Perth, introduced it to the market in 1922 and had great success with it, both domestically and on the export market. In the 1950s the firm hit upon the idea of bottling the whisky in ceramic decanters shaped like birds of prey.

The firm was taken over by the Scottish & Newcastle brewing concern in 1981. It has the whisky produced by INVERGORDON DISTILLERS and sells it mainly in its own pubs. The business of marketing the bottlings in the highly popular ceramic decanters is owned by LOMBARD.

BENMORE

Blended Scotch from UD.

The firm Benmore Distillers once operated the distillery DALLAS DHU. The blend is sold mainly in Belgium.

BENNACHIE

Scottish vatted malt, 10 and 12 years old, 86 proof, from Bennachie Scotch Whisky Co.

A balanced blend of Speyside malts that betrays its aging in sherry casks despite its smokiness. It has been on the market since 1993.

This whisky bears the name of a mountain near Aberdeen, at the foot of which there was a distillery in the 19th century. It was called Bennachie, but later changed its name to Jericho, taking its water from a river called the Jordan. It was closed in 1913 and has nothing to do with the present-day Bennachie firm. Bennachie was founded in Inverurie, near Aberdeen, in 1993, and also produces the following blends: DONS DRAM, JOCK, THE MURRAYFIELD, THE SCOTTISH NATIONAL TARTAN, and UNION GLEN. One of the first Bennachie brands, POT LID, has already been taken off the market.

BEN NEVIS

Scottish single malt (Highlands, Fort William) from NIKKA distillers.

A rather strong, full-bodied malt with a small but devoted following.

Original bottling: 21 years old, 111.2 proof; 26 years old, 116 proof (distilled 1967), 109.2 proof (distilled 1968), and 121 proof (distilled 1972).

Cadenhead: 17 years old (distilled 1977), 119.6 proof; the 22-year-old, 92 proof, has probably all been sold.

Signatory: Still has a grain from 1963.

James MacArthur: 27 years old, 108 proof (grain).

The distillery was built in 1825 by the legendary LONG JOHN Macdonald. In 1955 it fell into the hands of the more-infamous-than-legendary Joseph W. Hobbs, who made a fortune smuggling liquor during Prohibition and lost it again. In the 1930s

BEN NEVIS DISTILLERY
— ESTABLISHED 1825 —

he went to Scotland, bought a few distilleries (BRUICHLADDICH, GLENESK, Glenury-Royal), and established a cattle ranch on which the employees

ran around dressed as cowboys. In the 1950s he bought the distilleries LOCHSIDE and Ben Nevis, outfitted both with PATENT STILLS, and produced both malt and grain whiskies that were turned into blends on the spot. Hobbs was not particularly successful with these and disappeared from the scene. Ben Nevis reverted to Long John distillers in 1981. They removed the patent stills and shut the business down in 1986. The Japanese firm NIKKA acquired the distillery in 1989, and it has been in production again since 1991 (see DEW OF BEN NEVIS).

(Tel. 1379 70 24 76)

BENRIACH
Scottish single malt (Speyside, Elgin) from SEAGRAM.

A light, malty whisky that has been bottled officially since 1994.

Original bottling: 10 years old, 86 proof.

Gordon & MacPhail:

Vintages 1969, 1980, 1981, 1982, 80 proof.

Cadenhead: 17 years old (distilled 1978, sherry cask), 119.4 proof.

The distillery was opened in 1898 but closed again 2 years later, for the boom times of the waning century were followed by a depression that, among other things, shut down 30 Scottish distilleries within 10 years. It was not until 1965 that Benriach was renovated and reopened by Glenlivet. Since 1977 the firm has belonged to Seagram, which runs it through its CHIVAS & GLENLIVET GROUP. Almost the entire production goes into blends. The malt has therefore been available most of the time only from independent bottlers. Benriach has 4 stills and is one of the few operations still using its own malting floors; the water comes from nearby springs.

(Tel. 1542 78 34 00)

BENRINNES
Scottish single malt (Speyside, Aberlour) from UD.

A distinguished whisky, medium-heavy and well balanced.

Original botling: 15 years old, 86 proof.

Gordon & MacPhail: Vintages 1969, 1970, 1978, 80 proof.

Cadenhead: Most recently had a 15-year-old from 1980, aged in sherry casks, at 119.4 proof.

Signatory: 20 years old (distilled 1974, sherry cask), 86 and 107 proof.

Adelphi: Vintage 1979, 129.2 proof.

The distillery was founded as Lyne of Ruthrie Distillery in 1834 and has been known by its present name since 1838. In 1922 it was taken over by DEWAR's and thus came into the hands of its present owner by way of the DCL. The malt is the basis for the blends of the firm A. A. Crawford (see CRAWFORD's 3 STAR), which also held the license until 1992. Benrinnes has 6 stills and distills its product 3 times. The water comes from Scurran Burn and Rowantree Burn.

(Tel. 1340 87 12 15)

BEN ROLAND
A 5-year-old premium blended Scotch from Phillips Newman & Co., owners of the British retail chain Unwin's.

BENROMACH
Scottish single malt (Speyside, Forres) from GORDON & MACPHAIL.

An elegant malt with a medium body. One connoisseur has described it as "very drinkable," but unfortunately it is difficult to obtain.

Gordon & MacPhail: Vintages 1968, 1969, 1970, 1971, and 1972, all 80 proof.

Cadenhead: 18 years old (distilled 1976), 130 proof; 27 years old (distilled 1966), 107.2 proof; 28 years old (distilled 1965), 95.2 proof.

Benromach was built in 1898, and in the 1930s it belonged to the adventurer

J. W. Hobbs (see BEN NEVIS). Beginning in 1953 it became part of the DCL. The distillery was run by J. & W. Hardie, who used the malt for their blend THE ANTIQUARY. In 1983 it was closed, and since 1993 it has belonged to Gordon & MacPhail, who plan to reopen it in the next few years. Benromach has 2 stills; the water comes from Chapeltown.

BEN WYVIS

Scottish single malt (Northern Highlands, Cromarty Firth) from the INVERGORDON distillery of WHYTE & MACKAY (AMERICAN BRANDS).

From 1965 to 1977 there was a small malt distillery inside the Invergordon grain distillery. According to rumor, the malt was even bottled as a single at one time.

BERNHEIM DISTILLERY

U.S. distillery in Louisville, Kentucky, owned by UD.

Before the German-Swiss immigrant Isaac W. Bernheim opened this distillery around the turn of the century, he had already made a name for himself as the patent holder of the hip flask and a highly skilled whiskey dealer. Bernheim is considered to be one of the pioneers of the brand idea in the United States. He did not sell his product in casks or in whatever other containers lay at hand, as was the practice at the time, but rather in bottles marked with the brand name I. W. HARPER, which Bernheim had registered as early as 1875. During Prohibition the Bernheim distillery was one of the few that managed to survive by producing medicinal alcohol. It was taken over in 1937 by SCHENLEY, a firm that now belongs to UD. Of the more than 90 labels registered by the distillery, the new owners use only 3, all of which are produced by the same recipe: I. W. Harper, JAMES E. PEPPER, and OLD CHARTER. The mixture is composed of 86 percent corn, 8 percent barley malt, and 6 percent rye; the sour mash component amounts to 25 percent.

(Tel. 502 410-7410)

BERRY BROS. & RUDD

A London blending and trading house that began in 1690 as a grocery

B

business and has been highly successful internationally with its CUTTY SARK brand since the 1920s. Although it has this blend produced by ROBERTSON & BAXTER, it produces its other brands itself. Among these are the 12-year-old vatted malt called Berry's All Malt, at 80 proof, and the 8-year-old blend Berry's Best. Additional brands are BLUE HANGER, CHOICEST LIQUEUR, and ST. JAMES'S.

Berry Bros. & Rudd also bottles the malt THE GLENROTHES for HIGHLAND DISTILLERIES CO.

BIG T

Blended Scotch from the TOMATIN distillery of TAKARA SHUZO & OKURA.

Available as Black Label, Gold Label, and 12-year-old De Luxe.

BISSET'S

Blended Scotch from UD.

The Bisset firm was founded in Glasgow in 1828. In 1926 it acquired the ROYAL BRACKLA distillery, which it still operates as the licensee for UD. One can assume that one of the base malts for Bisset's blend is produced there.

B. J. HOLLADAY

Kentucky straight bourbon from Mc-CORMICK.

BLACK & WHITE

Blended Scotch, 80 proof, from James BUCHANAN & Co. (UD).

An old-fashioned—that is to say, well balanced but rather strong—Scotch that is now (like VAT 69) having a rather hard time contending against its lighter competitors. Although its sales figures have fallen, B & W is still one of the most successful Scotch brands in history. Placed on the market in 1884 as Buchanan's Blend, it was also known for a time as House of Commons, after Buchanan

43

had managed to stock the bar at Parliament with it. But everyone referred to it simply as Black & White, because of its dark bottle and white label. It was accordingly registered under that name in 1904.

The base malt is DALWHINNIE. Today its greatest sales are in South Africa, Canada, and Italy. Only recently it has also become possible to buy the whisky mixed with cola in a can.

BLACKBARREL
Scottish single grain, 86 proof, from William GRANT & SONS.

It is relatively certain that this whisky comes from Grant's GIRVAN distillery. A new brand created to popularize grain whisky, Blackbarrel is aged in bourbon casks like malt whisky. Though it is said to be triple-distilled, this is not correct: Blackbarrel is distilled continuously, though by a special process developed at Girvan. The result is a light and clean whisky that aims to appeal to a younger clientele.

BLACK BARREL
Blended Scotch from H. STENHAM LTD.

Like all Stenham Scotches, this one is available as a 3-, 5-, 8-, 10-, and 12-year-old, and like the others it is meant primarily for the Latin American and Southeast Asian markets.

BLACK BOTTLE
Blended Scotch, premium, 80 proof, from Gordon Graham & Co., a subsidiary of ALLIED DISTILLERS (ALLIED DOMECQ).

The brand has been around since 1879, and has been sold since roughly 1890 in a bottle resembling a POT STILL. The formula for the blend was changed in the early 1980s (most likely to make it lighter), and since that time Black Bottle has been one of the up-and-coming brands in Scotland.

Graham & Co. belonged for a time to the U.S. concern SCHENLEY, then was acquired by the British brewer Whitbread, which gave over its liquor interests in 1990 to Allied Distillers, the present owner.

Since the Graham firm reopened the IMPERIAL distillery in 1991, one can assume that one of the base malts comes from there.

BLACK BUSH

Blended Irish whiskey, premium, 80 proof, from the BUSHMILLS distillery, which belongs to IDG (PERNOD RICARD).

A full-flavored whiskey with a high percentage of malt (roughly 75 percent, mostly 8-year-old). One might call it the big brother of the lighter White Bush (see BUSHMILLS). Black Bush is one of the most popular Irish whiskeys internationally, and it is considered by many to be Ireland's best blend, a reputation that POWER's or JAMESON would, I'm sure, dispute. Black Bush is aged mainly in sherry casks.

BLACK PRINCE

1) Blended Scotch from BURN STEWART DISTILLERS.

Currently available in 2 premium bottlings, Select and 25 Years Old, and in 3 DE LUXE versions: a 17- and a 20-year-old, both in ceramic jars, and a 12-year-old Superior.

Black Prince was originally created by a Dutch firm for the U.S. (prewar) market. Since 1991 the brand has been one of the best horses in its present owner's stall.

2) U.S. firm in Clifton that has its brands produced by unidentified distilleries (see DRAKES and R. J. HODGES).

BLACK ROOSTER

Blended Scotch from Peter J. RUSSELL.

BLACK SHIELD

Blended Scotch from Peter J. RUSSELL.

BLACK STAG

Blended Scotch, 5 years old, from W. BROWN & SONS.

BLACKTHORN

A variant of the MANHATTAN, made with ¾ oz. Irish, ¾ oz. Noilly Prat, and a few dashes of anisette and Angostura.

IMPORTED

BLACK VELVET

Canadian Whisky

A BLEND

Distilled, Aged, and Blended under the
Supervision of the Canadian Government.
40% VOL.

The Black Velvet Distilling Company,
Toronto, Canada.

PRODUCT OF CANADA

750 ml

BLACK VELVET

Canadian blend from HEUBLEIN INC., a subsidiary of IDV/Grand Metropolitan.

Internationally, the 4th-best-selling Canadian, and a sumptuous whisky for its type. The brand was created in the 1950s and consists of single whiskies that are aged for 4 years after being blended.

BLACK WATCH

Blended Scotch from HILL, THOMSON & CO. (SEAGRAM).

Black Watch was formerly sold as 100 Pipers Black Watch (see 100 PIPERS) but is today a brand of its own.

BLADNOCH

Scottish single malt (Lowlands) from UD.

A light, fresh malt that is no longer easy to find.

Original bottling: 10 years old, 86 proof.

Gordon & MacPhail: Vintages 1984, 80 proof, and 1985, 116 proof.

Cadenhead: 15 years old (distilled 1980), 116 proof.

Adelphi: 11 years old (distilled 1984), 119.8 proof; 32 years old (distilled 1958), 92 proof.

James MacArthur: 10 years old, aged in sherry casks, 86 proof.

Signatory: 8 years old, 86 proof.

The distillery was built by the McCLELLANDS in 1817, and subsequently repeatedly sold, closed, and reopened. From 1973 to 1983 it belonged to INVER HOUSE DISTILLERS. It was then bought by ARTHUR BELL & SONS (see BELL'S), and finally went to UD, which closed it in 1993. Bladnoch is the southernmost distillery in Scotland. It has 2 stills, and the water comes from the Bladnoch River.

BLAIR ATHOL

Scottish single malt (Highlands, Pitlochry) from UD.

An everyday malt with a medium body.

Original bottling: 8 years old, 80 proof, and 12 years old, 86 proof.

Cadenhead: 24 years old (distilled 1966), 116.8 proof.

James McArthur: 18 years old, 100.8 proof.

Adelphi: Vintage 1976, 113.6 proof.

The distillery was built in 1798, then immediately closed for some time and only started up again in 1825. It belonged for many years to the Mackenzie firm (see THE REAL MACKENZIE), then was sold in 1933 to Arthur Bell & Sons (see BELL'S),

BLAIR ATHOL *distillery*, established in 1798, stands on *peaty moorland* in the *foothills* of the *GRAMPIAN MOUNTAINS*. An ancient source of *water* for the *distillery, ALLT DOUR BURN ~ 'The Burn of the Otter'* flows close by. This *single MALT SCOTCH WHISKY* has a *mellow deep toned* aroma, a *strong fruity* flavour and a *smooth* finish.

which still operates it. Since 1973 Blair Athol has had 4 stills; the water comes from the nearby Ben Vrackie.

(Tel. 1796 47 21 61)

BLAIRMHOR
Scottish vatted malt, 8 years old, 80 proof, from Carmichael & Sons, a subsidiary of INVER HOUSE DISTILLERS.

BLANTON'S
Kentucky straight bourbon, 93 proof, from the LEESTOWN DISTILLING COMPANY, owned by SAZERAC.

With this brand a new era in the history of bourbon began in 1984. The first and still the most successful of all SINGLE-BARREL BOURBONS was showered with awards from the start. It also opened up for bourbon exclusive market seg-

ments previously monopolized by Scottish single malts and cognacs of XO vintage and upward. One of the reasons it is so successful is its quality: Blanton's has a truly full body and a captivating balance. The rest is the result of clever marketing, which has emphasized the fact that each bottling is available—naturally—in only a limited quantity. For single-barrel bottlings only those casks with the best distillates are used, and only after they have fully aged (as a rule, for 10 to 12 years).

Most of Blanton's production (roughly 70 percent) is—no surprise—exported to Japan.

THE BLEND
Japanese blend with a high proportion of malt, from NIKKA.

The de luxe version of this brand is called The Blend Selection. Both versions were introduced in the 1980s.

BLENDED AMERICAN WHISKEY
A type of American whiskey often designated "A Blend" on the label. U.S. blends must contain at least 20 percent STRAIGHT WHISKEY; the rest is made up of neutral grain spirits. To mask the fact that the percentage of genuine whiskey is so small, at least in terms of color, a small addition of sherry is permitted.

Once the percentage of straight whiskey exceeds 51 percent, it is also

THE HOUSE OF

Seagram

FINE WHISKIES SINCE 1857

possible to call it blended bourbon or blended rye.

Blended Americans are lighter and cheaper than straights. They were relatively popular in the 1950s and 1960s, in large part thanks to enormous advertising by the Canadian spirit concern SEAGRAM. Even today, SEAGRAM'S 7 CROWN is the biggest-selling blend in the United States. In the 1970s this type of whiskey lost a considerable amount of the market share. People began to gravitate toward Canadian whisky, which—in terms of production and character—may well have been the model on which blended American whiskeys were based. (The Seagram firm could not care less; it is also one of the largest producers of Canadian.) At that time Americans were also beginning to prefer clear spirits, especially vodka—and why not? Blended American doesn't give you much more taste than vodka, and you certainly feel it more the next morning. (Seagram also produces vodka, needless to say.)

A list of brands is provided in the appendix.

BLENDED SCOTCH WHISKY

A mixture of MALT and GRAIN whiskies, the most popular type of whisky in the world.

Scotch whisky attained its worldwide stature in this diluted form, probably because the addition of the lighter-bodied grains takes away some of the intensity of the malt—the very quality that makes malt so attractive to connoisseurs. The quality of a blend depends not only on the percentage (5–70 percent) and age of the malt used, but also on its composition: the art of blending consists of putting together up to 50 different malts with 2 or 3 grains to create a balanced and, if possible, unmistakable whole. Lowland malts play a special role in blending; they serve to bond Highland and Islay malts, with their distinctive character, to more neutral grains.

The recipes for the many different brands are secrets known only to the blend masters, and they are often assed down from generation to generation. Nevertheless, a blend's taste changes over the years. A given single whisky may no longer be available, or the recipe may be changed in a deliberate attempt to adapt to changing public tastes. It used to be, for example, that buyers sought out deep-colored, smoky blends, but now the milder, less intense, and light-bodied brands predominate (see LIGHT WHISK(E)Y).

Although its sales have now fallen somewhat, blended Scotch is still the biggest-selling type of whisk(e)y in the world—much to the dismay of malt whisky lovers, who watch in horror as more than 90 percent of the entire malt production disappears into blends. But they should recognize that it is the success of blended Scotch that keeps most malt distilleries in operation; without it, malt would have remained as little known as, say, Armagnac.

The history of blended Scotch begins with the invention of the PATENT STILL in 1830. It was that still that made it possible to produce grain whisk(e)y, but it would be a few more decades before mixtures of malts and grains could make their way. The pioneers in the practice of blending were A. Usher (see USHER'S GREEN STRIPE), Wm SANDERSON, and W. P. Lowrie (see LOWRIE'S). The first brands were VAT 69, DEWAR'S, HAIG, WHITE HORSE, and BLACK & WHITE. (See also SCOTCH WHISKY.)

BLENDED WHISK(E)Y
The majority of the whiskies that now reach the market are blends—mixtures of malt or straight whiskey with either grain whisk(e)y or neutral spirits. The majority of these are created in accordance with the Scottish practice (see BLENDED SCOTCH WHISKY, BLENDED AMERICAN WHISKEY, CANADIAN WHISKY, IRISH WHISKEY, JAPANESE WHISKY, etc.).

BL GOLD LABEL See BULLOCH LADE & Co.

BLOOD & SAND
A tall drink related to the WHISKEY SOUR. Pour 3/4 oz. Scotch, 3/4 oz. vermouth rosso, 1/2 oz. cherry brandy, and 1 1/2 oz. orange juice over ice in a shaker. Shake vigorously and strain.

BLUE HANGER
Blended Scotch, 91.2 proof, from BERRY BROS. & RUDD.

BLUE HANGER
BLENDED
SCOTS WHISKY

BERRY BROS & RUDD LTD
Established in the XVII Century
at 3 St James's Street, London

This brand has been in existence since the beginning of the century; it was named after William "Blue" Hanger, a Berry customer widely considered to have been one of the best-dressed men of the 18th century.

B.N.J. See BAILIE NICOL JARVIE.

BOBBIE BURNS

A Scotch MANHATTAN with a dash of Benedictine instead of Angostura (see also ROBBIE BURNS).

BOILER MAKER

The name for a classic American drinking ritual in which one chases a shot of rye with a can of beer. According to Humphrey Bogart's son Stephen, the custom was followed religiously on the actor's yacht. Today it doesn't necessarily have to be rye—it is said that tequila delivers just as well. The Scottish variant is known as A HALF AND A NIP.

BOND 7

Australian blended whiskey from GILBEY (IDV/Grand Metropolitan).

IDV continues to sell the brand i Africa and Latin America, but produc tion has ceased (see AUSTRALIAN WHISKEY).

BOOKER'S

Kentucky straight bourbon from JIM BEAM Brands (AMERICAN BRANDS).

Booker's arrived on the market in 1989 as the first of the so-called SMALL-BATCH BOURBONS, but in fact i is a SINGLE-BARREL BOTTLING (that is a single-cask bottling). It is 6 to 8 years old as a rule and ranges from 120 to 126 proof.

This whiskey comes exclusivel from casks that have aged in the cente of the warehouse, where the tempera ture, ventilation, and light condition are optimal. It is one of the few bour bons that are not filtered before bot tling. One senses as much, for despite its high alcohol content, Booker's i gentle and balanced. Bourbons of this quality should be drunk neat, yet Booker Noe, Jim Beam's former stillman and the man after whom the brand was named, insists that Booker's is best with ice and a splash of water. He calls the mixture "Kentucky tea."

BOSTON SOUR

A WHISKEY SOUR with egg white.

BOSWELL'S RESERVE

Blended Scotch, 12 years old, from Brodie Crawford & Co. (see BRODIE'S SUPREME).

The brand was introduced in 1995, on the 200th anniversary of the death of the Scottish travel writer James Boswell.

Born in 1740, Boswell wrote, among other books, a biography of his friend Samuel Johnson, the great English man of letters. It was Johnson, in turn, who maintained that "no other invention has given mankind as much pleasure as a good pub."

BOTTLED IN BOND

A law passed in the United States in 1897 established that under certain conditions a whiskey could be stored in bond. It is necessary that the whiskey be aged for at least 4 years, have an alcohol content of 100 proof, and derive from only a single distillation. Although at first these regulations were meant to provide tax relief

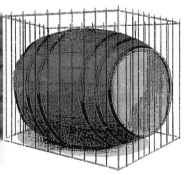

for distillers, the designation "bottled in bond" became to some extent a guarantee of quality, for at that time the notion of allowing whiskey to age for longer periods was foreign to many producers, and merchants tended routinely to dilute their product with tea, sherry, or anything else that came to mind.

Today the designation "bottled in bond" indicates above all that the whiskey comes from a single year and was not blended from distillates of different ages (see OLD TAYLOR).

BOTTLING

Before it is placed in bottles, whisk(e)y is filtered (see FILTRATION) and diluted with water to a drinking strength of from 80 to 86 proof (see ALCOHOL CONTENT). This takes place either after a blend is created or, in the case of MALT and STRAIGHT WHISKEY, after the barrels destined for bottling have been mixed together. Since every barrel produces a whisk(e)y like no other, a number of different ones—even from different years—are combined so as to obtain the most consistent possible product.

Whisk(e)y is bottled either in the distillery itself (this is the rule in Ireland and in the United States; in Scotland, only in the case of GLEN-FIDDICH and SPRINGBANK) or in huge plants to which it is transported in either barrels or steel tanks.

One should also be aware of so-called INDEPENDENT BOTTLERS, especially with regard to malt whiskies. These are firms that buy malts from individual distilleries and bottle them themselves. They are generally more flexible and more open to experiment than the producers, and they often come up with fresh ideas. In the last few years, for example, they have introduced SINGLE-BARREL BOTTLING. In this case the whisk(e)y is bottled undiluted and generally unfiltered, always from a single cask.

It has been the norm to sell whisk(e)y in bottles only since the end of the 19th century. Earlier, producers supplied dealers and taverns with the fresh distillate, leaving it up to them whether to let it age longer or to tinker with it—diluting it with water, for example, or adding color-

ing and flavoring agents such as saffron or tea. By the time the consumer ultimately acquired its product—in casks, stoneware jars, or other refillable containers—the distillery could no longer guarantee its quality. This practice was abandoned once quality-conscious producers switched to aging their whisk(e)y themselves and marketing it in labeled bottles. A label ensured that one was buying a recognizable product of guaranteed quality—in other words, a brand. The first brands, still with us today, were POWER's in Ireland (1894); CANADIAN CLUB in Canada (1884); OLD FORESTER in the United States (1874); and—probably—VAT 69 in Scotland (1882).

BOURBON
A type of American whiskey no longer defined by the place of its origin—Bourbon County, Kentucky, where in fact there isn't a single whiskey distillery left—but rather by the specific process by which it is produced. Theoretically, bourbon can

distilled anywhere in the United States, so long as it is done according to rules established by law in 1964: the whiskey must be distilled from a mash containing at least 51 but less than 80 percent corn, and it must be aged a minimum of 2 years. (If the proportion of corn in the mash is higher than 80 percent, the resulting distillate is CORN WHISKEY.) The remainder of the mash is made up of 5 to 15 percent malted barley, which promotes the fermentation, and 5 to 15 percent rye, which gives the whiskey its flavor. In some brands—MAKER'S MARK, OLD FITZGERALD, OLD RIP VAN WINKLE, REBEL YELL, W. L. WELLER—the rye is replaced by wheat, to make the bourbon milder. The higher the percentage of corn—75 to 78 percent is common—the sweeter the whiskey. (The grain mixture is called the "mashbill.")

Today bourbons are made by the SOUR MASH process. So the designation "sour mash" on a label is not an additional mark of quality, though some firms try to imply that it is. The amount of alcohol in the raw distillate cannot exceed 80 percent by volume, a regulation justified by the recognition that the hotter the still the less taste in the product. Today distillers gener-ally strive for 65 percent by volume.

Like all straight whiskeys, bourbon is distilled twice: first in a columnar apparatus related to the PATENT STILL, which in the United States (unlike in Scotland) consists of a single copper pipe. The first distillate ("low wines") has an alcohol content of between 55 and 60 percent by volume. This is distilled again, either in liquid form in a "doubler" or in the form of steam in a "thumper." Both of these resemble a POT STILL in shape. The result of the second distillation is called the "white dog" and has an alcohol content of 62 to 65 percent by volume.

THE ORIGINAL SOUR MASH
OLD CROW
KENTUCKY STRAIGHT BOURBON WHISKEY

The fresh distillate is stored in oak barrels that have been partially charred inside. The charcoal gives it its typical vanilla and caramel flavors. The barrels can be used only once. New barrels naturally have a stronger effect than old ones, and so bourbon does not have to age as long as Scotch, for example. The used barrels are either exported to Scotland and Ireland or used for other spirits. If the distillate is aged for less than 4 years, that fact must be indicated on the label, so the absence of an age on a label means the bourbon is at least 4 years old. Most brands are made up of single whiskeys from 4 to 6 years old; the better ones, of 6- to 8-year-olds. Aging for over 10 years is uncommon. Europeans tend to be confused by the fact that different ages of the same bourbon are sometimes given different names (as is the case at HEAVEN HILL DISTILLERS, for example).

Bourbon is distilled with soft mineral-free water that has percolated through limestone—the kind of water abundant in Kentucky. It is unquestionably the best-known U.S. whiskey, and like so many of the truly American contributions to civilization—rhythm and blues, peanut butter and Coca Cola—it is a product of the American South. The settlers of that region began growing corn and distilling it in around 1770; a census taken shortly after Kentucky attained statehood in 1792 counted more than 2,000 distilleries.

Even so, bourbon was for a long time overshadowed by RYE WHISKEY, the

most popular type of whiskey in the United States until the turn of the century. By the end of Prohibition, Canadian and Scotch whiskies had come to dominate the market, and even after World War II, when bourbon was perceived as part of "the American way of life" and had conquered the rest of the world, the United States in fact consumed more Canadian whisky than bourbon. That is still the case today, although bourbon has recently regained some of its image after a slump in the 1970s and 1980s, especially since the arrival of the so-called SINGLE-BARREL and SMALL-BATCH bourbons. These noble whiskeys are now considered acceptable by even the most demanding palates and are especially prized in the lucrative markets of the Far East.

BOURBON DELUXE

Kentucky straight bourbon from JIM BEAM Brands (AMERICAN BRANDS).

This brand has recently become available as a blended American as well.

BOURBON HIGHBALL

Pour 1¾ oz. bourbon over ice in a tall glass, fill with ginger ale, and garnish with lemon peel. Lemon-flavored sodas (7-Up, for example) can be used instead of ginger ale (see also HORSE'S NECK).

BOURBON SUPREME

Kentucky straight bourbon from SHERMAN.

A small brand originally produced in Pekin, Illinois, by the American Distilling firm.

BOURBONTOWN CLUB

Kentucky straight bourbon from KENTUCKY BOURBON DISTILLERS.

BOWMORE

Scottish single malt (Islay) from MORRISON BOWMORE DISTILLERS (SUNTORY).

One of the greatest names on the malt scene, considered by many the quintessential Islay, since it combines the peaty strength of the southern Islay malts with the mildness of those from the north. Bowmore is a top brand internationally, showered with honors, and is expected to attain even greater stature, although some claim that earlier bottlings were considerably better (stronger) than the current ones. This may be in part because Bowmore, like all Morrison malts, is now diluted to drinking strength and bottled in Glasgow, where the water cannot compare with the peaty Islay spring water.

Original bottling: In addition to the simple version, Legend, with no indication of age, 80 proof, Bowmore is available at 10 and 12 years old, each 80 proof; at 17, 21, and 25 years old, each 86 proof; also as Mariner, 15 years old, 86 proof; Moonlight, 22 years old, 86 proof; and Seadragon, 30 years old, 86 proof.

There are also a few limited editions: a 21-year-old sherry-cask bottling from 1972, 98.2 proof; a 20-year-old single-barrel bottling from 1973, 113.6 proof; and the legendary Black Bowmore, a sherry-cask bottling from 1964, at 98 and 100 proof, bottled at 29, 30, and 31 years of age, a delight for which any connoisseur would willingly go into debt.

Cadenhead: 12 years old (distilled 1983), 122 proof; 14 years old (distilled 1981), 118.6 proof.

The distillery was built in 1779, and beginning in 1963 it belonged to the Stanley P. Morrison firm, which developed into Morrison Bowmore. In 1989

the Japanese whisky concern Suntory bought 35 percent of Morrison Bowmore, and since 1994 it has been the majority shareholder. Bowmore has 4 stills and its own malting floors. It is the only Islay distillery that makes generous use of sherry casks. The water comes from the Laggan River.

(Tel. 1496 81 04 41)

BOW STREET See JAMESON.

BRACKLA See ROYAL BRACKLA.

BRAES OF GLENLIVET (BREVAL)
Scottish single malt (Speyside, Tomintoul) produced by the CHIVAS & GLENLIVET GROUP for SEAGRAM. A strong malt that is not being bottled officially at the moment. Chivas intends to market it in future under the name Breval, so as to avoid confusion with THE GLENLIVET.

Cadenhead: 8 years old (distilled 1987), 125.4 proof.

Signatory: 15 years old, 86 proof; 1979, 100 proof.

The computerized distillery was built in 1973–74. Its 6 stills are copies of those of STRATHISLA; the water comes from Pitilie Burn (see ALLT-Á-BHAINNE).

BRAZILIAN WHISKEY
The Brazilians are not only very fond of whiskey—especially since the 1950s—but they are also among the largest alcohol producers in the world. Of course, this is in part because alcohol is used there as fuel as well. The country continues to import a great deal of Scotch, but it also produces domestic whiskeys; for example, DRURY'S, GREGSON'S, and OLD EIGHT.

BRETON'S HAND & SEAL
Canadian blend from the Glenora Distillery, property of Great Northern Distillery, a subsidiary of HEUBLEIN INC. (IDV/Grand Metropolitan).

A new brand from a new distillery in Cape Breton, Nova Scotia. Glenora is a so-called micro-distillery, which is to say that most of the work is done by hand and the output is relatively small. Currently this whisky is available only in Atlanta, Chicago, and Denver.

BREVAL See BRAES OF GLENLIVET.

BRISTOL VAT
Blended Scotch from AVERY'S OF BRISTOL LTD.

BRITANNIA BLENDED WHISKEY
Blended American from MONTEBELLO.

BRODIE'S SUPREME
Blended Scotch from Brodie Crawford & Co., a trading firm in Surrey particularly oriented toward the export business. Other Brodie brands are BOSWELL'S RESERVE, FIRTH HOUSE,

and McDowall. In addition there are the vatted malt THE GLENMOY and ROYAL LORD CANADIAN RYE.

BROKER'S RESERVE

Blended American from HOOD RIVER, a firm that has been in existence in Portland, Oregon, since 1934 and has its whiskey produced by an unidentified distillery.

BROOKLYN

A MANHATTAN variant based on rye whiskey. Stir ¾ oz. vermouth rosso, 1 oz. rye whiskey, and a few dashes of Maraschino in ice and strain into a cocktail glass.

BROOKSTONE

Blended American from SAZERAC.

BRORA

Scottish single malt (Northern Highlands) from AINSLIE & HEILBRON (UD).

A strong and highly intriguing malt that is unfortunately no longer produced.

Original bottling: 22 years old (distilled 1972), 117.6 proof ("Rare Malts Selection").

Gordon & MacPhail: Vintage 1972, 80 proof.

Cadenhead: 13 years old (distilled 1982), 119.8 and 120.8 proof.

The history of this distillery is somewhat complicated. It was built in 1819, and until 1969 it was known as CLYNELISH. In that year its owners opened a second distillery on the same property, which was also called Clynelish. The old Clynelish was closed, and in 1975 it was reopened under the name Brora, then closed down again in 1983. It has since served as a warehouse for the new Clynelish distillery. Thus Brora is the malt produced in the old distillery between 1975 and 1983. Clynelish, on the other hand, is the whisky produced either in the old distillery before 1969 or since that date in the new one. In both cases the water comes from the Clynemilton Burn.

BROWN, W. & SONS

Scottish trading firm founded in Glasgow in 1976. It bottles its main brand, GLEN STUART, exclusively for export, and also bottles the brands ANCIENT PRIVILEGE, BLACK STAG, CAIRNDEW MIST, and DIPLOMATIC PRIVILEGE.

BROWN-FORMAN

U.S. producer in Louisville, Kentucky, one of the largest spirit concerns in

"GUARDING A GOOD THING IN ARIZONA"

against Prohibition. He published a pamphlet called "The Holy Bible Repudiates Prohibition." It includes quotations from the Bible that place alcohol in the proper light, as a gift from God.

During Prohibition the Browns did a thriving business in medicinal alcohol and bought the EARLY TIMES DISTILLERY, in Louisville, Kentucky, which is the firm's headquarters to this day.

There is another Early Times distillery in Shively, Kentucky, where the brands Early Times and Old Forester are produced. In addition, the firm owns JACK DANIEL'S in Tennessee and CANADIAN MIST in Canada.

Brands: CANADIAN MIST, EARLY TIMES, GENTLEMAN JACK, JACK DANIEL'S OLD NO. 7, OLD FORESTER, and SOUTHERN COMFORT.

In the near future Brown-Forman plans to issue a SMALL-BATCH BOURBON (Woodford Reserve), to be produced at the Labrot & Graham Distillery, currently under renovation.

BROWN FOX

A digestif cocktail. Stir 1½ oz. bourbon with ¾ oz. Benedictine on ice in a tumbler.

BRUICHLADDICH

Scottish single malt (Islay, Argyll) from

the world. The majority owners are the Brown family, descendants of Scottish immigrants who began trading in whiskey in 1870. Two years later they brought out their first brand, OLD FORESTER, and went down in the history of bourbon as the inventors of original bottling. They were the first to offer their whiskey in labeled bottles— at a time when most distillers sold their product in casks and left it up to middlemen or barkeeps to mix it and sell it as they chose.

George Brown, the head of the firm around the turn of the century, was heavily involved in the fight

Invergordon Distillers (Whyte & Mackay, American Brands).

One of the milder Islay malts, with only a hint of peat. Bruichladdich is often suggested as a beginner's Islay, but since it is by no means typical of the island it would seem more logical to present a first-timer with Bowmore.

Original bottling: 10 and 15 years old, 80 proof; 21 years old, 86 proof; 25 years old, 90 proof ("Stillman's Dram").

Gordon & MacPhail: Vintage 1964 90 and 100.8 proof.

Dun Eideann: 19 years old (distilled 1970), 92 proof.

The distillery was founded in 1881 and for a time belonged to Joseph W. Hobbs (Ben Nevis). Since 1968 it has been operated by Invergordon. It has 4 stills (since 1975); the water comes from the surrounding hills. When Bruichladdich was shut down in 1995, much of its original equipment was still being used.

(Tel. 1496 85 02 21)

BUCHANAN, JAMES & CO.

Scottish producers since 1884. The founder, James Buchanan (1849–1935), spent his apprenticeship in the Mackinlay house. He was not only one of the pioneers of the blending industry, but also one of the first to recognize the power of advertising. With it, he managed to make his Black & White one of the most successful brands to this day. In 1894 he built the Convalmore distillery (now closed) with W. P. Lowrie (see Lowrie's), the firm that had previously supplied him with malts. He later took over Lowrie altogether. At Convalmore and at the Glentauchers distillery, which he acquired in 1898, Buchanan experimented around 1910 with continuously distilled malt whisky. It was a failure for obvious reasons, but his attempts illustrate the pioneering spirit of those years. In 1915 he formed Scotch Whisky Brands

Ltd. with John Dewar, and in the following years that concern acquired additional distilleries, among them Port Ellen and Benrinnes. Buchanan further distinguished himself as the owner of a stable of racehorses, as a philanthropist, and later as Lord Woolavington of Lavington.

In 1925 Buchanan & Co. joined the DCL, and it now belongs to UD, for which it operates the 2 distilleries Dalwhinnie and Glentauchers.

In addition to the 12-year-old de luxe blend Buchanan's Reserve, 86 proof, which is based on Dalwhinnie and is sold almost exclusively in Latin America, the firm continues to produce Black & White and a vatted malt called Strathconon.

BUCKTROUT'S GOLD LABEL

Blended Scotch that was once bottled by Bucktrout & Co. exclusively for the Channel Island of Guernsey. The firm started out as a tobacco, wine, and spirit business. It is unlikely that it is still bottling the brand itself.

BUENA VISTA

Blended Irish whiskey, 80 proof, from the Midleton Distillery of IDG (Pernod Ricard).

A highly unusual name for an Irish whiskey, but you won't find it in Ireland anyway. The brand is produced exclusively for the Buena Vista Café in San Francisco. This bar is thought to have initiated the Irish coffee boom in the early 1950s. To this day the drink is still so popular there that they serve roughly half a million Irish coffees a year, and obviously it pays them to do their own importing. (See also Dunphys.)

BULLEIT

Kentucky straight bourbon, 90 and 101 proof, from the Leestown Distilling Company, owned by Sazerac.

A private label—that is to say, one of the regular whiskeys from Leestown that appears with a different label. Originally Bulleit was bottled solely for an attorney in Lexington, Kentucky, but he has recently begun exporting the whiskey to the Far East, and you even find it sometimes in Germany. Bulleit is the name of a Kentucky county.

BULLOCH LADE & CO.

A firm established in Glasgow in 1855. Until 1920 it operated a number of distilleries, among them Caol Ila, in which it produced its famous

blend BL Gold Label, first marketed in 1857. The brand was for a time so successful that supplies could not meet the demand. But World War I did the business in. Bulloch Lade miscalculated with an advertising campaign and was taken over by the DCL. Today it is part of UD, for which it runs Caol Ila and produces the blends BL and King Arthur.

BUNNAHABHAIN
[Gaelic for "river mouth"]

Scottish single malt (Islay, Port Askaig) from Highland Distilleries Co.

A relatively light malt by Islay standards, but that has not always been the case. It was only when the producers abandoned the original spring in the surrounding peat in favor of water piped down from nearby hills that Bunnahabhain lost the strength typical of the island's malts.

Original bottling: 12 years old, 80 proof.

Signatory: 26 years old (distilled 1969, sherry cask), 105.2 and 106.6 proof.

The distillery was built in 1881–82 and has been a part of Highland Distilleries since 1887. It has 4 stills, and the aging takes place in part in sherry casks. Bunnahabhain is a base malt for The Famous Grouse.

(Tel. 1496 84 06 46)

BUNRATTY EXPORT POTCHEEN
Irish spirit from the firm Bunratty Mead & Liqueur Co.

Potcheen in Gaelic means whiskey that is distilled illegally, or untaxed (see Poitín). Bunratty's brand cannot even be sold in Ireland, but since the firm pays its taxes there the term is a misnomer in any case. Far milder than true bootleg liquor, the whiskey is available mainly in duty-free shops and in the upscale London department store Fortnum & Mason.

BURBERRY
Blended Scotch bottled by Burn Stewart for the clothing store Burberry. Available as a premium, as

a 12-, 15-, or 25-year-old de luxe, and as a 15-year-old vatted malt.

BURNSIDE

Scottish single malt (Campbeltown), 15 years old, 92 proof, from EAGLESOME (J. A. MITCHELL).

A malt from the SPRINGBANK distillery has been available under this name for some time. Apparently it acquired the rights to the name from the old Burnside distillery, which operated in Campbeltown from 1825 to 1924.

BURN STEWART

Blended Scotch from BURN STEWART DISTILLERS.

Available as a 12-year-old de luxe blend; its main markets are France, South Africa, Japan, and Taiwan.

BURN STEWART DISTILLERS

This Glasgow firm came into being in 1988 as the result of a management buyout. It owns 2 malt distilleries, DEANSTON (acquired from INVERGORDON DISTILLERS in 1990) and TOBERMORY (since 1993), and has in addition to Burn Stewart a number of other brands in its program: BLACK PRINCE, BURBERRY, DRUMGRAY, GLEN

BLAIR, HIGHLAND ROSE, OLD ARGYLL, OLD ROYAL, SCOTTISH LEADER, and the single malt liqueur WALLACE.

In 1994 Burn Stewart began a joint venture with a Chinese spirit producer.

BUSHMILLS

Irish brand and distillery in County Antrim (Northern Ireland), owned by IDG (PERNOD RICARD).

The Old Bushmills Distillery is considered to be the oldest whiskey distillery in the world. The date 1608, given on the label as the year of its founding, refers only to the distilling license that was granted at that time to the entire area around the village of Bushmills. The first distillery to carry the name dates from 1784. The rest of Bushmills' history is difficult to reconstruct, for in 1941 the firm's records—along with large quantities of whiskey—were destroyed in a German bombing raid. We do know that the distillery was bought in 1921 by Samuel Boyd, a wealthy Belfast wine and spirit dealer who shrewdly wrote temperance tracts on the side. His successors

acquired the Coleraine Distillery as well in 1936, and ran the business under various owners (for a time, Seagram) until 1973. The year before, the firm IDG had taken over Bushmills; it is now part of the French spirit empire Pernod Ricard.

The distillery currently produces malt whiskey exclusively, securing the grain for its blends from the other IDG distillery, Midleton.

It produces the following brands: Bushmills Malt is a single malt of the Scottish type, although here the grain is not dried over peat. This, and the Irish practice of distilling 3 times, make Bushmills whiskeys somewhat milder than their Scottish cousins. Bushmills Malt is marketed in 2 versions: a 5-year-old was put out in 1992 solely for the Italian market; it is 80 proof and for all its gentleness betrays its long aging in sherry casks. The 10-year-old came out in 1984 and has since become one of the great Irish whiskey brands internationally. It too is light-bodied, and 80 proof, but it is aged mainly in bourbon casks.

A single-barrel malt at cask strength is sometimes available from Cadenhead. Recently they had a 16-year-old at 116.8 proof; this whiskey has a fullness not otherwise associated with Bushmills.

Another malt called Bushmills Millennium will be marketed in a limited edition for the year 2000. It has been aging since 1975 in sherry casks, but before it is bottled it will also spend some time in bourbon casks, for 25 years in sherry casks would doubtless rob it of too much of its true character.

Bushmills Original (formerly Old Bushmills) is a light, simple blend, 80 proof, also called White Bush because of its white label. It is the oldest brand from the house of Bushmills and consists essentially of 3-year-old grain whiskeys and 6-year-old malts (roughly 30 percent). Its older variant is called Black Bush. Bushmills 1608 is a very well-balanced 12-year-old de luxe blend with roughly 90 percent malt. It is available only in duty-free shops worldwide and is 86 proof. There is a new 16-year-old bottling of single malt called Three Woods, which is aged in bourbon, oloroso, and port casks successively.

The distillery also produces a blend called Coleraine.

(Tel. 1265 73 15 21)

BUSH PILOT'S PRIVATE RESERVE
Straight Canadian, 13 years old, 86 proof, from Robert Denton, a small firm in Michigan.

This is probably the only Canadian that is marketed as an undiluted single-barrel bottling. It is distilled from corn, for the most part, and yet its taste is amazingly dry.

I have not been able to discover which distillery produces this whisky but it is bottled for a Canadian association that charters sport airplanes.

C

"Honestly," Mrs. Morse said,
"I wouldn't close an eye if I didn't go to bed
full of Scotch."

Dorothy Parker,
Big Blonde

CABIN HOLLOW

Kentucky straight corn whiskey, 100 proof, from BARTON DISTILLING (Canandaigua).

A true cowboy whiskey that is sold almost exclusively in Alabama.

CABIN STILL

Kentucky straight bourbon, 80, 86, and 90 proof, from HEAVEN HILL DISTILLERS.

A pleasantly dry bourbon that was formerly produced by STITZEL-WELLER and then belonged to UD, which sold the remaining casks in 1992 to Heaven Hill. At the moment, the bourbons are still being bottled out of the original casks, but in future Heaven Hill plans to produce the brand itself.

CADENHEAD, WM

Scotland's oldest INDEPENDENT BOTTLER (founded in 1842). The firm uses the bottling plant of the SPRINGBANK distillery, which, like Cadenhead itself, belongs to the J. A. MITCHELL family.

Cadenhead is rightly proud of having prepared the way for the SINGLE-BARREL BOTTLINGS so popular today —of selling, in other words, the only "true" whisky. Cadenhead has always carried only unfiltered malts and, since 1991, exclusively at cask strength. (Until then the were diluted to 92 proof.) What ma ters to them is the individuality of th given distillate and not the continuit of a specific brand.

Until 1994 the firm also produce various malts (for example, ARDBEC TALISKER) under the Duthie's label

In addition, Cadenhead also has few blends (PUTACHIESIDE, HIELAN MAN, MOIDART) and has very consid erable holdings of Demerara rum stored in oak barrels. Its headquar ters are in Aberdeen, but in Edin burgh it has a small shop that i typical of Cadenhead: uncluttere but well organized, run by 2 devote specialists.

(172 Canongate, Tel. 131 556 58 64, Fax 55 25 27)

CAIRNBAAN
Blended Scotch from EAGLESOME, a subsidiary of J. & A. MITCHELL. The base malt is SPRINGBANK.

CAIRNDEW MIST
Blended Scotch from W. BROWN & SONS.

CALDWELL'S
Blended American from M. S. WALKER.

CALGARY TRAIL
Canadian blend from PHILLIPS.

CALVERT
Blended American from JIM BEAM BRANDS (AMERICAN BRANDS).

Not to be confused with LORD CALVERT, the Canadian from the same firm.

CAMBUS
Scottish single grain from the Cambus distillery of UD.

Light, Delicate, Exquisite.

PURE

CAMBUS
Patent Still
Scotch Grain Whisky

7 Years Old.   Matured in Wood

The Whisky with an individuality—totally different in all odeurs in peculiar delicacy and charm of flavour—mild and mellow. A sound, natural, wholesome stimulant, that ministers to good health and neither affects the head nor the liver.

Cambus is not a Pot Still Whisky.

Ask your Wine Merchant for CAMBUS.
3/6 · Bottle, 42/- a Case

THE DISTILLERS CO., LTD.
EDINBURGH.

The distillery was opened at Alloa (Lowlands) in 1806 and was refitted for grain production in 1936. It was absorbed into the DCL in 1877 and was, until its closing in 1993, one of the highly respected producers of UD blends. Cambus is still being bottled in small quantities as a single. Cadenhead recently had a 31-year-old at 106.4 proof.

CAMERON BRIG (CHOICE OLD)
Scottish single grain from UD.

One of the few grains regularly available on the market. The standard bottling is said to have aged for 9 years in the cask; however, its intense color leads many experts to suspect a generous addition of caramel.

One also occasionally finds a vintage bottling from 1959 at 106.4 proof.

The whisky comes from the Cameron Bridge distillery in Fife. That concern has been operated since 1824 by the Haigs (see JOHN HAIG & Co.), who experimented there with PATENT STILL variants as early as 1830. In the 1920s it changed over completely to the production of grain whisky, and then in 1989 it also began making gin.

CAMPBELL DISTILLERS
Scottish producer with headquarters in Kilwinning, Ayrshire. The firm was

originally a family business that began producing blends in 1879. It acquired the ABERLOUR distillery in 1945. Until 1974 it called itself House of Campbell, but then the French concern PERNOD RICARD took it over. Under its new owner it acquired the WHITELEY firm in 1982, and with it the distillery EDRADOUR and various blends. A few years later it also bought the distillery GLENALLACHIE.

Since 1988, under its present name, the concern has been responsible for its French owner's Scotch interests. (A listing appears under the heading PERNOD RICARD.)

CAMPBELTOWN
Scottish whisky region. That Campbeltown is considered even today a separate production center for malt whisky doubtless has to do with its history, for this town in the south of the Mull of Kintyre peninsula was one of the most important centers for Scotland's whisky industry up until the 1920s. Of the more than 30 distilleries that once operated here only 2 are still open: GLEN SCOTIA and SPRINGBANK. Even though the latter produces 2 different malts (see LON-

GROW), it is impossible to identify a special Campbeltown flavor.

CAMPBELTOWN LOCH
Blended Scotch from EAGLESOME, a subsidiary of J. A. MITCHELL.

It is certain that the base for this 10-year-old premium brand comes from SPRINGBANK.

CANADA HOUSE
Canadian blend from JIM BEAM Brands (AMERICAN BRANDS).

A smaller brand for the U.S. market.

CANADIAN AGE
Blended American from the LEESTOWN DISTILLING COMPANY, owned by SAZERAC.

An unusual name for a U.S. whiskey; however, this one is produced solely for the Canadian market.

CANADIAN CLUB
Canadian blend from HIRAM WALKER & SONS (ALLIED DOMECQ).

Canada's grand old brand has been around since 1884. It was this label that set the light, clean style for Canadian and established its worldwide fame (see CANADIAN WHISKY). Today CC, as it is often called, is the second-biggest-selling Canadian.

Unlike most Canadian brands, this one is blended before aging in barrels—for 6 years in the case of the standard version and 12 years for the De Luxe Canadian Club Classic.

CANADIAN DELUXE
Canadian blend from David SHERMAN.

CANADIAN GOLD
Canadian blend from KASSER LAIRD.

CANADIAN HOST
Canadian blend from BARTON (Canandaigua).

The Kentucky firm Barton imports this whisky in bulk, bottling it in its own plants for the U.S. market.

CANADIAN HUNTER
Canadian blend, 80 proof, from SEAGRAM.

One of the many Canadians produced exclusively for the U.S. market, though of course the American buyers are assured that Canadian Hunter was created especially for the fearless adventurers of Canada's northern wilderness.

CANADIAN LAKE
Canadian blend from MAJESTIC.

CANADIAN LEAF
Canadian blend from MAJESTIC.

CANADIAN LTD.
Canadian blend from BARTON (Canandaigua).

This brand belongs to the Barton subsidiary GLENMORE, formerly part of UD. Even today the whisky is distilled in the Canadian UD distillery VALLEYFIELD (this is known as "contract distilling") but bottled by Barton in the United States and marketed there exclusively.

CANADIAN MIST
Canadian blend from BROWN-FORMAN.

The U.S. concern acquired this brand in the early 1970s and soon made it the best-selling Canadian in the United States. By now Canadian Mist is the largest-selling whisky of its type worldwide.

Since 1995, the 8-year-old Canadian Mist 1885 Special Reserve 21 has been available in addition to the pleasing standard version. This de luxe edition was created to celebrate the centennial of the completion of the Canadian Pacific Railroad.

CANADIAN PEAK
Canadian blend from MAJESTIC.

CANADIAN RESERVE
Canadian blend from CONSOLIDATED, produced by Canadian Lake, a subsidiary of HIRAM WALKER & SONS.

CANADIAN SPRINGS
Canadian blend from SHERMAN.

This brand is produced in Canada and bottled and marketed in the United States.

CANADIAN SUPREME
Canadian blend from BARTON (Canandaigua).

Imported and bottled exclusively for the U.S. market.

CANADIAN WHISKY
Canadian blend is relatively mild tasting. At best it is distinguished by a sharp, rye-derived fruitiness. It lacks the intensity of a Scotch or bourbon, which may be one of the reasons why it is so successful. With its roughly 200 million bottles a year, Canada is the third-largest whisky producer in the work. The most successful brands are CANADIAN MIST, CANADIAN CLUB, CROWN ROYAL, BLACK VELVET, and SEAGRAM'S V.O. (There is a complete brand listing in the appendix.)

Canadian is the classic basis for a MANHATTAN cocktail, but it is also ideal for tall drinks.

History: The history of Canadian whisky is essentially dominated by two names: SEAGRAM and HIRAM WALKER & SONS.

Hiram Walker (1816–99), who had made a fortune producing vinegar and had built a small town in southern Ontario called Walkerville, began distilling whiskey in 1854. As was customary at the time, he started out by selling his distillate fresh from the still. It was then colored with all manner of additives and marketed as whisky. A farsighted man, Walker soon recognized that times were changing, and that the future belonged not to the raw rotgut of the woodsman but to drinks better suited to the tastes of people in the growing industrial cities. He began to experiment and finally developed the methods that are still used today and that give Canadian its typically mild, dry flavor: slow, intense distilling and diluting with neutral spirits.

In addition, while other producers were still selling their wares by the cask, leaving it to others to retail it in pitchers or carafes, Walker began marketing his Canadian Club in labeled bottles. He thus became one of the pioneers of brand whiskies. Canadian Club was an immediate success, especially in the major cities of the United States, and it set the style for Canadian blends up to the present day.

The story of the Seagram firm begins in 1883, when Joseph E. Sea-gram, the son of an English immigrant, acquired a distillery in Waterloo, Ontario. With his brand Seagram's V.O., launched in 1916, he soon became the largest producer of rye whisky in the country. In the 1920s the British whisky giant DCL took over the Seagram firm and soon became involved in another Canadian whisky concern by the name of Bronfman. The Bronfmans had emigrated from Bessarabia at the end of the 19th century, and at this time—the Prohibition era—they were making a small fortune smuggling alcohol into the United States. Whatever DCL may have hoped to gain by such a connection, in 1928 it got cold feet, sold the Seagram firm to the Bronfmans, and withdrew from Canada altogether. The Bronfmans, who have called their firm Seagram ever since, were more farsighted, rightly suspecting that

DISTILLER. MILLER

Joseph E. Seagram.
Waterloo, Ontario, Canada.

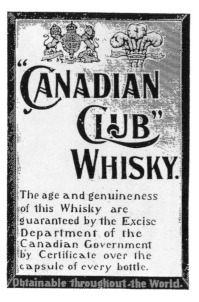

"CANADIAN CLUB" WHISKY.

The age and genuineness of this Whisky are guaranteed by the Excise Department of the Canadian Government by Certificate over the capsule of every bottle.

Obtainable throughout the World.

moonshine produced at home in those years Canadian whisky was the genuine article. It is therefore largely the Bronfmans' doing that more Canadian than domestic whiskey is consumed in the United States even today, and after World War II their firm became the largest spirit concern in the world (see SEAGRAM). The popularity of Canadian in the United States also explains why so many Canadian brands are owned by U.S. firms and marketed solely below the border. Other producers in addition to Seagram and Hiram Walker (now part of ALLIED DOMECQ; see also CORBY) are GILBEY's (an IDV subsidiary), JIM BEAM Brands (see ALBERTA), and the ever-present UD (see SCHENLEY).

Production: Canadian is called a rye whisky, but it is nothing like the straight rye from the United States. For, with but a few exceptions (see BUSH PILOT's), Canadian is always a blend of various straight whiskies in small quantities (3 to 5 percent; almost never more than 10 percent) and highly refined grain or neutral spirits. It could be argued that Canadian is in fact only a neutral spirit flavored with a little bit of whisky. Yet the Canadians take great pains in their blending. Each blend contains from 15 to 20 different whiskies of 6 or 7 basic types. The many variations

repeal of Prohibition was just around the corner.

Under the direction of Samuel Bronfman (1890–1971), the firm bought up huge reserves of whisky, and when Prohibition was finally voted out in 1933 Seagram flooded the American market with Canadian blends. The firm was able to capitalize on the fact that most whiskey producers in the United States had gone bankrupt and that the Canadian whisky smuggled into the country during Prohibition had acquired a good reputation. Little wonder: to thirsty Americans trying to make do with the kind of

come about as follows: various different types of grain can be distilled—either rye (raw or malted), corn, or barley (raw or malted), or any combination thereof. Further, various different yeasts are introduced and different distilling methods applied. Most Canadian distilling appears to be accomplished in continuous stills, but here they are more sophisticated than elsewhere, being combined as needed with other columnar stills, finishing stills, POT STILLS, rectifiers, etc.

The various whiskies thus produced are either immediately blended, diluted, and set to age or, as is more common, permitted to age first as single whiskies and blended only afterward. Aging, too, can be accomplished in different ways, using either old bourbon barrels, brandy or sherry casks, or new barrels. The minimum age prescribed is 3 years. Better brands age for 4 or 5 years and select ones for 6 to 8 years; only rarely are Canadians aged 12 years or longer. Producers desirous of saving

time and cutting costs are permitted to add so-called flavorings (a maximum of 2 percent by volume). These aromatic substances might be sherry, juices, or even fermented fruit juices (notably plum wine), and they are meant to mask, by the addition of both color and taste, the immaturity of the whiskies and the high percentage of neutral spirits.

Canadian is generally 80 proof and often higher for export.

C. & J. MCDONALD
Blended Scotch from the BELL'S (UD) subsidiary of the same name, which also has other brands in its program: HEATHWOOD, McDONALD'S SPECIAL BLEND, and QUEEN'S CHOICE.

CANTRELL & COCHRANE
Irish subsidiary of ALLIED DISTILLERS (ALLIED DOMECQ), with headquarters in Dublin. Since 1993, C. & C. has owned the brand TULLAMORE DEW; it also produces the liqueurs CAROLANS and IRISH MIST.

CAN-Y-DELYN
Whisky herb liqueur, 80 proof, from HALLGARTEN LIQUEURS.

CAOL ILA
Scottish single malt (Islay) from UD.

Another hot tip from the island of Islay, relatively light-bodied but with an intense peat flavor. Caol Ila has always been difficult to get, and even the official bottling that has been on the market since 1988–89 is rarely seen, for the whisky has always been in great demand as a blending malt.

Original bottling: 15 years old, 86 proof ("Flora and Fauna" series, aged in sherry casks).

Gordon & MacPhail: Vintage 1966 (sherry cask); vintages 1972, 1974, 1981, all 80 proof, and also in the cask-strength series at 125.2 proof, 13 years old (distilled 1980).

Cadenhead: 21 years old (distilled 1974), 116.8 proof.

Signatory: 16 years old (distilled 1980), 119.4 proof.

James MacArthur: 17 years old, 86 proof (aged in sherry casks).

The distillery was built in 1846. It was acquired by Bulloch Lade & Co. in 1863, by Robertson & Baxter in 1920, by the DCL in 1927, and by way of the latter became part of UD. In 1972–74 it was completely renovated, and since that time it has had 6 stills. The water comes from Loch Nam Ban.

(Tel. 1496 84 02 07)

CAPERDONICH
Scottish single malt (Speyside, Rothes) from the Chivas & Glenlivet Group of Seagram.

A light, fruity, and malty whisky that goes almost exclusively into the Seagram blends (Chivas Regal, for example), and is thus available only from independent bottlers.

Gordon & MacPhail: Vintages 1968, 1979, 1980, 1982, all 80 proof.

Cadenhead: 14 years old (distilled 1977), 121 proof; 16 years old (distilled 1977, sherry cask), 117.2 proof.

The distillery was built as a second plant for the Glen Grant distillery in 1898 and was for a long time called simply Glen Grant No. 2. The 2 distilleries, facing each other across the main street of Rothes, were connected by a pipeline. Caperdonich was shut down between 1902 and 1965, when it was renovated by its new owner, Glenlivet, and enlarged to accommodate 4 stills. The water comes from the Caperdonich spring. In 1977 the distillery was acquired along with Glenlivet by Seagram.

(Tel. 1542 78 33 00)

CAPTAIN COLLINS

A COLLINS based on Canadian.

CARDHU

[Gaelic for "black rock"]

Scottish single malt (Speyside) from UD.

The ideal beginner's malt: gentle, malty, and uncomplicated. Cardhu is today a top international brand, the most sought-after product from UD.

Original bottling: 12 years old, 80 proof.

Cadenhead sometimes bottles the whisky under the (English) name Cardow.

Before John Cumming acquired a license for his distillery in 1824, he was a notorious Highland bootlegger. His reputation is still a source of pride to the present management, as one gathers from the framed judgments against him hung prominently in the office. Cardhu was rebuilt in 1884, and some years later John Walker (see JOHNNIE WALKER) bought the distillery, whose product has since been a component of the Johnnie Walker blends. Cardhu has 6 stills; the water comes from the Mannoch hill and Lyne Burn.

(Tel. 1340 81 02 04)

CAROLANS

Irish whiskey cream liqueur, 34 proof, from CANTRELL & COCHRANE (ALLIED DOMECQ).

After Bailey's, this brand, introduced in 1979, is the best-selling whiskey liqueur of its type.

C

CARSEBRIDGE
Scottish grain whisky from the distillery of the same name near Sterling. It belonged to the DCL and for a time was the largest distillery in Scotland, but it was shut down in 1983. Its whisky was sometimes bottled as a single, and with luck it is still possible to find a 1965 at 115.6 proof.

CARSTAIRS WHITE SEAL
Blended American from SAZERAC.

CASK STRENGTH
This designation is occasionally used as a synonym for single-barrel (see SINGLE-BARREL BOTTLING).

THE CASTLE COLLECTION
A small shop in Tomintoul, Speyside, has recently been bottling various malts under this name. So far, they include ALLT-Á-BHAINNE, GLENTURRET, and GLENALLACHIE.

Distilled 10/79
Bottled 2/93

Number 1

Cask No. 026329

THE CASTLE COLLECTION

ALLT-Á-BHAINNE
Aged 13 Years

Bottled In Scotland For
The Whisky Castle
Tomintoul

70cl.   43% vol.

CASTLE PRIDE
Blended Scotch from ANGUS DUNDEE.

CATTO'S
Blended Scotch from James Catto & Co., a subsidiary of INVER HOUSE DISTILLERS.

The standard version is called Catto's Rare Old Scottish Highland; the DE LUXE, Catto's 12 Years Old Scottish Highland.

James Catto (1829–1908) began in 1861 as a tea and spirits merchant in Aberdeen but soon devoted himself very successfully to the blending of whisky. In 1920 the firm was sold to GILBEY, and since 1990 it has belonged to Inver House.

CELTIC CROSSING
This rather strange new product from Gaelic Heritage is a blend of Irish malt whiskey and cognac. It comes in either a crock or a bottle and is sold mainly on the U.S. market, though it is also available in duty-free.

CENTURY
Vatted malt produced by the CHIVAS & GLENLIVET GROUP (SEAGRAM).

The Century of Malts, as this brand is called in full, is a blend of 100 single malts, and came out in 1996 especially for the duty-free market.

CHAIRMAN'S
Blended Scotch from ELDRIDGE, POPE & Co., one of the biggest brewers in Dorset.

It is altogether common in Great Britain for brewers to produce their own whisky brands (see BEER).

CHAIRMAN'S RESERVE
Blended Scotch, de luxe, from the CHIVAS & GLENLIVET GROUP (SEAGRAM).

CHARRED KEG
Kentucky straight bourbon from MAJESTIC. Also available as a blended American.

CHEQUER'S
Blended Scotch from John McEWAN & Co. (UD), which is probably based on LINKWOOD and is mainly sold in Latin America.

CHIEFTAIN'S CHOICE
Scotch whiskies from Peter J. RUSSELL.

Under this name there are 3 malts from various regions (not further identified and probably vatted), a series of old single malts (a 21-year-old and a 32-year-old Speyside, a 26-year-old Highland, and a 30-year-old Lowland), and finally 3 premium blends (8, 12, and 18 years old).

CHINESE WHISKY
Until recently, cognac was the only Western spirit to find any notable success in China—such success, in fact, that Rémy Martin recently moved its head-quarters from Paris to Hong Kong. For the future, however, people are counting on an enormous potential for whisky imports, especially for blended Scotch. (The market leader at the moment is JOHNNIE WALKER.)

Given this gigantic market (the number of alcohol consumers is estimated to be 800 million, and wages are paid in part in alcohol), the big spirit concerns are attempting to secure a foothold in China through joint ventures with native producers, not only for production reasons but also with the intention of producing tax-favored, native whiskies. As always, the first to become involved was SEAGRAM, which has been distilling its SEAGRAM'S 7 CROWN in China since 1988. In the meantime, UD, HIRAM WALKER & SONS (ALLIED DOMECQ), and PERNOD RICARD have moved in the same direction, though without having introduced any new brands.

CHIVAS & GLENLIVET GROUP
Scottish subsidiary of the spirit giant SEAGRAM, responsible within the concern for the Scotch business.

CHIVAS REGAL
Blended Scotch from the CHIVAS & GLENLIVET GROUP (SEAGRAM).

A very balanced, 12-year-old de luxe blend,

available in more than 150 countries and one of the 5 biggest-selling Scotch whiskies in the world.

Base malts: STRATHISLA, THE GLENLIVET, LONGMORN, and GLEN GRANT.

Chivas is also available as a 15-year-old. The 18-year-old is called Chivas Imperial, and the top of the line is the 21-year-old ROYAL SALUTE.

James Chivas got his start as a whisky dealer in Aberdeen in 1841 and soon made a name for himself as a producer as well. His first blend was called Glen-Dee. He later introduced Royal Strathythan, with which he became purveyor of Scotch to the Hapsburg court in Vienna. In 1891, finally, Chivas Regal came on the market, and it soon proved to be an export hit. Seagram took over the firm in 1949, entrusting it with the running of the STRATHISLA distillery. In 1957 it began construction of the distillery GLEN KEITH, and a short time later it added a bottling plant near Paisley.

CHOICEST LIQUEUR
Blended Scotch from BERRY BROS. & RUDD.

CLAN ARDOCH
Blended Scotch from HALL & BRAMLEY.

CLAN CAMPBELL
Blended Scotch from CAMPBELL DISTILLERS (PERNOD RICARD).

In addition to the standard bottling, which had the greatest growth on the European blended-Scotch market in the 1980s, the producer added in the early 1990s a Clan Campbell Highlander, 12 years old, and a Clan Campbell Legendary, 21 years old. The 12-year-old Clan Campbell Special Reserve in a ceramic jar (bottled by Muir Mackenzie) comes from the precursor firm, HOUSE OF CAMPBELL. Although it is no longer produced, it is still possible to find.

CLAN MACGREGOR
Blended Scotch from Alexander MacGregor, a subsidiary of WILLIAM GRANT.

Created in the 1970s for the U.S. market, where it is relatively successful.

CLAN MUNRO
Blended Scotch from WILLIAM LAWSON, a subsidiary of Martini & Rossi (Bacardi Ltd.).

CLAN MURDOCK
Blended Scotch from MACDONALD MARTIN DISTILLERS.

CLAN ROY
Blended Scotch from T. & A. McCLELLAND LTD., a subsidiary of MORRISON BOWMORE DISTILLERS (SUNTORY).

CLANSMAN
Blended Scotch from GLEN CATRINE, designated mainly for the Latin American market.

CLASSIC CLUB
Kentucky straight bourbon from MAJESTIC. Also available as a blended American and a blended Scotch.

THE CLAYMORE

Blended Scotch from WHYTE & MACKAY (AMERICAN BRANDS).

An inexpensive brand, highly successful in its native market. Introduced by the DCL in 1977 solely for the British market, it was sold in 1986 by the DCL's successor, UD, to the present owners.

CLEMENTINE'S

Kentucky straight bourbon, 101 proof, from BARTON DISTILLING (Canandaigua).

This brand is bottled exclusively for the Japanese market.

CLUB

Blended Scotch from Justerini & Brooks (IDV/Grand Metropolitan).

This brand, the first blend from J & B, was introduced in the 1880s and is now available only in the firm's stores in Edinburgh and London.

CLUB 400

Blended American from MAJESTIC.

CLUNY

Blended Scotch from John E. McPherson & Co., a subsidiary of INVERGORDON DISTILLERS (WHYTE AND MACKAY, AMERICAN BRANDS).

Bottled as a standard and as a 12-year-old and 21-year-old blend and exported mainly to the United States, Canada, Australia, Scandinavia, and Italy.

The wine and spirits firm of McPherson was founded in Edinburgh in 1857. It was taken over by SCOTTISH & NEWCASTLE BREWERIES in 1961, and since 1985 has belonged to Invergordon.

CLYNELISH

Scottish single malt (Northern Highlands) from UD.

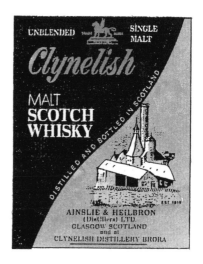

C

A strong, full malt with a definite character, one that is highly prized by the happy few who know it.

Original bottling: 14 years old*, 86 proof ("Flora & Fauna" series); 22 years old, 117.98 proof ("Rare Malts Selection").

Gordon & MacPhail: 12 years old, 80 and 114 proof.

Cadenhead: 23 years old (distilled 1965), 114.2 proof; 13 years old* (distilled 1982), 131.6 proof.

Signatory: 28 years old (distilled 1965), 101.4 proof (aged in sherry casks).

Adelphi: 11 years old (distilled 1984), 122 proof.

The bottlings listed come from 2 different distilleries. Those marked with an asterisk (*) are from the Clynelish distillery opened in 1969; the remainder, from the older one (1819). It is not certain which one produced the Gordon & MacPhail bottlings. The history of the name is recounted under BRORA.

The first Clynelish distillery belonged for a time to the firm AINSLIE & HEILBRON, which used its malt for its blends. Ainslie continued to operate it under the later owner, DCL. The present distillery has 6 stills; the water comes from Clynemilton Burn.

(Tel. 1408 62 11 31)

COCKBURN & CAMPBELL
Renowned Scottish wine dealers in Leith, owned by the brewery Young

& Co. since 1972. Of its original 6 whisky brands only 2 remain: THE ROYAL AND ANCIENT and Special Malt.

COCKBURN & MURRAY
Blended Scotch, 8 years old, de luxe, from Peter J. RUSSELL.

This small whisky and wine dealer was acquired in 1953 by Russell, which also markets a vatted malt from C. & M., THE SEVEN STILLS.

COCKBURN'S OF LEITH
This firm, established in 1796, supplied whisky to both Charles Dickens and Sir Walter Scott. It made its name, however, with the port wine house that it opened in Porto in 1815. For a time Cockburn's belonged to DRAMBUIE; then in 1993 it was taken over by the Scottish Wine Company, which has preferred to continue all of its business under the name Cockburn's.

In addition to a vatted called Cockburn's Highland Malt, the firm also produces the 8-year-old blend Cockburn's O.V. 8, as well as the brands THE DOMINIE and OLD DECANTER.

COLEBURN
Scottish single malt (Speyside, Elgin), from UD.

A light and well-balanced malt that is now available only from independent bottlers.

Gordon & MacPhail: Vintages 1965 and 1972, 80 proof.

Cadenhead: 17 years old (distilled 1978), 124 proof.

John MacArthur: 12 years old, 86 proof.

The distillery was built in 1897 and was closed down in 1985. In its time it furnished the base malt for the Usher blends (see USHER'S GREEN STRIPE).

COLERAINE
Blended Irish whiskey, standard, 80 proof, from the BUSHMILLS distillery, owned by IDC (PERNOD RICARD).

A small brand with a great name. Today one can buy Coleraine only in Northern Ireland, but in the 19th century it was considered one of Ireland's best whiskeys. Even in the bar of the British House of Commons you could then find a 10-year-old malt from the Coleraine distillery, which was established in 1820 right next to Bushmills. Like most Irish distilleries, it failed to survive the period of Prohibition in the United States. It was closed in the 1920s and later sold to Bushmills. In the late 1930s it was started up again, and then in 1978 it was shut down for good. Production was transferred to Bushmills, where the brand is bottled only in small quantities, as a sort of sideline to BUSHMILLS ORIGINAL.

In 1993 another 396 bottles of a 34-year-old Coleraine malt came on the market. It was bottled at cask strength (114.2 proof) and is said to be of quite extraordinary quality.

COLONEL LEE
Kentucky straight bourbon, bottled in bond, 100 proof, from BARTON DISTILLING (Canandaigua).

A passable everyday bourbon, but beware: Barton also bottles a less desirable light whiskey under the same name.

COLLINS
A collins is a mixed drink related to a fizz. A base spirit is blended with lemon juice and sugar and topped with soda. The name changes depending on the type of whisk(e)y used: A Sandy Collins uses Scotch, a Colonel Collins bourbon, a Mike Collins Irish, and a Captain Collins Canadian.

Collinses are served on ice in a tall glass and are excellent thirst quenchers.

COLONEL COLLINS
A COLLINS using a bourbon base.

COLUMBA CREAM
Scottish whisky cream liqueur, 34 proof, from the firm John Murray (Clagary, Isle of Mull).

The brand is relatively new to the market and is said to be based on 4-year-old malts.

CONNEMARA
Irish single malt, 80 proof, from COOLEY DISTILLERY.

Probably the peatiest Irish whiskey and, unlike most, distilled only twice. The brand has been produced only since the early

1990s and is still in the developmental stage, so to speak (see PURE POT STILL).

CONSOLIDATED
U.S. firm founded in Chicago in 1933, which has its brands produced by various different distilleries (see BAKER STREET, CANADIAN RESERVE, TOM HANNAH).

CONSULATE
Blended Scotch from WILLIAM GRANT & SON, bottled solely for the U.S. market.

CONTINUOUS DISTILLATION See PATENT STILL.

CONVALMORE
Scottish single malt (Speyside, Dufftown) from William GRANT & SONS.

A complex, balanced digestif malt whose aroma has been described by one author as like that of "a wheat field after a summer rain."

Gordon & MacPhail: Vintage 1969, 80 proof.

Cadenhead: 17 years old (distilled 1977), 130.6 proof, and 31 years old (distilled 1962), 97.8 proof.

The distillery was opened in 1894 and was operated for a long time by the LOWRIE firm, producing many of the malts for its blends. After Lowrie was taken over by BUCHANAN, they experimented briefly with continuous distilling of malt whisky there. By way of Buchanan, Convalmore fell to UD, which sold it to the Grants in 1990. Closed down in 1985, it now serves merely as a warehouse.

COOLEY DISTILLERY

The only Irish-owned distillery in Ireland was reopened only a few years ago, and it will be fascinating to see whether the owner, John Teeling, is successful in his attempt to break the monopoly of the IDG (Irish Distillers Group) and raise Irish whiskey to world-class stature once again. Blocked in his bid to take over IDG by the French spirit concern PERNOD RICARD in 1986, Teeling purchased a state-owned spirit factory in Cooley, Dundalk, in 1987. In 1989 he began producing POT STILL and GRAIN whiskeys. With its acquisition of the competitors A. A. Watt and John LOCKE (see KILBEGGAN), the Cooley Distillery secured

the rights to the old Irish brands THE TYRCONNELL and LOCKE's. The IDG, in turn, tried to take over Cooley but was prevented from doing so by Irish laws protecting competition. Thus Cooley was finally able to place on the market its malt Tyrconnell in 1992, and in the following year the blends Kilbeggan and Locke's. It has meanwhile added the brands AVOCA, CONNEMARA, ERIN'S ISLE, INISHOWEN, and MILLARS SPECIAL RESERVE to its portfolio.

The distillery is near Dundalk, County Westmeath, and uses the warehouses of the nonworking distilleries Kilbeggan and Tullamore (see TULLAMORE DEW). Unlike most other Irish whiskeys, Cooley products use peated grains and are distilled only twice.

The management in Dublin sees its main opportunity in the export business and is working to that end with firms like HEAVEN HILL

DISTILLERS and UD. Its chief brand, Kilbeggan, has meanwhile become the second-best-selling Irish in Germany, one of the most important export markets for Irish whiskey.

CORBY
Canadian producer with headquarters in Montreal. The firm was established in 1857 in the vicinity of Toronto by Henry Corby. Since the 1930s it has belonged to the ALLIED DOMECQ subsidiary HIRAM WALKER & SONS, in whose distillery in Windsor, Ontario, the Corby brands are produced: McGUINNESS, MEAGHERS 1878, SILK TASSEL, ROYAL RESERVE, and WISER'S.

CORBY'S
Blended American, 80 proof, from BARTON DISTILLING (Canandaigua), with 30 percent bourbon.

CORIO
Australian blended whiskey from the distillery of the same name near Melbourne. The brand was one of the last stocks belonging to the group UD, which redistilled its whisk(e)y into gin in 1995 and then shut the distillery down (see AUSTRALIAN WHISKEY).

CORK DISTILLERIES See MIDLETON, PADDY, and IDG.

CORN BASE
Japanese blend of the bourbon type, 8 years old, from NIKKA.

CORN CRIB
Kentucky straight corn from BARTON DISTILLING (Canandaigua).

CORNEY & BARROW
Blended Scotch from the renowned London wine and spirit shop Corney & Barrow, founded in 1780. When C & B still belonged to the CATTO firm, it did its own production; today this is contracted out to Peter J. RUSSELL, and most of the brand goes to the Japanese market.

In 1994 C & B combined with Whighams of Ayr, another traditional firm, which made a name for itself with its DUART CASTLE whisky.

CORN WHISKEY
U.S. whiskey of the most primitive kind. Corn whiskey is distilled from a mash consisting of more than 80 percent corn and aged in either used or untreated barrels—usually for only a short time, so that it has little color. Its alcohol content is very high, as a rule, and its taste is sweet and simple. In many respects it resembles MOONSHINE, and as with moonshine one finds corn whiskey most readily in the South. GEORGIA MOON is probably the best-known brand. Others are CABIN HOLLOW, CORN CRIB, GOLDEN GRAIN, McCORMICK, J. W. CORN, Mellow Corn, and OLD DISPENSARY.

COUNTRY CLUB
Kentucky straight bourbon from KASSER LAIRD.

COUNTY
American blended from SHERMAN.

CRABBIE'S
Blended Scotch from John Crabbie & Co. (MACDONALD MARTIN DISTILLERS),  an old Edinburgh producer (established in 1801) that for a time owned its own grain distillery and was sold by UD to its present owner in 1994.

Crabbie also puts out a Green Ginger Cordial that is very popular in Scotland and is essential in the preparation of a WHISKY MAC.

CRAGGANMORE
Scottish single malt (SPEYSIDE) from D. & J. McCallum (UD). (See also MCCALLUM'S PERFECTION.)

A distinctly noble malt, in which malt and peat are exquisitely balanced. Despite its obvious quality, Cragganmore is still relatively unknown. This is in part because the distillery's production is rather small and in part because it has been marketed officially only since 1988–89.

Original bottling: 12 years old, 86 proof (from the series "Classic Malts").

Gordon & MacPhail: Vintages 1976, 1977, 1978, all 80 proof, and 17 years old (distilled 1976), 107.6 proof.

Cadenhead: 13 years old (distilled 1982), 121.8 proof.

Cragganmore was opened in 1869 by a former MACALLAN manager and belonged for a time to WHITE HORSE. The distillery has 4 stills; the water comes from the hill Craggan More. The malt is an essential component in the McCallum blends.

(Tel. 1807 50 02 02)

CRAIGELLACHIE
Scottish single malt (Speyside) from WHITE HORSE (UD).

An unusual malt that is both smoky and fruity and, in some bottlings, also very peaty.

Original bottling: 14 years old, 86 proof ("Flora & Fauna" series).

The Best of Speyside

MALT CRAGGANMORE

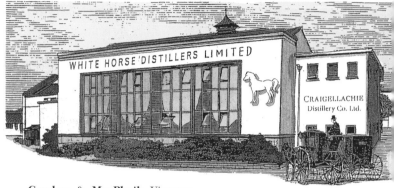

Gordon & MacPhail: Vintages 1974, 1977, 80 proof.

Cadenhead: Recently had a 15-year-old at 92 proof.

Signatory: 17 years old (distilled 1978, sherry cask), 86 proof.

The distillery was built in 1891 by a consortium that included, among others, Peter Mackie, the founder of White Horse. A large part of the Craigellachie output disappears into that blend to this day. In 1927 the distillery became part of the DCL, by way of which it ended up belonging to UD. It has 4 stills; the water comes from Little Convall Hill.

(Tel. 1340 88 12 12)

CRAWFORD'S 3 STAR

Blended Scotch, 80 proof, from A. & A. Crawford, a subsidiary of UD (the licensees in Great Britain are WHYTE & MACKAY).

The brand was introduced in 1900 and was for a time the number-1 blended Scotch in Scotland. The de luxe version, Crawford's 5 Star, is no longer on the market. The firm of A. & A. Crawford was an independent blending house from 1860 to 1944. It was later sold to the DCL, and even later to UD, for which it operated the distillery BENRINNES until 1992.

CRESCENT

Japanese blend, de luxe, from KIRIN-SEAGRAM. Like all blends from this house, Crescent is a mixture of na-

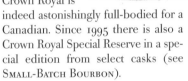

tive and Scottish whiskies. By Japanese standards it is rather dry and smoky.

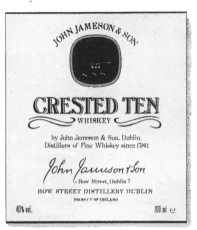

CRESTED TEN

Blended Irish whiskey, 80 proof, from the MIDLETON distillery of IDG (PERNOD RICARD).

This well-balanced premium brand from the house of JAMESON has been on the market since 1963. It enjoys a particularly high reputation among Dublin's businesspeople and is therefore anathema in the simpler pubs (which are generally the better ones in Ireland), where it is considered a "yuppie whiskey."

CROWN ROYAL

Canadian blend from SEAGRAM.

This 10-year-old de luxe is generally considered to be the best the Canadian whisky industry has to offer. It was created in 1939 on the occasion of a state visit by the British king and queen, supposedly by Seagram boss Samuel Bronfman himself. Crown Royal is indeed astonishingly full-bodied for a Canadian. Since 1995 there is also a Crown Royal Special Reserve in a special edition from select casks (see SMALL-BATCH BOURBON).

CUMBRAE CASTLE

Blended Scotch from MACDUFF INTERNATIONAL.

A relatively new brand, designated mainly for export.

CUSTODIAN

Blended Scotch from Denham, a subsidiary of RED LION BLENDING. Its chief market is Venezuela.

CUTTY SARK

Blended Scots whisky produced by Lang Bros. (see LANG'S) for BERRY BROS. & RUDD.

A light blend without caramel coloring; the leading Scotch in the United States.

In addition to the standard bottling, there is a premium called Cutty Sark Imperial Kingdom, a 12-year-old

Cutty Sark Emerald (formerly Cutty 12), an 18-year-old Cutty Sark Discovery, and a Cutty Sark Golden Jubilee, which contains malts as much as 50 years old. All Cutty blends are 86 proof.

The base malts come most likely from BUNNAHABHAIN and certainly from Glenrothes.

Cutty Sark came on the market in 1923 and was the first of the now-popular light scotches (see LIGHT WHISK(E)Y). Immediately after Prohibition it enjoyed tremendous success in the United States, for even during those years large quantities of it had reached the country illegally. It appears that Cutty Sark was created especially to gain a foothold in this hotly contested market. Its light body and color represented precisely the kind of whisky that the American public had become accustomed to, thanks to the generous—and lucrative—diluting practiced by illegal spirit merchants, and it is the one that they still prefer today.

Cutty Sark was the name of a witch in a poem by Scotland's national poet, Robert Burns. The name was also made famous as that of what was once the fastest sailing ship in the world—the one pictured on the label. Fast boats were precisely what Caribbean whisky smugglers needed in order to land their cargo safely on the American coast. One of the most famous of these so-called rumrunners, William McCoy, worked as an agent for Berry Bros. & Rudd. Even today the slang phrase "the real McCoy" is used as a synonym for genuine whisky.

CWS (CO-OPERATIVE WHOLESALE SOCIETY)

British bottler with its own store label and a huge bottling plant in Manchester that is also used by other producers. CWS has its own brands (HEATHERDALE, HIGHLAND ABBEY, MAJORITY) produced for it by INVERGORDON DISTILLERS.

D

"Sippin' whisky," Gage said,
"the secret of my survival."

William Boyd,
Stars & Bars

D

DAILUAINE

[Gaelic for "green valley"]

Scottish single malt (Speyside, Carron) from UD.

A veritably sumptuous malt for all occasions.

Original bottling: 16 years, 86 proof ("Flora and Fauna" series).

Gordon & MacPhail: Vintages 1971, 1974, 80 proof.

Cadenhead: 27 years old (distilled 1962), 101.6 proof; 27 years old (distilled 1966, sherry cask), 91.4 proof.

The distillery was founded in 1854 and later considerably enlarged. Beginning in 1898 it was associated with TALISKER, and even today the 2 form the basis for the JOHNNIE WALKER blends. In 1916 the distillery was bought by the DCL.

Dailuaine has 6 stills; the water comes from Bailliemullich Burn.

DALLAS DHU

Scottish single malt (Speyside, Findhorn) from UD.

A compact and very harmonious malt, a good aperitif.

Original bottling: 24 years old (distilled 1970), 119.8 proof ("Rare Malts Selection").

Gordon & MacPhail: Vintages 1969, 1971, 1974, each 80 proof.

Cadenhead: 18 years old (distilled 1977), 118.4 proof.

Signatory: 18 years old (distilled 1974), 121.6 proof.

Dallas Dhu was designed in 1898 by Charles Doig, an architect from Elgin who specialized in distillery design and was probably the inventor of the pagoda-style roofs that one sees so often above malting floors. The distillery was finally closed in 1983 and later turned into a museum where one can study traditional whisky-making methods. It is also possible to buy there a blend called RODERICK DHU, a brand that was already popular at the turn of the century.

Dallas Dhu is also still available itself, although supplies are running out and prices have risen to the point that only true connoisseurs buy it for its intended use rather than for display in a locked cupboard.

DALMENY

Blended Scotch, standard and de luxe, from J. Townend & Sons, an old wine and spirit dealer in Hull that purchased this brand, created in the late 19th century, in the 1930s. The blend is bought from an unnamed producer in Scotland and sold mainly to restaurants and supermarkets.

DALMORE

Scottish single malt (Northern Highlands) from WHYTE & MACKAY (AMERICAN BRANDS).

A very elegant whisky or, in the words of Wallace Milroy, "another really good malt," which by no means enjoys the popularity it deserves. Also one of those malts that are not harmed by long aging; on the contrary, the extremely rare bottlings aged 50 or over are becoming quite famous.

Original bottling: 12 years old, 80 proof; 26 years old, 90 proof ("Stillman's Dram").

Cadenhead: 30 years old (distilled 1963), 109 proof; 19 years old (distilled 1976), 117.4 proof.

After making a fortune in the tea and opium trade in Hong Kong, Alexander Matheson began distilling whiskey in Dalmore in 1839. The distillery was taken over by the Mackenzie family in 1886, mainly supplying the firm of WHYTE & MACKAY. Since that time Dalmore has been one of the base malts for the Whyte and Mackay blends.

The distillery has 8 stills; the water comes from the Alnes River. Bourbon and sherry (oloroso) barrels are used in the aging.

(Tel. 1349 88 23 62)

DALWHINNIE

Scottish single malt (Highlands, Inverness-shire) from James BUCHANAN & Co. (UD).

A gentle, aromatic, and very sensuous malt.

Original bottling: 15 years old, 86 proof (from the series "Classic Malts").

Gordon & MacPhail: Vintage 1970, 80 proof.

Cadenhead: Most recently a 27-year-old from 1966 at 91 proof.

Dalwhinnie was opened as the Strathspey Distillery in 1897 and took its present name only some years later. In 1926 it was acquired by the DCL, and since that time the whisky has been an important component in the BUCHANAN Blends—for example, BLACK & WHITE—and in Haig's DIMPLE (PINCH).

The distillery has 2 stills; the water comes from Lochan an Doire-Uaine.

(Tel. 1528 52 22 40)

DAVID NICHOLSON 1843

Kentucky straight bourbon, 7 years old, 90 and 100 proof. A very scarce private label that the firm Rip Van Winkle (see OLD RIP VAN WINKLE) bottles for a business in St. Louis.

DAVIESS COUNTY

Blended American from SHERMAN.

The brand used to be produced by MEDLEY, a Daviess County, Kentucky, firm that is no longer in business.

DCL (DISTILLERS COMPANY LTD.)

Today the name DCL is solely of historic importance—but such importance that it is necessary to say a few words about it here. The business was created in 1877 from the merger of 6 grain distilleries, and new firms continued to be added over the following years. What had begun as only an association to promote the interests of its members gradually developed into the most influential whisky concern in Scotland. It expanded to Ireland, Australia, and Canada, and in the late 1920s even the great names BUCHANAN, DEWAR, HAIG, HIRAM WALKER, and WHITE HORSE were part of the DCL. For a time the firm controlled over 40 percent of the entire production of Scotch. In addition it was a major factor in the British gin industry (Gordons, Tanqueray, Booth) and was indispensable as the most important yeast producer in the country. (Even today most malt distilleries use descendants of DCL yeast cultures.)

But sheer size does not make a company invulnerable. In the 1970s, when other spirits began to be fashionable and made inroads on the Scotch market, the DCL, a clumsy colossus, was incapable of reacting appropriately.

The first crack had appeared in the facade in the early 1960s, when the concern became entangled in the so-called Thalidomide tragedy. Its subsidiary firm DCL Biochemicals had been responsible for the manufacture and distribution of the effective ingredient in the medication Thalidomide, and the many lawsuits filed continued to create bad press until the early 1970s. The next blow came from Brussels: new regulations issued by the European Commonwealth forced the DCL to take its best-selling JOHNNIE WALKER off the British market, thereby giving the lead—which they still hold today—to the competing brands BELL'S and THE FAMOUS GROUSE. The DCL therefore entered into the economic crisis that plagued Great Britain in the 1980s considerably weakened, and the great distillery die-off began: between 1983 and 1985 some 2 dozen DCL opera-

tions were shut down. In other words, the old fortress was ripe for attack, and attempts to take it by storm were not long in coming. The ultimate victor was the Irish brewing giant Guinness, which took over the DCL in 1986 and a year later renamed it UNITED DISTILLERS (see UD). The renaming may have been to some degree belated revenge on the part of the Irish, for the DCL had swallowed up an Irish concern of the same name in the 1920s.

DEANSTON

Scottish single malt (Southern Highlands) from BURN STEWART DISTILLERS.

A light, smooth malt for every
time of day.

Original bottling: 12, 17, and 25
years old, each 80 proof.

Cadenhead: 18 years old (distilled
1977), 109.4 proof.

Deanston is a relatively young distillery, opened only in 1965. In 1972 it
was bought by INVERGORDON DIS-
TILLERS, which closed it in 1982 and
sold it to the present owners 8 years
later. Since 1990 it is again in operation, with 4 stills and water from the
River Teith.

(Tel. 1786 84 14 39)

DEFENDER

Blended Scotch, which is produced
by the firm Dalaruan, in Glasgow, in
3 versions: as Very Classic Pale and as
a 5- and 12-year-old Success, all at 80
proof.

The brand was created in
1989 and is sold primarily in
France, Japan, and Spain. The
blending house of Dalaruan is
a cooperative undertaking
of several firms, among
them ROBERTSON & BAXTER,
Asbach, Osborne, Taittin-
ger, and Takahashi. It bears
the name of a historic distillery that once stood in
CAMPBELTOWN and was torn
down in the 1930s.

D

DE LUXE

The upper price category, especially in blended Scotch and bourbon (see PREMIUM, STANDARD), but one that does not necessarily guarantee a brand's quality. It is true that de luxe Scotches contain a minimum of 35 percent malt whiskies, but there are some standard blends that contain even more than that.

DERBY SPECIAL

Blended Scotch from KINROSS WHISKY Co., which is offered in 3- and 5-year-old versions and a 12-year-old DE LUXE.

DER FALCKNER

German blended whiskey, 80 proof, from C. W. Falckenthal, a firm established in Luckenwalde, near Berlin, in 1759 and known primarily as a producer of liqueurs. Der Falckner was already a familiar name in the German Democratic Republic, and the eastern German states are still its main market. Falckenthal recently added another whiskey called EDEL FALCKE; both are distilled exclusively from native grain.

DEWAR'S

Blended Scotch from the house of John Dewar & Son, a subsidiary of UD.

The history of this brand is in many respects the history of blended Scotch itself. At the age of 23, John Dewar (1806–80) started working as a clerk in a wine and spirit shop in Perth. Eighteen years later he set up business for himself, selling his own blends. Dewar was one of the first to market his whisky in bottles instead of in jars or casks, as was the practice at the time. His 2 sons, John Alexander and Tommy, proved to be equally shrewd market strategists. In 1885 they opened a branch in London, exploiting the popular romantic notion of Scotland as the place where "noble savages" wore funny costumes day in and day out, and played strange music on weird-looking instruments. The kilt and bagpipe were essential elements of all of their advertising, and these stereotypes remained the images of Scotch whisky well into the 1970s. (Much of the supposedly typical Scottish folklore was invented specifically for the visit to Scotland by George IV in 1822—the first by a British monarch in 200 years—and based on the works of the novelist Sir Walter Scott.) The Dewar's brand was registered in 1891.

In order to meet the increasing demand, the Dewars began building the

"Among the distinguished passengers"

distillery ABERFELDY in 1896, and by 1923 they had acquired 8 additional distilleries, among them AULTMORE, BENRINNES, GLEN ORD, Lochnagar, and Pulteney (see OLD PULTENEY). After earning fortunes, the brothers went into politics—one as a Tory, the other as a Liberal—and became the first in the line of whisky barons to be knighted. Tommy Dewar is also remembered as the third man in Great Britain to own an automobile. The first was the tea magnate Thomas Lipton; the second, the Prince of Wales. In 1915, together with James BUCHANAN & CO.,

the brothers formed Scotch Whisky Brands Ltd., thereby gaining control of the greatest store of whisky in Scotland. The firm's entry into the DCL, where Dewar's would play a major role, followed in 1925.

Today Dewar's belongs to UD, for which it holds the licenses to Aberfeldy and Glen Ord.

A large portion of the base malts for the Dewar's blends doubtless comes from Aberfeldy. The main brand is Dewar's White Label, 87 proof, one of the great brands worldwide and one available in 140 countries. At the moment Germany is not one of them, although White Label is the best-selling Scotch in the United States. The de luxe version is the 12-year-old Dewar's Ancestor, also 87 proof. If you're lucky, you may also still find Dewar's Pure Malt, an extremely elegant, 12-year-old vatted malt produced, unfortunately, only between 1975 and 1982.

DEW OF BEN NEVIS

Blended Scotch, produced from whiskies from the BEN NEVIS distillery, owned by NIKKA.

Available as "Extra Special" premium and as 12- and 15-year-old de luxe.

DEW OF THE WESTERN ISLES

Blended Scotch from SPEYSIDE DISTILLERY.

DIMPLE

Blended Scotch from John Haig & Co. (UD).

An exceptional blend, 80 proof, that is one of the leading de luxe brands worldwide. In addition to the well-known 12-year-old, there is also a 15-year-old de luxe and a standard version called Dimple Royal Sovereign. The base malts are Glenkinchie and Dalwhinnie.

The name Dimple comes from the shape of the bottle in which this whisky has been sold since 1893. In the United States the brand name is Pinch; not so charming, perhaps, but signifying much the same thing.

DINER'S

Scotch whisky that the firm Red Lion Blending has produced by its subsidiary Douglas Denham for the credit-card company Diner's Club.

Diner's is available exclusively to club members as a 5-, 8-, 12-, or 21-year-old blend and as a 15-year-old vatted malt. These are aged in the barrel for 4 years between blending and bottling.

DIPLOMATIC PRIVILEGE

Blended Scotch from W. Brown & Sons.

DIRECTOR'S SPECIAL

Blended Scotch from H. Stenham Ltd.

Like all Stenham Scotches, it is available as a 3-, 5-, 8-, 10-, or 12-year-old, and like the rest it is meant primarily for the Latin American and Southeast Asian markets.

DOCTOR'S SPECIAL

Blended Scotch from Hiram Walker & Sons (Allied Domecq).

Before this brand was acquired by its present owner, it belonged to R. Macnish (see Grand Macnish), which first introduced it in the 1920s. Today it is marketed almost exclusively in Scandinavia.

D

THE DOMINIE

Blended Scotch from COCKBURN'S OF LEITH.

DONS DRAM

Blended Scotch, 5 years old, 80 proof, from BENNACHIE.

This relatively new brand is also known in its homeland as "The Official Aberdeen Football Club Scotch Whisky."

DOUBLE Q

Blended Scotch, bottled for the German market by the firm Dethleffsen in Flensburg. It is one of the 10 highest-selling whiskies in Germany. Just who the Scottish producer might be is unknown.

DOWLING

Kentucky straight bourbon, 8 years old, 86 proof, and 10 years old, 100 proof, from HEAVEN HILL DISTILLERS (the Stonegate Distillery pictured on the label is a fiction).

A regional brand now offered only in the vicinity of Lawrenceburg, where it is more popular than many of the big-name brands.

The name comes from that of a family of Scottish immigrants who began distilling here in 1889 but sold their distillery with the onset of Prohibition and moved the operation to Mexico. There, needless to say, the spirit business would soon experience a boom.

In the old Dowling family home in Lawrenceburg 2 charming ladies run a pleasant bed-and-breakfast

DRAKES

Blended Scotch produced for the U.S. market by BLACK PRINCE.

D

DRAM
A British apothecary's measure equal to ⅛ ounce (3.9 grams); also a "sip" or a "trifle." In Scotland, the common term for a glass of whisky. It has nothing to do with the size of the glass; on the contrary, a "wee dram" can be a major dose.

DRAMBUIE
[Gaelic for "the drink that satisfies"]

Scottish whisky and herb liqueur, 80 proof, from the Drambuie Liquor Company, a firm established by the MacKinnons in 1906. They were descendants of the family that was supposedly given the recipe for Drambuie in 1746 by Bonnie Prince Charles, in gratitude for their having hidden him after his defeat by the English (see MOIDART).

Drambuie is the oldest and surely one of the finest whisky liqueur brands. One of its components is the malt TEANINICH.

DREAM OF BARLEY
Blended Scotch from ALLIED DISTILLERS (ALLIED DOMECQ).

DRUMGRAY
Scottish whisky cream liqueur from BURN STEWART DISTILLERS.

DRUMGUISH
Scottish single malt (Northern Highlands) from SPEYSIDE DISTILLERY & BONDING CO.

A light, malty whisky, astonishingly well developed given its young age.

Original bottling: 3 years old, 80 proof.

Drumguish comes from the Speyside Distillery, which was started up in 1990 and is the newest addition to the family of Scottish malts. The distillery has only 2 stills and gets its water from the River Tromie.

DRURY'S
Brazilian blended whiskey from IDV/Grand Metropolitan.

Like most Brazilian whiskies, Drury's consists of Scottish malt diluted with native distillates.

DUART CASTLE
Blended Scotch from Whigham's of Ayr, a trading house with a rich tradition that began in the small town of Ayr as a wine dealership, under the grand name of Alexander Oliphant & Co. In 1994 the firm merged with the London wine dealers CORNEY & BARROW.

Duart Castle was also once available as a vatted malt.

DUBLINER
Irish whiskey cream liqueur, 34 proof, from IDV/Grand Metropolitan.

DUFFTOWN
Scottish single malt (Speyside, Dufftown) from UD.

D

A simple aperitif whisky, on the sweet side. Michael Jackson calls it "a good, no-nonsense Highland whisky."

Original bottling: 15 years old, 86 proof ("Flora & Fauna" series); one sometimes still finds bottlings by the former owner, Arthur Bell & Sons (see BELL'S), which offered both an 8- and a 10-year-old.

Cadenhead: 12 years old (distilled 1979), 119.4 proof.

Signatory: 13 years old (distilled 1979), 86 proof.

James MacArthur: 17 years old, 117 proof.

Dufftown, one of the 8 distilleries in the village of the same name, was opened in 1896 and taken over a year later by Peter Mackenzie & Co. (see THE REAL MAC-KENZIE). In 1933 Mackenzie was acquired, in turn, by Arthur Bell & Sons, for whose blends this whisky has been used ever since. Bell has been a part of UD since 1985. The distillery has 6 stills and gets its water from Jock's Well.

(Tel. 1340 82 02 24)

DUGGAN'S
Blended American from Duggan's Distillers.

DUMBARTON
Scottish grain distillery belonging to George BALLANTINE & SON (ALLIED DISTILLERS, ALLIED DOMECQ).

This distillery, built in 1938 by HIRAM WALKER & SONS, produces the majority of the grains for the Allied Distillers blends. The complex also includes the malt distillery INVER-LEVEN, the first to be outfitted with LOMOND STILLS.

DUNCAN TAYLOR
Blended Scotch produced for the U.S. market by STAR LIQUOR.

THE DUNDEE
Blended Scotch, the most important brand from ANGUS DUNDEE.

DUN EIDEANN
The independent bottler SIGNATORY occasionally presents its SINGLE-BARREL BOTTLINGS under this name.

DUNHEATH
Blended Scotch produced for the U.S. market by KASSER LAIRD.

DUNHILL OLDMASTER
Blended Scotch, 86 proof, that the London men's furnishings shop has had produced by IDV since 1981. It is of

The unusual name has a complex etymology: "brose" is a kind of groats, but it can also mean any sort of drink; the recipe itself is said to have been the invention of an earl of Atholl; and in the early 19th century there was a distillery on Athol Street in the village of Dunkeld (Southern Highlands).

DUNPHYS

Blended Irish whiskey, standard, 80 proof, from the MIDLETON distillery of IDG (PERNOD RICARD).

A small, inexpensive brand with a somewhat unusual history: when IRISH COFFEE became fashionable in the United States in the early 1950s, the people at Cork Distilleries (see PADDY) got the bright idea of creating

extraordinary quality and is available exclusively at Dunhill branches and in duty-free shops—needless to say, at a premium. If you want to spend even more, you can buy Oldmaster in the Crystal Decanter version, in the limited Celebration Edition, or in the very limited Centenary Cast version. Since 1993 there has also been a Gentlemen's Speyside Blend, which is not so subtle. One of the base malts is STRATHMILL.

DUNKELD ATHOLL BROSE

Scottish whisky herb liqueur, 70 proof, from GORDON & MACPHAIL. An addictive mixture of 12-year-old malts, herbs, and honey based on an 18th-century recipe. Originally it contained oatmeal instead of herbs.

a special brand for the purpose. It was not to cost too much, so as to make the buyer feel that he was not wasting whiskey that was somehow too good. And that's what Dunphys tastes like; the British whisky journalist Murray suggests that one "keep it in the coffee cup."

Since the waning of the Irish coffee boom in the United States, the brand has been available only in Ireland.

DUTHIE'S See CADENHEAD, WM.

DYC

Spanish blended whisky from the DISTILERIAS Y CRIANZA, Segovia, a subsidiary

of HIRAM WALKER & SONS (ALLIED DOMECQ).

DYC has enjoyed great popularity in its homeland since 1963. Although it is marketed almost exclusively in Spain, it has been one of the 25 best-selling whiskies worldwide for years. It is produced by the Scottish method—that is, with peat-dried malt and aged in bourbon barrels. At times it was composed of Spanish grain and imported malt from the Scottish LOCHSIDE distillery, which has belonged to Distilerias y Crianza since 1972.

DYC is available as a standard and as an 8-year-old blend, both 80 proof.

E

Doctor Dohmler saw that there were tears
in the corners of his eyes and
noticed for the first time
that there was whiskey on his breath.

F. Scott Fitzgerald,
Tender Is the Night

EAGLE OF SPEY

Scottish single malt, 10 years old, 80 proof, from J. & G. Grant (see GLEN-FARCLAS, GLEN DOWAN).

A second label for Glenfarclas, aged exclusively in new oak barrels.

EAGLE RARE

Kentucky straight bourbon from SAZERAC's LEESTOWN DISTILLING Co. The brand was formerly produced by SEA-GRAM and is now marketed in 2 versions: as a 10-year-old at 101 proof and, for export, as a 15-year-old at 100.7 proof.

Both are extremely palatable digestif bourbons, and it is astonishing, given their quality, that they are so little-known.

EAGLESOME'S

Blended Scotch from Eaglesome, a firm that runs a small grocery business in Campbeltown. It belongs to the J. A. MITCHELL family, and comes in various blends: in addition to Eaglesome's, which is also sold as a 12-year-old de luxe blend, there are ALLAN's, CAIRNBAAN, CAMPBELTOWN LOCH, and OLD SPENCER.

EARLY TIMES DISTILLERY

U.S. distilleries in Louisville and Shively, Kentucky, owned by BROWN-

FORMAN. The old Early Times Distillery was founded in Louisville in 1860 by John H. Beam, an uncle of the famous Jim. During Prohibition it passed to Brown-Forman, which uses it as the firm's headquarters and as the bottling plant for the whiskeys—OLD FORESTER and Early Times—distilled in the distillery of the same name in Shively, Kentucky.

Early Times is thought to be one of the oldest bourbon brands and is now marketed in 2 versions—both of them using the Scottish spelling of whisky, without an "e."

Early Times Kentucky Straight Bourbon is a light, balanced whiskey at 80 and 86 proof. In the 1950s it was

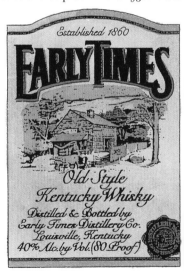

a best-seller in the United States, but today it is produced solely for export.

Early Times Old Style Kentucky Whisky came onto the market in the 1980s as a replacement for the straight bourbon version and was an immediate success. It is 80 proof and is aged in old barrels, which is why it cannot be sold as bourbon. Early Times Old Style is a light and dry whiskey, not as sweet as a bourbon but also not as flat as a blended or "light" whiskey.

In the Early Times Distillery 2 different grain mixtures are used: for the Early Times whiskeys the mash is made up of 79 percent corn, 11 percent rye, and 10 percent barley malt; for Old Forester it is 72 percent corn, 18 percent rye, and 10 percent barley malt. In both the sour mash component is 20 percent.

(Tel. 502 585-1100)

EATON'S SPECIAL RESERVE
Blended Scotch from Douglas LAING & CO.

ECHO SPRING
Kentucky straight bourbon from HEAVEN HILL DISTILLERS.

A minor brand rarely found north of Kentucky.

EDEL FALCKE
German blended whiskey, 80 proof, from C. W. Falckenthal (see DER FALCKNER). Edel Falcke is the successor brand of Oldmaster, which Falckenthal brought out in the early 90s as a "malt whiskey." Once it became known that Oldmaster was in fact a blend, it was taken off the market and replaced by Edel Falcke.

EDRADOUR
Scottish single malt (Southern Highlands) from CAMPBELL DISTILLERS (PERNOD RICARD).

A light, charming malt from sherry barrels.

Original bottling: 10 years old, 80 proof.

Cadenhead: 19 years old (distilled 1976), 98.4 proof.

Signatory: 19 years old (distilled 1976), 98.6 proof.

Edradour was first documented in 1837 but is possibly older. In 1933 the distillery was bought by Wm WHITELEY, and since that time it has supplied one of the base malts for that

firm's blend HOUSE OF LORDS. Edradour has been available from Campbell Distillers as a single malt only since 1982.

Edradour is the smallest and most traditional distillery in Scotland. After the fashion of the old farmhouse distilleries, its 3 employees produce as much whisky in a year as other distilleries do in a week. Edradour has 2 stills and gets its water from a spring on Ben Vrackie.

(Tel. 1796 47 35 24)

EILEANDOUR
Scottish vatted malt, 10 years old, from ISLE OF ARRAN DISTILLERS.

ELDRIDGE, POPE & CO.
This English brewery was founded in Dorchester, Dorset, in 1833, and since 1907 has been bottling its own whiskies, CHAIRMAN'S and OLD HIGHLAND BLEND.

ELIJAH CRAIG
Kentucky straight bourbon, super premium, from HEAVEN HILL DISTILLERS.

Bourbon at its best: rich, round, and pleasantly sweet. Available as a 12-year-old at 94 proof and, since 1995, also as a SINGLE-BARREL BOURBON 18 years old and 90 proof.

The brand is named after the Baptist preacher Elijah Craig (1743–1808), who was also a distiller and is often called the inventor of bourbon.

Some, however, maintain that that legend was deliberately circulated in the late 19th century to annoy the temperance advocates, who could not imagine that a man of the cloth could have been responsible for the existence of the devil's brew.

ELMER T. LEE
Kentucky straight bourbon from SAZERAC'S LEESTOWN DISTILLING CO.

Although 90 proof, a velvety soft SINGLE-BARREL BOURBON that came on the market in 1992 and is named after the distiller's master stillman, who still looks in once a week to see that things are being done right.

EL VINO CONNOISSEUR'S BLEND
Blended Scotch, de luxe, 7 years old, which has been sold by the famous London wine shop El Vino since the end of the 19th century. After blending it is aged in the barrels in which the shop imports its sherry. There is also a 13-year-old BUNNAHABHAIN bottled under the name El Vino Islay Malt.

Both bottlings are available in the firm's London wine bars—for example, the highly recommended El Vino Bar in Fleet Street or Old Wine

Westering Home.

Shades in Martin Lane. They can also be ordered by mail:

El Vino Co. Ltd., Vintage House, 1 Hare Place, London EC4.

EMBLEM
Japanese blend, premium, from KIRIN-SEAGRAM.

A dry and rather smoky blend of native and Scotch whiskies.

EMMETS CLASSIC CREAM
Irish whiskey cream liqueur, 34 proof, from IDV/Grand Metropolitan.

ERIN'S ISLE
Blended Irish whiskey, standard, 80 proof, from COOLEY DISTILLERY.

A young whiskey, with respect to both the amount of time it has been on the market and what is inside the bottle. Erin's Isle is an inexpensive brand that is bottled and marketed by INVERGORDON DISTILLERS.

EVAN WILLIAMS
Kentucky straight bourbon from HEAVEN HILL DISTILLERS.

The British whisky doyen Michael Jackson predicted in 1987 that Evan Williams would be the coming brand on the bourbon market, and since the early 1990s it has indeed been one of the top sellers. This is not surprising, for all of the Evan Williams versions are bourbons with no sharp edges: medium heavy, soft, and sweet. The Black Label, 7 years old and 90 proof, now ranks third in the United States. In addition there are the 8-year-old Green Label at 86 proof, the 10-year-old Evan Williams 1783, and a Single Barrel Vintage at 86.6 proof, which is generally 8 or 9 years old. The label gives only the year it was distilled; the first was from 1986, and the 1987 is currently available.

The brand was created in 1960 and named after one of Kentucky's first distillers. Evan Williams opened his distillery in Louisville in 1783, but 20 years later he was forced to close it down because of complaints from his neighbors.

EZRA BROOKS

Kentucky straight bourbon from SHERMAN.

A rather traditional whiskey, medium heavy and smooth on the palate, available in 2 versions: Ezra Brooks Gold Label, at 90 proof, and Old Ezra Rare Old Sippin' Whiskey, either 7 or 12 years old and 101 proof. (For old-fashioned Kentucky folk the designation "sippin' whiskey" is virtually the highest compliment you can pay to a brand.)

This old brand was bought in the 1950s by MEDLEY and marketed as a

competitor to JACK DANIEL'S. The design of the bottle and label were modeled so closely after those of the competition that the producers of Jack Daniel's even took them to court—without success. Since then the brand has changed hands a number of times, finally landing with the Sherman firm in St. Louis, Missouri. Ezra Brooks is bottled there even now, but what distillery it comes from is a secret. The only thing that is certain is that it is produced in Kentucky.

I've always found that good whiskey,
taken in moderation as an appetizer,
is the best of tonics.

Eugene O'Neill,
Long Day's Journey into Night

THE FAMOUS GROUSE

Blended Scotch from Matthew Gloag & Son, a subsidiary of HIGHLAND DISTILLERIES CO. A pleasantly aromatic whisky for any time of day and, in addition, the Scots' favorite blend and one of the top 10 best-selling blends worldwide.

The premium is 80 proof; the 15-year-old de luxe, 86 proof.

In 1896, after being active in the wine business in France for some years, Matthew Gloag returned to his native Perth, took over his grandfather's wine and spirit shop, and began producing his own blend. He called it The Grouse Brand, and was soon so successful with it that he tacked on the word "Famous." In the 1920s, Famous Grouse was exported in quantity to the Caribbean, and smugglers brought it from there to the United States. When Prohibition was repealed, the Gloags already had

a foot in the door and could establish their whisky on the American market. In 1970 the firm was sold to Highland Distilleries, whose ambitious advertising campaign in the 1980s made the brand num-

ber 1 in Scotland and number 2 in England (see also DCL).

The base malts are BUNNAHAB HAIN, THE GLENROTHES, HIGHLAND PARK, and TAMDHU.

FILTRATION

With the exception of most so-called SINGLE-BARREL BOTTLINGS, all whiskies are filtered before they are bottled, so as to get rid of any undesirable acidic esters or aromas picked up from defective barrels. Various methods are used:

Cold filtration: In this process used in Scotland, the whisky is chilled to just below freezing. Many of the undesired substances simply solidify and can then be filtered out mechanically.

Active coal filtration: This method is especially popular in Kentucky. The fresh whiskey passes through a layer of charcoal dust under pressure, and any bacteria are caught in it. Even a spoiled mash can be revived by the addition of active charcoal.

F

whiskey a special aroma and an extraordinary mildness. In the case of GENTLEMAN JACK the process is repeated after aging in the barrel. The used, whiskey-drenched charcoal is packaged and sold and is in great demand among barbecue fanatics.

FINDLATER'S FINEST

Blended Scotch, 5 and 21 years old, from Findlater, Mackie Todd & Co., a subsidiary of INVER-

Charcoal filtration: This method, known as the Lincoln County process, is prescribed for the production of TENNESSEE WHISKEY. Before being aged in barrels, the fresh distillate is filtered drop by drop through a layer of oak charcoal roughly 10 feet (3 meters) thick, at the bottom of which it passes through a woolen cloth. This removes all of the undesirable aromatic substances.

The process is called "charcoal mellowing" or "leaching" and takes from 10 to 12 days. It is very time-consuming and costly, but it gives the

GORDON DISTILLERS (WHYTE & MACKAY, AMERICAN BRANDS). It is possible that Alexander Findlater's father—one of the hated tax men whose job it was to track down moonshiners—occasionally brought home some of his catch and thereby helped to develop his son's taste. In any case, the son began dealing in whisky in Dublin at the age of

26, moved to London in 1850, and there made a name for himself with the blends that he started marketing under his own name in 1863.

Findlater, which has been a part of Invergordon since 1990, also puts out a vatted malt by the name of MAR LODGE.

FINE FARE
Blended Scotch from the supermarket chain of the same name. Available as a 5-year-old blend and a 12-year-old vatted malt.

FINE OLD SPECIAL
Blended Scotch from Joseph Holt. This Scotch is available only in the vicinity of Manchester, where the Holt firm has had its headquarters since 1849, selling whisky in addition to beer.

FIRTH HOUSE
Blended Scotch, 5 years old, from Brodie Crawford & Co. (see BRODIE'S SUPREME).

FIVE STAR BLEND
Blended American from LAIRD & CO.

FLEISCHMANN'S PREFERRED
Blended American from BARTON DISTILLING (Canandaigua).

An old brand that formerly came from the Fleischmann Distillery in Owensboro, Kentucky. In the 1980s it was acquired by GLENMORE DISTILLING, which has in turn been a part of Barton since 1995.

FLORIAN

A variant of the whiskey sour. Shake 1½ oz. bourbon, a few dashes of Chartreuse Verte, one dash of Angostura, a bar spoon of powdered sugar, and ¾ oz. orange juice with ice and strain.

FORFARS
Blended Scotch from ANGUS DUNDEE.

FORTNUM & MASON
The prestigious department store near Piccadilly Circus offers a series of whiskies under its own label: there is a Fortnum & Mason Choice Old, as well as an 8-year-old Blended Scotch, a 12-year-old Vatted Malt, and a 21-year-old Single Malt, the producers of which are not disclosed.

Fortnum & Mason also sells a special bottling of 21-year-old LINKWOOD malts.

FOUR ROSES
Kentucky straight bourbon and blended American from SEAGRAM.

One of the great old bourbon brands, registered in 1888, available in the United States only as a blended whiskey. The bourbon versions are produced exclusively for export, in the same distillery near Lawrenceburg in which the brand was produced even before Prohibition. Originally it was called the Old rentice Distillery, and it produced a ew additional brands now marketed by other firms (see BENCHMARK, EAGLE RARE). It was built in 1910–12 in an impressive mixture of styles ranging from Spanish mission to a Disneyland version of Spanish mission. In 1943 the Seagram concern took over the distillery, along with the Four Roses brand, which is now offered in 4 versions. The standard bottling is 80 proof and is one of the best-selling bourbons in Europe; in addition there are the Premium Black Label at 86 proof and the super-premium Platinum, also at 86 proof. Recently Seagram has also brought out a Single Barrel Reserve, with no indication of age, at 86 proof—to say nothing of the attractive

yellow cans filled with Four Roses Cola.

The various brands produced by most U.S. distilleries are generally simply different ages of the same whiskeys. Seagram operates differently, using a method more like that used in Canada or Ireland. The various Four Roses versions are combinations of distillates of different mixtures of grains (75 percent corn, 21 percent rye, and 4 percent barley malt, or 60 percent corn, 36 percent rye, and 4 percent barley malt) and different yeast cultures. The sour mash component is the only constant; it is always 25 percent.

(Tel. 502 839-3436)

FRASER'S SUPREME

Blended Scotch from Strathnairn Whisky, a subsidiary of GORDON & MACPHAIL.

FRISCO SOUR

A variant of the WHISKEY SOUR that includes, in addition to bourbon, ½ oz. of Benedictine.

FROM THE BARREL

Japanese blend, 102.8 proof, from NIKKA, available since 1985. Even though the name and the alcohol content would suggest as much, this is not a SINGLE-BARREL BOTTLING.

G

Oh many a peer of England brews
Livelier liquor than the Muse,
And malt does more than Milton can
To justify God's ways to man.

A. E. Housman,
A Shropshire Lad, XVII

GAIRLOCH

Blended Scotch from McMullen & Sons, one of the many British breweries that own a private brand and sell it in their own pubs.

Gairloch has been around since 1904 and is produced by ROBERTSON & BAXTER, which makes use of first-class malts such as GLENGOYNE, THE GLENROTHES, HIGHLAND PARK, and THE MACALLAN.

GALE'S

Blended Scotch, 8 years old, from George Gale & Co.

The Gale firm, owners of the South English Hampshire Brewery, is one of the few producers willing to reveal which whiskies go into their brands. The malts are THE GLENLIVET, BEN NEVIS, DUFFTOWN, GLEN GRANT, BUNNAHABHAIN, HIGHLAND PARK, and DALMORE; the grains come from STRATHCLYDE, DUMBARTON, CAMERON BRIG, and NORTH BRITISH.

Gale's is sold mainly in the pubs associated with the Hampshire Brewery.

GAMEFAIR

Scottish vatted malt, 10 years old, from Hynard Hughes.

A small brand that has been produced by the Hynard family since 1926 and is drunk mainly in the area around Leicester (see also HYNARD'S FINEST).

GARNHEATH

Scottish distillery in Moffat, Airdrie (Lowlands), built in 1965 by INVER HOUSE DISTILLERS. The distillery was also called Moffat or Inver House Distillery. It had 5 patent stills and 1 pot still, the largest malting house in the world at the time, 32 warehouses, and a blending and bottling plant. It produced mainly grain whisky, but also a malt called GLEN FLAGLER. The entire complex was closed down in 1985, but the Glen Flagler brand is still in existence (see KILLYLOCH).

GENTLEMAN JACK

Tennessee sour mash, 80 proof, from BROWN-FORMAN's Jack Daniel distillery.

Gentleman Jack was introduced in 1988, and unlike its stablemate Jack Daniel's, it is filtered a second time through charcoal after it has aged (see FILTRATION). This and the lower ALCOHOL CONTENT make for a noticeably milder but still substantial premium whiskey.

The words "Single Whiskey" on the label are obviously meant to suggest some connection to SINGLE-BARREL BOTTLING or SINGLE MALT, but in fact there is none.

ESTᴰ 1870

GEORGE
Dickel
TENNESSEE
Sour Mash
WHISKY
OLD No 8 BRAND

DISTILLED & CHARCOAL MELLOWED AT
GEORGE A. DICKEL & CO. TULLAHOMA
TENNESSEE

40% Alc/vol (80 Proof)

GEORGE DICKEL

Tennessee sour mash from the George Dickel Distillery, Tullahoma, which belongs to UD.

A very elegant whisky—they use the Scottish spelling—and a well-kept secret overshadowed by the other great Tennessee whiskey, Jack Daniel's.

Of the two Dickel versions, Old No. 8, at 86.8 proof and with a black label, is the younger (4 to 6 years old) and a good example of the fact that age does not necessarily mean better quality, for the older Old No. 12, 90 proof and with a white label, is no competition for its younger brother in terms of elegance and fullness.

Since 1994 Dickel has also offered a kind of SMALL-BATCH BOURBON called Special Barrel Reserve, 10 years old and 86 proof. The old George Dickel whiskies from the pre-

Prohibition era were often called "mellow as moonlight," and if that description doesn't mean anything to you, just taste this version.

These earlier whiskies were known by the name Cascade Whisky. Cascade was the name of the distillery in which George Dickel (1818–88) began distilling his whisky in about 1880. After Prohibition, which was already in force in Tennessee in 1908, the name was bought by Schenley, which built a new distillery close to the original one in 1958. The whisky began to be marketed under its present name only in the 1960s. Dickel was absorbed into UD along with Schenley in 1987.

The distillery is near Tullahoma, a town in deepest Tennessee, and is operated with the same attention to tradition as is the Jack Daniel distillery only a few miles away. (See also TENNESSEE WHISKEY.)

GEORGIA MOON

Kentucky straight corn whiskey from HEAVEN HILL DISTILLERS.

This brand name was obviously chosen to evoke the notion of MOONSHINE. Like true moonshine, Georgia Moon is marketed in jelly jars, and the label proudly proclaims: "aged less than fifty days" (often it's less than thirty). Accordingly, it is almost as clear as water and does indeed taste more like rotgut than bourbon as we know it.

Georgia Moon is the best-known corn whiskey in the United States and, as such, almost the only one available north of Kentucky.

GERMAN WHISKEY

Whiskey became popular in Germany only in the 1960s, but as early as 1913 the Germans had been experimenting with producing similar spirits. At the Institut für Gärungsgewerbe (Institute for Fermentation Trades) in Berlin, they tried making whiskey "in the American way." They aged 90-proof potato spirits for several years in charred oak barrels from Slavonia, and it is said that the resulting whiskey was very similar to bourbon. But what happened to it is not recorded. The next attempt was made in 1958, when in Bingen the Racke firm started producing a German variant

of Scotch, diluting imported malt with native grain distillates (see RACKE RAUCHZART). The time was right, for in the early post-war years the Germans were increasingly eager to experience foreign delights. Hollywood had played its part in glamorizing the American lifestyle, and soon even German films would show both elegantly dressed gentlemen and toughs drinking quantities of whisk(e)y. Im-

ported spirits were still considered luxury goods at the time. Racke Rauchzart was able to capitalize on whisk(e)y's upscale image and in fact managed to hold onto its position as the market leader against Scottish and American competition into the 1970s, in large part because of its low price.

Bourbon had become popular in Germany in the 1960s, but neither Racke's imported brand Old Red Fox nor the imitation bourbon Jacob Stück Whiskey, from the house of Jacobi, survived for long.

Today Racke Rauchzart is still one of the 5 best-selling whiskey brands in Germany. Well below it is DER FALCKNER, which is distilled exclusively from native grain by the Falckenthal firm, near Berlin. Since 1995 there has also been a German malt whiskey; it is marketed under the somewhat ominous name PIRATEN (Pirates') WHISKEY, and comes from Franconia.

GIBSON'S FINEST
Canadian blend from VALLEYFIELD distillery, a property of UD.

In addition to the 12-year-old premium there is also the de luxe version, Gibson's Finest Sterling Edition. This brand has no connection to the former Gibson firm (see BARTON DISTILLING).

GILBEY'S
Indian blended whisky from Gilbey (IDV/Grand Metropolitan).

Versions: Gilbey's Green, Heritage, Old Gold, White.

The firm of W & A Gilbey began as wine dealers in London in 1857. In 1872 it opened its first gin distillery there. (Gilbey's gin is currently number 5 on the world market.) Since 1887 Gilbey has also been in the whisky business (see GLEN SPEY, KNOCKANDO, STRATHMILL), and in the Canadian market it has been highly successful with its BLACK VELVET brand since 1945.

The merger between Gilbey and Justerini & Brooks (see J & B) in 1962 produced the IDV concern, which was later acquired by Grand Metropolitan. Within that organization, Gilbey is also now responsible for the whiskey liqueur BAILEYS ORIGINAL IRISH CREAM.

The name is used as a whisky brand only on the Indian market. (See also BOND 7, CATTO'S, REDBREAST.)

GILLON'S
Blended Scotch from John Gillon & Co., a subsidiary of UD. Currently available only in Italy. The Gillon firm was founded in 1917 and had already changed hands several times before it was acquired by the DCL in

1925. It was given the license for the Glenury distillery (see GLENURY-ROYAL), which it held until that facility was torn down in 1993.

Gillon also produces a blend called KING WILLIAM IV.

GIRVAN
Scottish distilling complex belonging to the firm William GRANT & SONS.

This Lowlands distillery, established in 1963, produces the grain whisky for the various Grant blends, which are created there. Within the complex there is also a malt distillery called LADYBURN. Girvan also became available only recently as a single, namely from

Cadenhead: 15 years old (distilled 1979), 126.2 proof (see also BLACK-BARREL).

GLAYVA
[Gaelic for "very good"]

Scottish whisky herb liqueur, 70 proof, with a ginger and anise flavor, from INVERGORDON DISTILLERS (WHYTE & MACKAY, AMERICAN BRANDS), on the market since 1974.

GLEN ALBYN
Scottish single malt (Highlands, Inverness).

This malty whisky with a medium-heavy body is now available only from independent bottlers—and only small quantities are left.

Gordon & MacPhail: Vintages 1963, 1965, 1972, 1973, all 80 proof.

Cadenhead: 27 years old (distilled 1964), 102.8 proof; 30 years old (distilled 1964), 93.4 proof.

Signatory: 15 years old (distilled 1980), 86 proof.

The distillery, established in 1846, was appropriated by the U.S. Navy in World War I for the manufacture of mines. Subsequently the firm MACKINLAY took it over, using the malt mainly in its blends. In 1972 Glen Albyn was acquired by the DCL, which closed it down in 1983. Today there is a supermarket where it once stood.

GLENALLACHIE
Scottish single malt (Speyside, Aberlour) from CAMPBELL DISTILLERS (PERNOD RICARD).

A light and very elegant malt that is unfortunately extremely difficult to find.

Original bottling: 12 years old, 80 proof (produced under the former owners, INVERGORDON DISTILLERS).

The Castle Collection: 18 years old (distilled 1976), 86 proof.

The distillery was built in 1967–68 by Mackinlay McPherson, a subsidiary of SCOTTISH & NEWCASTLE BREWERIES. In 1989 it was acquired by Invergordon, and in 1989 by Campbell Distillers, which is currently not bottling the whisky.

GLEN AVON

Scottish single malt (Speyside), 8, 15, 21, and 25 years old, and also vintages 1953, 1955, 1958, and 1962, from Avonside Whisky Ltd., a subsidiary of GORDON & MACPHAIL.

There was once a Glen Avon distillery in Scotland, but it closed down well over a century ago. For decades Gordon & MacPhail has been aging this whisky in its own warehouses but declines to say what distillery produces it.

GLEN BAREN

Scottish vatted malt, 5 and 8 years old, from KINROSS WHISKY CO.

GLEN BLAIR

Scottish vatted malt from BURN STEWART DISTILLERS. The firm's best-selling vatted.

GLENBURGIE

Scottish single malt (Speyside, Forres) from J. & G. STODART (ALLIED DISTILLERS, ALLIED DOMECQ).

A scarce, soft, somewhat sweet malt.

Original bottling: 5 years old, very scarce; the designation "Glenlivet" on its label is confusing.

CONNOISSEURS CHOICE

Connoisseurs Choice, a range of single malts from various districts of Scotland.

The distilleries situated in the area of the valley of the River Spey produce some of the finest malt whiskies.

GRAMPIANS

SINGLE SPEYSIDE
MALT SCOTCH WHISKY

DISTILLED AT

GLENBURGIE

DISTILLERY

PROPRIETORS: Jas. & Geo. Stodart Ltd

DISTILLED 1968 DISTILLED

SPECIALLY SELECTED PRODUCED AND BOTTLED BY

GORDON & MACPHAIL

ELGIN · SCOTLAND
PRODUCT OF SCOTLAND

75cl   40%vol

Gordon & MacPhail: Vintages 1948, 1960, 1967, 1968, all 80 proof; 8 years old, 80 proof; 1966, 115.2 and 122.4 proof; 1984, 118.4 proof.

Cadenhead: 28 years old (distilled 1963), 115.6 proof;

13 years old (distilled 1978), 119.6 proof.

The distillery was founded in 1829 and was originally called Kilnflat. In 1930 it was bought by HIRAM WALKER & SONS and assigned to its subsidiary Stodart, which continues to operate it to this day. Since that time the majority of its whiskies have gone into the BALLANTINE's blends. Glenburgie has 2 stills, and the water comes from local springs.

From 1958 to the early 1980s the distillery also had 2 LOMOND STILLS, with which it produced a malt called GLENCRAIG.

(Tel. 1343 85 02 58)

GLENCADAM

Scottish single malt (Eastern Highlands) from George BALLANTINE & SON (ALLIED DISTILLERS, ALLIED DOMECQ).

A full and malty digestif whose flavor reminded one inspired writer of "wet wool." Glencadam is currently unavailable.

Gordon & MacPhail: Vintage 1974, 80 proof.

Cadenhead: 11 years old (distilled 1980), 122.4 proof.

The distillery was opened in 1825 and since 1954 has belonged to HIRAM WALKER & SONS, now part of the Allied group. The lion's share of its malts goes into the Ballantine's blends. Glencadam has 2 stills; its water comes from Loch Lee.

(Tel. 3562 22 17)

GLEN CALDER

Blended Scotch, 80 proof, from GORDON & MACPHAIL.

A blend with a high proportion of malt, one of the few available also in vintage bottlings—in this case, 1949.

GLEN CARREN

Scottish vatted malt, 10 years old, from HALL & BRAMLEY.

GLEN CATRINE

Blended Scotch from Glen Catrine Bonded Warehouse Ltd.

This firm was formerly only a blender and bottler, but since 1985 it has owned its own distilleries. At that time it took over the distillery LOCH LOMOND from INVERGORDON DISTILLERS, and in 1993 it began construction of a grain distillery.

In 1994 it acquired the assets of the bankrupt Gibson International (see BARTON DISTILLING), including the distilleries GLEN SCOTIA and LITTLEMILL.

In addition to Glen Catrine it produces the following brands: CLANS-

---

man, Glenshiel, High Commissioner, Inchmurrin, Old Rhosdhu, and Scots Earl. Of the large number of former Gibson blends only a few are still in existence: Highland Mist, House of Stuart, and Howard MacLaren de Luxe. (See also Old Court, Royal Culross, Scotia Royale.)

GLEN CLOVA

Blended Scotch from Invergordon Distillers (Whyte & Mackay, American Brands).

GLENCOE

Scottish vatted malt, 8 years old, 114 proof, from Red Lion Blending.

GLEN CORRIE

Scottish vatted malt from William Grant & Sons.

GLENCRAIG

Scottish single malt (Speyside, Forres) from J. & G. Stodart (Allied Distillers, Allied Domecq).

This whisky comes from the Glenburgie distillery. For a time (1958–80) that facility was outfitted with 2 Lomond stills, and Glencraig was distilled only in them.

Gordon & MacPhail bottled it at that time and is currently offering a vintage 1970.

GLENDARROCH

Blended Scotch, 12-year-old de luxe, from William Gillies & Co., a trading house in Glasgow (not to be confused with A. Gillies; see Glen Scotia). This Scotch takes its name from

a former Highland distillery that was operated for a time by the Gillies family. The distillery was also called Glenfyne; it was closed in 1937 and now houses a fish farm and a cabinetmaking operation.

Gillies & Co. also owned the Oban distillery for a short time.

GLEN DEVERON

Scottish single malt (Speyside, Banff) from the MacDuff distillery, property of Wm Lawson (Bacardi).

The ideal malt for beginners: soft, clean, and malty.

Original bottling: 12 years old, 80 proof, for export also at 86 proof, and as a 5-year-old at 86 proof.

Gordon & MacPhail: The firm bottles Deveron under the name of the distillery, MacDuff, and currently offers a 1975 at 80 proof.

Cadenhead: Also labeled MacDuff, a 16-year-old (distilled 1978) at 111.6 proof and a 20-year-old (distilled 1975) at 117.8 proof.

MacDuff was built in 1962–63 and has changed owners several times. For a while it belonged to the Morrison family (see MORRISON BOWMORE DISTILLERS), then in 1972 it was sold to Wm Lawson, a firm taken over in 1980 by the Luxemburg concern General Beverage. General Beverage controls the Italian producer Martini & Rossi and since 1995 has been part of the Bacardi empire. The majority of the MacDuff malts are destined for the Lawson blends. The distillery has 4 stills and the water comes from the Gelly Burn.

(Tel. 1261 81 26 12)

GLEN DEW
Scottish vatted malt, 5 years old, from Mitchell Bros., Glasgow. Currently an extremely scarce brand that incorporates the malt NORTH PORT.

GLEN DOWAN
Blended Scotch from J. & G. GRANT.

THE GLENDRONACH
Scottish single malt (Speyside, Huntly) from ALLIED DISTILLERS (ALLIED DOMECQ).

An elegant whisky that is treasured above all by lovers of mild malts.

Original bottling: Traditional, 12 years old, 80 and 86 proof. The bottlings Sherry Cask (12 and 18

years old) and Original, which were put out in the 1980s and first made the malt popular, are no longer produced.

The distillery was opened in 1826 and for a time belonged to the WILLIAM GRANT family. Since 1960 it has been owned by TEACHER's, which firm, which uses Glendronach in its blends. Wm Teacher & Sons has been a part of Allied since 1976.

Glendronach still operates in the traditional manner. It has its own malting floors, and its 4 stills are fired with coal; the water comes from a spring 4 miles east of the distillery. Glendronach is only lightly peated and is aged in new oak barrels and sherry casks.

(Tel. 1466 73 02 02)

GLENDROSTAN
Blended Scotch, 8 and 12 years old, from Longman, a subsidiary of INVERGORDON DISTILLERS (WHYTE AND MACKAY, AMERICAN BRANDS).

GLEN DRUMM
Scottish vatted malt from Douglas LAING & CO.

GLEN DRUMMOND
Scottish vatted malt from INVER HOUSE DISTILLERS.

GLENDULLAN
Scottish single malt (Speyside, Dufftown) from MACDONALD GREENLEES LTD. (UD).

An opulent digestif malt that deserves to be better known.

Original bottling: 12 years old, 86 proof ("Flora & Fauna" series), also in the "Rare Malt Selection"; the pre-UD bottling from the DCL, also 12 years old, is now valued as a rarity.

Cadenhead: 25 years old (distilled 1965), 102.2 and 104.8 proof; 17 years old (distilled 1978), 130.6 proof.

James MacArthur: 11 years old, 86 proof.

The distillery was built in 1897–98 by Wm Williams, a precursor firm of the present-day licensee Macdonald Greenlees. The DCL took over the operation in 1927 and in the 1970s added a new distillery with 6 stills. The water comes from the Conval Hills. The major part of the malt is used in the OLD PARR blends.

(Tel. 1340 82 02 50)

GLEN ELGIN
Scottish single malt (Speyside, Elgin) from WHITE HORSE (UD).

A pleasant, mild malt for every occasion.

Original bottling: The 12-year-old version at 86 proof is sadly no longer available. A new one with no age designation is marketed almost exclusively in Japan.

Gordon & MacPhail: Vintage 1968, 80 proof.

Cadenhead: Recently the firm had a 22-year-old from 1971 at 100.6 proof.

The distillery was opened in 1900. It is one of 9 distilleries in the environs of Elgin, an important whisky center.

Glen Elgin has 6 stills; the water comes from springs next to Millbuies Loch. The whisky is one of the base malts for the White Horse blend.

(Tel. 1343 86 02 12)

GLENESK
Scottish single malt (Highlands, Montrose) from UD.

A well-balanced malt that is now difficult to find.

Original bottling: Until 1985 Glenesk was bottled by Wm SANDERSON & SON as a 12-year-old at 86 proof; since then it has been offered by UD in the "Rare Malt Selection" under the name Hillside.

Gordon & MacPhail: Vintage 1982, 80 proof.

G

Cadenhead: 13 years old (distilled 1982), 133 proof.

A distillery with a confusing history. It was established under the name Highland Esk in 1897 in what had once been a flax mill, then 2 years later the name was changed to North Esk. During World War I it was used as a barracks, and once the war was over it was closed. In 1938 it was bought by an American firm, refitted as a grain distillery, and called Montrose.

In 1964 the distillery was acquired by the DCL, which 10 years later changed it back to malt production and named it Hillside. Beginning in 1980 it was called Glenesk and supplied the base malt for the blend VAT 69, but since 1985 it has served only as a malt house for other UD distilleries.

GLENFAIRN
Scottish vatted malt from INVERGORDON DISTILLERS (WHYTE & MACKAY, AMERICAN BRANDS).

GLENFARCLAS
[Gaelic for "valley of green grass"]

Scottish single malt (Speyside) from J. & G. Grant.

To describe this extraordinary malt one has no choice but to resort to the hackneyed adjectives "classic" or "quintessential," for it has everything one could want in a Highland malt: strength, mildness, and charac-

ter. Even lovers of heavier, peatier whiskies are impressed by Glenfarclas's complexity and finesse. Tommy Dewar (see DEWAR's) called it "the king of whiskies." Michael Jackson refers to it simply as "nectar."

Glenfarclas is available at various different ages, all of which have their admirers. Although it would be difficult to choose, there are a number of authorities who feel that the 15-year-old is the best of all.

Original bottling: 10 years old, 80 proof; 12 years old, 86 proof; 15 years old, 92 proof; 17 years old, 86 proof; 21, 25, and 30 years old, 86 proof; as Glenfarclas 105 there is an 8-year-old at 120 proof, for a long time the only cask-strength malt officially bottled.

In addition, the vintages 1961, 1970, 1971, 1976, and 1978 are available, all 86 proof.

Cadenhead: 13 years old (distilled 1980, sherry cask), 92 proof; 14 years old (distilled 1980), 117.4 proof.

Signatory: 24 years old (distilled 1969), 113 proof; 21 years old (distilled 1964), 108.2 proof; 36 years old (distilled 1959), 105.2 proof.

Glenfarclas is one of the few independent family operations in the

Scottish whisky industry. The distillery was probably established in 1836, and it is certain that it has been in operation since 1844. Since 1865 it has been owned by the J. & G. Grant family (no relation to the GLENFIDDICH Grants), and it is now being operated by the 5th generation. The distillery has 6 stills; the water comes from Ben Rinnes. Up until only a few years ago, bourbon and sherry casks and new oak barrels were used for aging, but now the firm has begun using sherry casks exclusively.

See also EAGLE OF SPEY, HIGHLAND CATTLE.

(Tel. 1807 50 02 09)

GLENFERN
Blended Scotch from UD.

GLENFIDDICH
Scottish single malt (Speyside, Dufftown) from William GRANT & SONS.

Far and away the best-selling malt worldwide, Glenfiddich is also a good beginner's whisky, light and pleasant to the palate, with increasing complexity in its older versions.

Original bottling: Special Reserve without age designation, 80 proof;

Excellence, 18 years old, 86 proof; Ancient Reserve, 18 years old, 86 proof; Wedgwood, 21 years old, 86 proof, in a porcelain decanter; Stag's Head, 30 years old (distilled 1963), 103.4 proof; and a number of other bottlings marketed especially in duty-free shops in the Far East. The 500 bottles of a 50-year-old that were placed on the market a few years ago are purely collectors' items. Currently there is also a 15-year-old Cask Strength.

Cadenhead: 15 years old (distilled 1979), 116.6 proof.

Ever since it was built in 1886–87, the distillery has belonged to the William Grant family, which introduced the whisky to the world market in 1963 as the first single malt. Other producers laughed at the notion, just as they laughed at what seemed at that time a highly eccentric triangular bottle, which is now the Glenfiddich trademark. In those boom years for blended Scotch, malt whisky was considered unmarketable outside of Scotland because of its intensity. It took about 10 years before the competition realized how large the market for single malts really is, but by that time the

Grants had already staked out the territory; today 35 percent of the malts exported come from the Glenfiddich distillery. Malt drinkers around the world like to dismiss the brand as being too "mainstream," but they should at least respect the firm's courage; without it, most of our favorite tipples would be buried in anonymous blends. And in addition, the older versions of Glenfiddich are anything but boring.

By now the largest distillery in Scotland, Glenfiddich has a total of 28 stills. The water comes from the Robbie Dubh Springs. The entire process, from malting to bottling, takes place on the distillery premises. The whisky is aged in bourbon and sherry barrels.

(Tel. 1340 82 03 73).

GLEN FLAGLER
Scottish Lowland malt from the GARNHEATH distillery, an INVER HOUSE DISTILLERS property.

The distillery was closed in 1985, but the remaining stores are being mixed with other malts and offered as vatted malt under the name Glen Flagler Pure Malt Special Reserve (8 years old, 80 proof). In 1994 the independent bottler SIGNATORY placed on the market another 350 bottles of Glen Flagler as a single malt (23 years old, distilled in 1970, 100.2 proof).

GLENFORRES
Scottish vatted malt, 12 years old, from Wm WHITELEY (PERNOD RICARD). One of the base malts comes from the EDRADOUR distillery, which for a time was called Glenforres.

GLENFOYLE RESERVE
Blended Scotch, 12 years old, from Longman, a subsidiary of INVERGORDON DISTILLERS (WHYTE & MACKAY, AMERICAN BRANDS).

GLEN FRASER
Scottish single malt, 8, 12, 15, and 21 years old, 80 proof, from GORDON & MACPHAIL.

The bottlers refuse to tell which distillery produces this smoky malt; they will say only that it comes from the Highlands.

GLENGALWAN
Scottish vatted malt from INVER HOUSE.

GLEN GARIOCH
Scottish single malt (Eastern Highlands) from MORRISON BOWMORE DISTILLERS (SUNTORY).

A good, middle-grade malt, especially peaty for a Highland.

Original bottling: 8 years old, 86 proof; 10 years old, 80 proof; 12 years old, 80 proof; 15 years old, 86 proof; 21 years old, 86 proof; 1984, 80 and 110 proof.

The distillery was established in 1798 and operated for a time by Wm Sanderson & Son. The Morrison family took it over in 1970. Up to the time it closed in 1995 it ran 4 stills, taking its water from Perock Hill. Glen Garioch had its own malting floors and used bourbon and sherry casks for aging.

(Tel. 1651 87 27 06)

GLEN GARRY

Blended Scotch from John Hopkins & Co., a subsidiary of UD, which is exclusively exported to Spain.

After making his money for a time as a cognac importer in Glasgow,

John Hopkins switched to producing blended whisky. In 1878 he introduced the brand Glen Garry and 2 years later, Old Mill (now owned by Whyte & Mackay).

For a time, Hopkins & Co. owned the distilleries Speyburn (1897–1916) and Tobermory (1890–1916). The firm was acquired by the DCL in 1916. Today it belongs to United Distillers, for which it has operated the Oban distillery since 1992.

GLEN GHOIL

Blended Scotch from Hall & Bramley, available since the late 19th century.

GLENGLASSAUGH

Scottish single malt (Speyside, Banff) from Highland Distilleries Co.

A charming middleweight, whose unusual aroma led a well-known writer to say that this whisky smelled like freshly made beds.

Original bottling: The 80-proof version, without age designation, and

the 12-year-old at 86 proof are almost impossible to find.

Gordon & MacPhail: Vintage 1983, 80 proof.

Cadenhead: 13 years old (distilled 1977), 119.6 proof.

Glenglassaugh was established in 1875 and has belonged to Highland Distilleries since the 1890s. It has been shut down repeatedly, most recently in 1986, but is currently in operation once more. It has 2 stills and gets its water from the spring of the River Glassaugh.

(Tel. 1261 84 23 67)

GLEN GORDON

Scottish single malt (Speyside), available at 15 years old, 80 proof, and in the vintages 1947 and 1958 from Glen Gordon Whisky Co., a subsidiary of GORDON AND MACPHAIL.

This is not the original bottling from a distillery but rather a so-called brand bottling; that is, the bottler acquires the whisky from an unnamed distillery and bottles it under his own label (see INDEPENDENT BOTTLERS).

GLENGOYNE

Scottish single malt (Southern Highlands) from LANG BROS. (ROBERTSON & BAXTER).

A light, malty whisky without any trace of peat.

Original bottling: 10 and 12 years old, 80 proof; 17 years old, 86 proof; 25 years old (distilled 1968), 102.2

proof; 25 years old (distilled 1969), 94 proof.

Cadenhead: The firm began stocking Glengoyne in 1996.

The distillery was created in 1833 from a small moonshine operation and has belonged to the Lang Bros. since 1876. For a time it was called Glen Guin. It has 3 stills, its own spring, and uses bourbon and sherry casks for aging.

(Tel. 1360 55 02 29)

GLEN GRANT

Scottish single malt (Speyside, Rothes) from the CHIVAS & GLENLIVET GROUP (SEAGRAM).

One of the great old single malt brands (second on the world market)

and a pleasant, balanced whisky that survives long aging with aplomb.

Original bottling: At least 2 different bottlings without age designation (5 to 9 years old), 80 proof; 5 years old, 80 proof (first on the important Italian market); 10 and 12 years old, 86 proof.

Gordon & MacPhail: Here there are numerous versions, 21 and 25 years old, but especially vintage bottlings reaching back to 1936. They are presented under license to Gordon & MacPhail—that is, with the original distillery label.

Cadenhead: 21 years old (distilled 1974), 109.2 proof.

The brothers John and James Grant, who opened the distillery in 1840, had learned their trade making moonshine and smuggling. James had also worked as a lawyer, so he had 2 skills that together promised a brilliant career. Glen Grant was the first of the distilleries in the village of Rothes—now there are 5—and the Grants were so successful with it that they began building a second one in 1897. It was called Glen Grant No. 2, was closed in 1902, and has been in operation again only since 1965 under the name CAPERDONICH. Glen Grant was already being bottled as a single malt around the turn of the century and can thus be considered one of the oldest brands of this type. At that time malts were sold as singles only within Scotland; the rest of the world only started to learn about them in the second half of the century. In this, as well, Glen Grant was a forerunner. Even before one of the other Grant families in the whisky business—WILLIAM GRANT & SONS—began worldwide marketing of its GLENFIDDICH, Glen Grant had also found its way into a foreign market, namely Italy. This was thanks to the Milan hotelier Armando Giovanni, who in the 1950s took several cases of this malt home with him and introduced it there. Today the 5-year-old Glen Grant alone has 70 percent of the Italian market share.

In 1953 the Grant firm merged with George & J. G. Smith, who operated the GLENLIVET distillery, and 20 years later the distillery LONG-MORN and the firm HILL, THOMSON & Co. were added. The resulting concern was renamed Glenlivet Distillers and was taken over in 1977 by the Canadian spirits giant Seagram, whose Scotch branch is now known as the Chivas & Glenlivet Group.

In that same year 6 new gas-fired stills were added to the 4 old ones, still fired by coal. In spite of the higher capacity this achieved, it is worrisome that the large number of young bottlings that are now placed on the market will in time thin out the reserves of the splendid old Glen Grants; the popular Seagram brands CHIVAS REGAL and PASSPORT already swallow up great quantities of them. The water comes from the Caperdonich Well.

(Tel. 1542 78 33 00)

GLENHAVEN

Independent bottler with headquarters in Glasgow, specializing in SINGLE-BARREL BOTTLINGS intended mainly for the U.S. market.

GLEN KEITH

Scottish single malt (Speyside, Keith) from the CHIVAS & GLENLIVET GROUP (SEAGRAM).

This malt is usually available only from the independent bottlers Gordon & MacPhail (distilled 1965, 80 proof), Cadenhead (22 years old, distilled 1973, 114.2 proof), James MacArthur (22 years old, 102.4 proof), and Signatory (distilled 1967, 92 proof). The lion's share goes into the blends of the Chivas & Glenlivet Group, which built this distillery in 1957–60 to satisfy the huge demand for world brands such as CHIVAS REGAL and PASSPORT. (For a time there was also a blend called Glen Keith.) The first of the original bottling came on the market in late 1994—with no age designation, but simply the legend: "Distilled before 1983," at 86 proof.

As the name suggests, the distillery is in Keith, one of the Speyside region's main whisky centers. The distillery was the first one in Scotland to fire its stills—at that time 3 of them—with gas and to run the entire production by means of microprocessors. Up until 1970 its whiskies were distilled 3 times, but then they went back to the usual 2. Today Glen Keith has 6 stills, and the water comes from the Balloch Hills.

(Tel. 1542 78 30 44)

GLEN KELLA MANX WHITE WHISKEY

Malt and blended whiskey from the firm Glen Kella Distillers on the Isle of Man.

It must have been his nostalgia for the vodka of his homeland that led the exiled Pole Lucian Landau to want to produce a "white," or clear, whiskey, distilled 3 times, on this island in the middle of the Irish Sea. He started experimenting in the early 1970s and finally came up with a process that is not only supposed to be quicker (and therefore cheaper) than the Scottish method, but in his opinion also produces superior results. What exactly goes on in his distillery—it has only a single still and gets its water from a nearby lake—is not disclosed. All that is certain is that

Scottish malt and grain whiskies stored there are blended and finally distilled one more time. The result is obviously quite satisfying, for the 12-year-old vatted Glen Kella—introduced to the market in 1990—is no longer produced, and the 8-year-old is supposedly so good that aging it any longer would be a terrible waste of time. Aside from that, since 1984 there has also been a blended Glen Kella, 3 and 5 years old, at 80 proof. Glen Kella's most important export country is Germany.

GLENKINCHIE

Scottish single malt (Eastern Lowlands) from John HAIG & Co. (UD)

A light malt, more aromatic than one might expect from a Lowlands product.

Original bottling: 10 years old, 86 proof (from the series "Classic Malts")

The distillery was established as Milton Distillery in 1825 and has been in operation under its present name since 1837. Glenkinchie is the chief component in Haig's DIMPLE blend. The distillery has 2 stills and gets its water from the Lammermuir Hills

(Tel. 1875 34 03 33)

GLEN KINDIE

Blended Scotch, 80 proof, from MONTROSE WHISKY.

GLEN LEVEN

Scottish vatted malt, 12 years old, from John HAIG & Co. (UD), consist-

ing of 6 malts, among them GLEN-
LOSSIE.

THE GLENLIVET

Scottish single malt (Speyside) from
George & J. G. Smith (SEAGRAM).

Glenlivet, the valley of the Livet
River, is considered the jewel of
Speyside, and the whisky that bears
its name is the oldest and most illus-
trious brand of the region.

It is a very elegant, malty whisky
that develops an astonishing fullness
with increasing age. Glenlivet is one of
the top international brands and the
number-1 malt in the United States.

Original bottling: 12 years old, 80
proof; 18 years old, 86 proof (currently available only in the United
States; 21 years old, 86 proof.

Gordon & MacPhail: Under the
name George & J. G. Smith's Glenlivet, a number of versions, including
12 years old, 80 proof; 15 years old,
80, 92, and 114 proof; 21 years old, 80
proof; vintage bottlings from 1943 to
1978, the last at 117.2 proof.

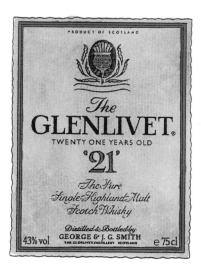

Cadenhead: 16 years old (distilled 1976, sherry cask), 92 proof.

Signatory: 21 years old (distilled 1973), 112 proof.

The official establishment of this distillery in 1824 marks the beginning of legal distilling in Scotland.

Like most Highland farmers, George Smith (1792–1871) distilled his own whisky and did not let the presence of British tax authorities prevent him from smuggling his product to the lucrative markets to the south. Smith was nevertheless the first to use the new tax laws of 1823 to turn his business into a perfectly legal operation. All of the care and energy that he had previously de-

voted to keeping his activities secret he now applied to the production of his whisky, developing the celebrated and frequently imitated brand Glenlivet. But before he could do so he first had to deal with his angry neighbors, who continued to work illegally. Moonlighting was still considered an act of resistance against hated British sovereignty; as the Scottish national poet Robert Burns put it, "Freedom and whisky go together." Smith finally prevailed because he enjoyed the support of the landed nobility eager to assert its authority over the recalcitrant Highlanders.

Over the following decades Glenlivet's reputation grew to such an extent that other producers also sold their products under that name and Glenlivet came to be known, ironically, as "the longest valley in Scotland." It was only in 1880 that a court decision ruled that whiskies that did not come from the Glenlivet distillery could use the name on their labels only as a geographical term, and such highly respected firms as GLEN GRANT and THE MACALLAN would do so up until fairly recently.

In 1953 the Smith firm merged with J. & J.

Grant, the owners of the Glen Grant distillery, and in 1973 the new firm acquired the distillery LONGMORN and the firm HILL, THOMSON & CO. The resulting concern was named Glenlivet Distillers, and in 1977 it was taken over by the Canadian liquor giant Seagram, which runs it today as its Chivas & Glenlivet Group.

The distillery has 8 stills and gets its water from Josie's Well.

(Tel. 1542 78 32 20)

GLENLOCHY

Scottish single malt (Highlands, Fort William) from UD.

A light, aromatic aperitif malt, the remaining stores of which will soon be used up.

Original bottling: Now only in the "Rare Malt Selection."

Gordon & MacPhail: Vintages 1974, 1977, 80 proof.

Cadenhead: Recently still had a 17-year-old at 117 proof.

Signatory: 30 years old (distilled 1963), 104.4 proof.

The distillery was built in 1898 and was acquired in 1953 by the DCL, which closed it in 1983 and converted it into apartments. It had 2 stills and took its water from the River Nevis.

GLENLOSSIE

Scottish single malt (Spey-

side, Elgin) from John HAIG & CO. (UD).

A very mild and malty digestif malt.

Original bottling: 10 years old, 86 proof (from the "Flora & Fauna" series).

Gordon & MacPhail: Vintages 1968, 1969, 1974, 1975, all 80 proof.

Cadenhead: 17 years old (distilled 1978), 114 proof.

The distillery dates back to 1876 and came under the control of the DCL in 1919. Haig has had the license since 1962 and uses the malt for its blends. Part of the same complex is the MANNOCHMORE Distillery, built in 1971. Both operations use water from the Bardon Burn. Glenlossie has 6 stills and in addition uses so-called purifiers, cylindrical apparatuses that clarify the fresh distillate and produce a milder taste.

(Tel. 1343 86 03 31)

GLEN LYON

1) Blended Scotch from Glen Lyon Blending, a subsidiary of MACLEAY DUFF (UD). The brand was formerly a vatted malt and is now exported mainly to South Africa.

2) Blended Scotch from INVERGORDON DISTILLERS (WHYTE & MACKAY, AMERICAN BRANDS).

GLEN MHOR

Scottish single malt (Highlands, Inverness) from UD.

A lightweight, somewhat on the sweet side, becoming increasingly difficult to find.

Gordon & MacPhail: 8 years old, 80 and 114 proof; vintages 1965, 80 proof; 1978, 124.4 proof; and 1979, 133.4 proof.

Cadenhead: 15 years old (distilled 1976), 121.8 proof; 19 years old (distilled 1976), 115.6 proof.

Signatory: 14 years old, 86 proof.

Glen Mhor was built in 1892 by Mackinlay & Birnie (see MACKINLAY's), taken over by the DCL in 1972, and closed in 1983. The distillery had 2 stills and the water came from Loch Ness. The site is now occupied by a large shopping center.

GLEN MIST

Scottish whisky herb liqueur from HALLGARTEN LIQUEURS, aged in old whisky barrels and relatively dry.

GLENMORANGIE
ESTABLISHED 1843
PRODUCT OF SCOTLAND
PORT WOOD FINISH
SINGLE HIGHLAND MALT WHISKY
Trade Mark
The GLENMORANGIE
DISTILLERY COY. TAIN, ROSS-SHIRE SCOTLAND
BOTTLED IN SCOTLAND

GLENMORANGIE

[Gaelic for "valley of calm"]

Scottish single malt (Northern Highlands) from MACDONALD MARTIN DISTILLERS (this company is now called Glenmorangie itself).

A fine, very well-balanced malt that has been the market leader in Scotland for years.

Original bottling: 10 years old, 80 and 114 proof; 18 years old, 86 proof; vintage 1963 (23 years old), 86 proof; The Native Ross-Shire Glenmorangie, 10 years old (distilled 1980), 115.2 proof; Port Wood Finish, without age designation (15 years old), 93.6 proof; Madeira Finish, without age designation (12 to 15 years old), 86 proof; Tain L'Hermitage 1978 (17 years old), 86 proof; Sherry Wood Finish (more than

12 years old), 86 proof; The Culloden Bottle, 25 years old (distilled 1971), 86 proof, a limited edition of 2,500 bottles commemorating the 250th anniversary of the battle of Culloden; vintages 1971 and 1979, both 80 proof.

The distillery was set up in a former brewery in 1843, on a spot where there is known to have been a distillery as early as the 17th century. In 1918 Glenmorangie was acquired by Macdonald & Muir, the precursor of Macdonald Martin, which introduced the malt as a single in 1920. (The fact that a Glenmorangie bottling from as early as 1880 has been spotted in the Vatican's cellars does not mean that the malt was already on the market outside of Scotland back then; it is rather an indication of the Holy See's extraordinary connections.)

The distillery is relatively small—it takes only 16 men to run it—but it has the tallest stills (8 altogether) in Scotland. There are also other oddities about Glenmorangie. Whereas experts generally agree that the softer the water, the better it is for whisky, at Glenmorangie they feel that the hard, mineral-rich water from the Tarlogie Hills above the distillery is what allows for the develop-

ment of the desired aromatic substances. The majority of the malt is aged exclusively in bourbon barrels, and these are not merely acquired at random. To ensure quality and a continuing supply, the company bought its own oak forest in Missouri and ships its new barrels to selected bourbon distillers (for example, MAKER'S MARK) for conditioning. It also experiments with other sorts of barrels: the 1963 spent a year in sherry casks, and the Port Wood Finish aged for 3 years in old ruby port casks from the COCKBURN & CAMPBELL firm. In 1995 2 special bottlings were introduced: a Madeira Finish and a Red Wine Finish; the latter was continued for only 5 years. Another experiment is currently under way in association with the Maker's Mark Distillery in Kentucky: a cask of Glenmorangie is aging in the Kentucky warehouse and a barrel of the American bourbon in Scotland. The producer hopes to determine what effects the different climates have on aging (see ALCOHOL CONTENT).

(Tel. 1862 89 20 43)

GLEN MORAY

Scottish single malt (Speyside, Elgin) from MACDONALD MARTIN DISTILLERS.

Like its sister distillery, Glenmorangie, Glen Moray was originally a brewery, but in this case the conversion was done only in 1897. It has been in the hands of the present owners since 1923. The distillery produces mainly the base malt for their HIGHLAND QUEEN blend. It has 4 stills, and the water comes from the River Lossie. Bourbon barrels are used for aging.

(Tel. 1343 54 25 77)

An elegant, malty whisky for every occasion.

Original bottling: 5 years old, 80 proof (exclusively for Italy); 12 years old, 80 proof; 15 and 17 years old, 86 proof; also vintage bottlings at 86 proof, currently 1962, 1963, 1966, 1967.

Cadenhead: The firm recently had a 27-year-old from 1962 at 110.2 proof.

Adelphi: 13 years old, 112 proof.

Dun Eideann: 14 years old (distilled 1980), 86 proof.

GLENMORE DISTILLING

U.S. distillery in Louisville, Kentucky, owned by BARTON DISTILLING (Canandaigua).

The distillery was established in 1890 by an Irish immigrant family by the name of Thompson, related to the Browns of BROWN-FORMAN. One of its first brands was KENTUCKY TAVERN, and somewhat later it introduced YELLOWSTONE. In the 1950s and 1960s both were among the most successful bourbons in the United

States. In 1970 the Thompsons acquired the firm Mr. Boston Distiller, known to barkeeps more for its OLD MR. BOSTON'S OFFICIAL BARTENDER'S GUIDE than for its spirits.

In the late 1980s Glenmore took over the distilleries MEDLEY and FLEISCHMANN, and in 1991 the concern was itself absorbed by UD. They sold the operation to Barton in 1995, who shut it down for the first time—only temporarily, it is said.

GLENMORISTON

Scottish vatted malt, a small brand from the house of BURN STEWART DISTILLERS.

THE GLENMOY

Scottish vatted malt, 10 years old, from Brodie Crawford & Co. (see BRODIE'S SUPREME).

GLEN NIVEN

Blended Scotch from Douglas Mac-Niven & Co., a subsidiary of MAC-DONALD MARTIN DISTILLERS.

GLEN ORD

Scottish single malt (Northern Highlands) from J. DEWAR & SONS (UD).

A very mild, medium-heavy malt that deserves to be better known. Obviously UD feels the same way, for since 1993 it has been pushing Glen Ord on the European market (most of it still disappears into the Dewar's blends). Up until then the brand was often distinguished by the confusing array of names under which it was presented over the years.

Original bottling: Glen Ord, 12 years old, 80 proof; until 1992 the same bottling was available from the licensee at the time, PETER DAWSON, as Glenordie, and before that the DCL marketed it as Ord.

Cadenhead: Ord, 31 years old (distilled 1962), 106 proof.

The distillery itself is called Ord or Muir of Ord and was established in 1838 (see also BAXTER'S BARLEY BREE). In 1924 it was taken over by the Dewars, and a year later it was acquired by the DCL. For a time the Dawson firm ran it, but since 1992 it has again been managed by J. Dewar & Sons. Ord has 6 stills and gets its water from Loch Nan Eun and Loch Nam Bonnach. The distillery also operates a large malt house that produces malt for other distilleries as well.

(Tel. 1463 87 04 21)

G

GLENROB
Blended Scotch from MAYERSON & CO.

GLEN ROSA
Blended Scotch from ISLE OF ARRAN DISTILLERS.

THE GLENROTHES
Scottish single malt (Speyside, Rothes) from HIGHLAND DISTILLERIES CO.

A brilliant malt, velvety, perfectly balanced, and far too seldom bottled as a single.

Berry Bros. & Rudd: Vintage 1979 (15 years old), 86 proof; vintage 1984 (11 years old), 86 proof.

These vintage bottlings are offered in limited quantities and in prize-winning packaging.

Gordon & MacPhail: 8 years old, 80 proof; 1978, 80 proof (Centenary Reserve Bottling).

Cadenhead: 16 years old, 92 proof.

Signatory: 27 years old (distilled 1966), 102.6 proof.

The distillery was built in 1878 and merged in 1887 with the BUNNAHABHAIN distillery to form Highland Distilleries. Today Glenrothes has 10 stills; its water comes from local springs. The whisky is used in the blends THE FAMOUS GROUSE and CUTTY SARK.

(Tel. 1340 83 12 48)

GLEN SALEN
Blended Scotch, produced for the U.S. market by HEAVEN HILL DISTILLERS.

GLEN SCOTIA
Scottish single malt (Campbeltown) from GLEN CATRINE Bonded Warehouse Ltd.

A mild but fresh, slightly salty whisky with a medium body.

Original bottling: 14 years old, 80 proof; currently it is also possible to buy bottlings that the former owner, Gibson, issued through A. Gillies & Co. (8 and 12 years old, 80 proof).

Cadenhead: 16 years old (distilled 1977), 115.2 proof.

Signatory: 27 years old (distilled 1966), 103 proof.

The distillery was established in 1832 under the name Scotia and has frequently changed hands over the years. For a time it belonged to HIRAM WALKER & SONS, and beginning in 1955 it was part of the firm A. Gillies, which was absorbed in 1970 into a concern called ADP. That owner closed the distillery in 1984, after renovating it at a cost of $1.5 million. In that year the DCL empire began to collapse, and in the confusion the ADP (see DCL, UD) also went under. A management buyout created the firm Gibson, which reopened Glen Scotia in 1989, but soon the distillery—except for SPRINGBANK, the last one left in Campbeltown—was threatened yet again. Gibson went bankrupt in 1994, and once again the lights were turned off in Glen Scotia. Gibson's assets were purchased by GLEN CATRINE, but the distillery is still closed. It has 2 stills and gets its water from the Crosshill Loch and from 2 drilled wells on the premises. It is said that the ghost of one of the former owners, who drowned in the nearby Campbel-

town Loch, continues to haunt the place.

(Tel. 1586 55 22 88)

GLENSHIEL
Scottish vatted malt, 12 years old, 86 proof, from GLEN CATRINE.

A new brand, exclusively for export; the base malts are likely GLEN SCOTIA, INCHMURRIN, and LITTLEMILL.

GLENSIDE
Blended Scotch from Tresher Ltd., available only in the shops of the British off-license chain Tresher's. Glenside was the name of a racehorse that won a spectacular victory in the Grand National Derby in 1911.

GLEN SLOY
Scottish vatted malt from Longman, a subsidiary of INVERGORDON DISTILLERS (WHYTE & MACKAY, AMERICAN BRANDS).

GLEN SPEY
Scottish single malt (Speyside, Rothes) from IDV/Grand Metropolitan.

A light malt whose aroma one writer compared to freshly mown fields. The same gentleman recommended that one drink Glen Spey with pudding—or in place of it. Both are difficult, for the malt is only rarely bottled as a single.

Original bottling: 8 years old, 80 proof, almost impossible to find.

Cadenhead: 13 years old, 124.6 proof.

James MacArthur: 21 years old, 110.8 proof.

Glen Spey was opened in around 1878 and was taken over in 1887 by the London gin producer GILBEY, which in turn became part of IDV in 1962. Most of the production goes into its blend J & B. The distillery has 4 stills, and the water comes from the Doonie Burn.

There is also a blended Scotch by the name of Glen Spey; it also belongs to IDV and is based mainly on STRATHMILL malt.

(Tel. 1340 83 12 15)

GLEN STUART
Blended Scotch from W. BROWN & SONS.

Available as a 5-year-old standard and as Pure Malt, or a vatted malt, 5, 8, and 12 years old.

GLENTAUCHERS
Scottish single malt (Speyside, Mulben) from ALLIED DISTILLERS (ALLIED DOMECQ).

A spicy, medium-weight malt.

Gordon & MacPhail: Vintage 1979, 80 proof.

Cadenhead: 16 years old (distilled 1977), 127.6 proof.

The distillery was built by W. P. LOWRIE and James BUCHANAN in 1897–98. It was one of the distilleries in which Buchanan experimented with continuously distilled malt whisky. Most of the time Glentauchers has supplied one of the base malts for Buchanan's BLACK & WHITE blend; whether this is still the case, after the distillery was closed in 1985 and sold to Allied in 1989, could not be determined. The only thing that is certain is that Glentauchers is again in operation. Whether the malt is still being marketed—and if so, how—is a mystery.

The distillery has 6 stills; it gets its water from various springs in the surrounding hills.

(Tel. 1542 86 02 72)

GLENTROMIE

Scottish vatted malt, 12 and 17 years old, from SPEYSIDE DISTILLERY.

This whisky consists mainly of Highland malts and is sold mainly in France, Japan, and the United States.

GLENTURRET

Scottish single malt (Southern Highlands) from HIGHLAND DISTILLERIES Co.

A quite astonishing, spicy malt.

Original bottling: 8 years old, 80 proof; 12 years old, 80 proof; 15 years old, 86 and 100 proof; 18 years old, 80 proof; 21 years old, 80 proof; 25 years old, 86 proof; vintages 1966, 1968, 1972, all 80 proof.

In addition there are special versions available only in 1¾-ounce (5-cl) miniatures: 10 years old, 114.2 proof; 5,000 days, 80 proof; 10,000 days, 80 proof.

Finally, there is also a Glenturret Malt Liqueur at 70 proof.

Signatory: 20 years old, 107 proof.

The Castle Collection: 13 years old (distilled 1979), 86 proof.

Glenturret vies with LITTLEMILL and STRATHISLA for the title of "oldest distillery in Scotland." It dates back to 1775. At that time it was called Hosh; it was given its present name only in 1875, by another distillery that had been opened in 1814 by a man with the resounding name

of Thomas McComish and closed down around 1850.

Glenturret was also later closed and turned into a warehouse. The fact that this wonderful whisky is again available today is solely thanks to James Fairlie, who built up the distillery again in the 1950s. Between 1981 and 1990 Glenturret belonged to the French liquor concern Cointreau, and since that time it has been a part of Highland Distilleries. It is one of the smallest in Scotland, has 2 stills, and gets its water from Loch Turret. It ages its malt in bourbon and sherry casks.

(Tel. 1764 65 65 65)

GLENUGIE
Scottish single malt (Eastern Highlands).

Not exactly a major brand, and today mostly a collectors' item, for production ceased in 1983 and supplies are running low.

Gordon & MacPhail: Vintage 1967, 80 proof.

Cadenhead: 12 years old (distilled 1980), 119.6, 119.4, and 116.2 proof; 13 years old (distilled 1978), 121.8 proof.

The distillery was founded in 1831 and for a long time belonged to LONG JOHN.

Its later owner, the brewing firm Whitbread, closed Glenugie in 1983, and today only a few of its metal buildings are still standing.

GLEN URQUHART
Blended Scotch, 80 proof, from GORDON & MACPHAIL.

John Urquhart was one of Gordon & MacPhail's employees from the time the business was founded in 1895. His descendants later took over the firm and continue to run it today.

GLENURY-ROYAL
Scottish single malt (Eastern Highlands) from UD.

An earthy, dry, and smoky whisky that is almost impossible to find. For that reason it is questionable whether there are many admirers left who follow the recommendation of the Scotch Malt Whisky Society that one drink Glenury with Greek olives.

Gordon & MacPhail: 12 years old, 80 proof.

Signatory: 15 years old (distilled 1978), 124.6 proof.

The distillery was established in 1825 and belonged for some years to Robert Barclay, a member of parliament to whose friendship with the queen—he called her simply "Mrs. Windsor"—the business owes the "Royal" in its name. Glenury was later bought by American interests, then in 1953 was acquired by the DCL, which used the whisky for its GILLON's blends. It was closed in 1985 and demolition was begun in 1993.

GLORIOUS 12TH
Blended Scotch, 12-year-old de luxe, from John Buckmaster & Sons, a London blending and trading house, on the market since 1980. The "Glorious 12th" referred to is the 12th of August, the day pheasant season opens.

GODFATHER
A digestif cocktail. Blend 1½ oz. bourbon and ¾ oz. Amaretto with ice in a goblet.

GOLD & GOLD
Japanese blend from NIKKA.

GOLD BLEND
Blended Scotch from KINROSS WHISKY CO.

GOLDEN AGE
Blended Scotch from John HAIG & Co. (UD).

This 12-year-old de luxe was introduced in 1979 as a substitute for DIMPLE, temporarily withdrawn from the British market. It currently has only a minor following.

GOLDEN CAP
Blended Scotch from J. C. & R. H. Palmer, a small brewery in Dorset that has been selling this brand in its pubs since the 1930s (see BEER).

GOLDEN GRAIN
Kentucky straight corn whiskey from BARTON DISTILLING (Canandaigua).

At 190 proof a powerful hit, and a favored punch base at college parties.

GOLDEN NAIL
A digestif cocktail. Mix 1½ oz. bourbon and ¾ oz. SOUTHERN COMFORT with ice in a goblet.

GOLDEN PIPER

Blended Scotch, 80 proof, from Lombard Scotch Whisky Ltd. (see LOMBARD's).

GOLD KING

Blended Scotch, de luxe, from Gold King Whisky, a small London firm that was formerly called John MaKay.

GOLD LABEL

Blended Scotch, 80 proof, from RED LION BLENDING.

GORDON & MACPHAIL

This Scottish producer and trading firm with headquarters in Elgin is considered the most important INDEPENDENT BOTTLER of malt whiskies, a designation that only Cadenhead might contest. While the latter became famous for reviving SINGLE-BARREL BOTTLING, it was Gordon & MacPhail who saw to it that SINGLE MALT survived the big boom in blended Scotch at all. In the postwar years especially, it was by no means customary for producers to bottle their own whiskies; almost their entire production disappeared into blends, and scarcely any whisky drinkers outside of Scotland were aware that there even was such a thing as single malt. In those dark years Gordon & MacPhail was the only bottler of single malt worth mentioning, and in fact a number of brands managed to survive as single malts only under the Gordon & MacPhail label. The firm's vast stock of old malts was what made the difference, for the gentlemen in Elgin were among the first to value aged malts and accordingly built up supplies early on. Even today there is no one who can offer as many old vintages—some going back to the 1930s—as Gordon & MacPhail.

In addition to its series "Connoisseur's Choice," which encompasses over 40 different brands, the firm has meanwhile issued a "Cask Strength" series—that is, undiluted and unfiltered single-barrel bottlings. Gordon & MacPhail also has a number of so-called Brand Malts; that is to say unofficial single-malt bottlings that for legal reasons cannot bear the names of their distilleries (see GLEN AVON

CONNOISSEURS CHOICE

Connoisseurs Choice, a range of single malts from various districts of Scotland.

In the Highlands are situated the greatest number of malt whisky distilleries.

SINGLE HIGHLAND MALT SCOTCH WHISKY
DISTILLED AT
KNOCKDHU
DISTILLERY
PROPRIETOR: James Munro & Son Ltd

DISTILLED 1974 DISTILLED

SPECIALLY SELECTED, PRODUCED AND BOTTLED BY
GORDON & MACPHAIL
ELGIN - SCOTLAND
PRODUCT OF SCOTLAND

75cl   40% vol

GLEN FRASER, GLEN GORDON, MAC-PHAIL'S). The firm also sometimes bottles under the name Speymalt Whisky.

Since it acquired BENROMACH in 1993, Gordon & MacPhail is also the proud owner of its own distillery.

The firm is also famous for its vatted malts: its special bottlings by region, offered under the names PRIDE OF ISLAY, etc., enjoy an excellent reputation. Some are even considered superior to the single malts in question. (Other Gordon & MacPhail vatteds are HIGHLAND FUSILIER and OLD ELGIN.)

Finally, the firm also offers a number of superb blends: AVONSIDE, BEN AIGEN, BEN ALDER, FRASER'S SUPREME, GLEN CALDER, GLEN URQUHART, IM-MORTAL MEMORY, JAMES GORDON'S, MONSTER'S CHOICE, OLD ORKNEY, ROYAL FINDHORN, SPEY CAST, and UBIQUE.

Gordon & MacPhail was founded in Elgin in 1895 by James Gordon and John MacPhail. Today it is operated by the Urquhart family, descendants of John Urquhart, who was an employee in the firm from the time of its founding. Like many of the now-famous whisky pioneers, the founders started as "Italian warehousemen." That was the name for grocers who stocked more than regional products, including tea, wine, and spirits. The main office of the firm is still in a side room off the original shop, and one first has to make one's way past cases filled with sausages and cheese to

MACPHAIL'S
highland malt scotch whisky
DISTILLED 1965
40% vol   70 cl

PRODUCT OF SCOTLAND

30

reach what was once aptly called the "whisky lover's temple."

(Tel. 1343 54 51 11)

GOVERNORS CLUB
Blended American from SHERMAN.

GRAIN WHISKY
A grain distillate used in the production of BLENDED SCOTCH WHISKY. It is produced primarily from corn, in PATENT STILLS, and is purer and more flavorless than MALT, PURE POT STILL, or STRAIGHT WHISK(E)Y (see also SCOTCH WHISKY).

In Scotland grain whisky is also occasionally bottled as a single. Currently there are 7 grain distilleries in operation in the country: CAMERON BRIG, DUMBARTON, GIRVAN, INVERGORDON, NORTH BRITISH, PORT DUNDAS, and STRATHCLYDE. (See also BEN NEVIS, BLACKBARREL, CAMBUS, CARSEBRIDGE, and LOCHSIDE.)

GRAND AGE
Japanese blend, super premium, from NIKKA, on the market since 1989.

GRANDE CANADIAN
Canadian blend from HEAVEN HILL DISTILLERS.

The Kentucky firm Heaven Hill imports this whisky in bulk and bottles it for the U.S. market.

GRAND MACNISH
Blended Scotch, standard and 12-year-old de luxe, from MACDUFF INTERNATIONAL.

This brand was created at the end of the last century by Robert McNish, who had been selling tea, tobacco, and whisky in Glasgow since 1863. Grand Macnish later changed hands a number of times. It finally ended up with HIRAM WALKER & SONS, and for a time disappeared completely. It was acquired by the present owner only in 1992 and again introduced to the international market, especially North and Central America (see also DOCTOR'S SPECIAL).

GRANT, J. & G. See GLENFARCLAS, GLEN DOWAN.

GRANT, J. & J. See GLEN GRANT.

With its WILLIAM GRANT'S, the family also owns one of the world's most successful blended Scotches. In addition, it has a number of brands that are produced by the subsidiary firm Quality Spirits International and sold around the world: CONSULATE, GLEN CORRIE, GREAT MACAULAY, HIGHLAND BIRD, HIGHLAND RESERVE, KING CHARLES, LOCH KINDIE, OLDMOOR, and THE SCOTTISH COLLIE.

GRANT, WILLIAM & SONS

Scottish producers with headquarters in Glasgow. Given the increasing concentration of the whisk(e)y industry in the hands of interlocking international companies, it is highly anachronistic that GLENFIDDICH, far and away Scotland's most successful malt brand worldwide, should still be in the hands of an independent family business. In fact this distillery is now being run by the 5th generation of William Grant's descendants. He opened it in 1887. A short time later he built the BALVENIE distillery, and today the Grants also own CONVALMORE, GIRVAN, and KININVIE. (See also LADYBURN, BLACKBARREL.)

GRANT'S ROYAL

Blended Scotch from WILLIAM GRANT & SONS.

A 12-year-old de luxe blend from the series WILLIAM GRANT'S.

GREAT COUNT O'BLATHER

Irish whiskey from B. O'Nolan, Strabane.

A small brand, highly prized in Dublin literary circles, where whiskey is also referred to as "oil of the sun."

GREAT MAC

Blended Scotch from MONTROSE WHISKY.

GREAT MACAULAY

Blended Scotch from William GRANT & SONS.

GREEN HIGHLANDER
Blended Scotch, 86 proof, from G. &
F. Greenall, Edinburgh.

GREEN SPOT
Irish PURE POT STILL WHISKEY, 80
proof, available from the Dublin trading house Mitchell & Son since the
1920s. The Mitchells used to buy the
freshly distilled whiskey from the
JAMESON distillery, age it themselves
in sherry casks, and bottle it as a 10-
year-old. Since the merger of the large
Irish distilleries (see IDG), Green
Spot has been bottled by Jameson itself without any designation of age. It
consists of 7- and 8-year-old whiskeys
and, together with REDBREAST, it is
one of the last representatives of the
once-famous pure pot still type—a full-
flavored, elegant whiskey of which
only roughly 6,000 bottles are placed
on the market each year.

It is very difficult to find outside
of Ireland, and the most stylish way
to buy it is in the Mitchells' own wine
and spirits shop on Kildare Street.

In the great days of Irish whiskey,
Mitchell & Son also offered other
brands: Blue Spot (7 years old), Yellow Spot (12 years old), and Red
Spot (15 years old).

(Tel. 1676 07 66)

GREGSON'S
Brazilian blended whiskey from IDV/
Grand Metropolitan.

GRIERSON'S NO. 1
Scottish vatted malt, 12 years old,
from Grierson's Ltd., a tradition-rich
London wine merchant that supplies
mainly hotels and restaurants.

No man is genuinely happy, married,
who has to drink worse whiskey
than he used to drink when he was single.

H. L. Mencken,
Prejudices: Fourth Series

HAIG & CO., JOHN

Scottish whisky house owned by UD.

The Haig dynasty, whose ancestors arrived in England with William the Conqueror and settled in the Lowlands in the 13th century, contributed materially to the industrialization of the Scottish whisky business. The development of the brew first distilled by Highlanders for their own consumption, as a by-product of their work in the fields, into the Scotch

whisky famous around the world today would not have been the same without them. Even though one might question the date of the firm's founding, which it claims was 1627, the Haigs can with some justification claim to bear the oldest name in the whisky business. They were first documented in connection with it in

1655, when one Robert Haig was called to account for himself to the local church authorities for distilling on Sunday.

The marriage of his great-great-grandson John (died 1773) to Margaret Stein not only brought into the family 2 of the largest distilleries in Scotland but also the—future—relationship with Robert Stein, who in 1826 would invent the PATENT STILL, which first made possible the production of GRAIN WHISKY (and with it the blending of whisky). That marriage was also extremely fruitful in other ways: 4 of the 5 sons founded their own distilleries, and 1 of the 2 daughters married John JAMESON.

The Haigs were then among the first to capitalize on the new technique and to fit out their Cameronbridge distillery with patent stills (1830, see CAMERON BRIG). At that time the business was run by the John Haig (1802–78) who was a driving force behind the merger of the large Lowland distilleries into the concern that would become the DCL in 1877. John Haig & Co. itself joined this group of more than 30 distilleries and numerous producers in 1919. Ever since the DCL has been controlled by UD, Haig has been responsible as an independent firm for the distilleries CAMERON-BRIDGE, GLENKINCHIE, GLENLOSSIE, and MANNOCHMORE.

In addition, Haig produces the 2 blends HAIG GOLD LABEL and DIMPLE.

HAIG GOLD LABEL
Blended Scotch, 80 proof, from the house of HAIG & CO. (UD).

Gold Label is one of the oldest and most successful blended Scotch brands—"Don't be vague, ask for Haig" was a famous advertising slogan—but cannot be considered a mass-market product in terms of quality. The 12-year-old de luxe version is called DIMPLE. (For its history, see HAIG & CO.)

In Great Britain the brand is distributed by WHYTE & MACKAY.

HAIR OF THE DOG
This anti-hangover drink takes its name from an old adage first cited by the English poet John Heywood in 1546. It claims that the best cure is a hair of the dog that bit you the night before. Shake well 1½ oz. Scotch, 1 tablespoon honey, and 1 tablespoon cream with ice cubes, strain, and serve without ice.

A HALF AND A NIP
A popular way to drink (blended) whisky in the British Isles. One follows a small whisky (a "nip") with a glass of beer (a "half"). The custom dates back to the time when even in Scotland virtually no one drank malt whisky. It is virtually immaterial what the quality of the whisky is, the main thing is that it burn enough that one has reason to quench the fire; conversely, it adds pep to the glass of beer. The American variant is called a BOILER MAKER.

HALL & BRAMLEY
A tradition-rich Scottish blending and trading house that was established in Glasgow in 1860 and has managed to maintain its independence to the present day. Its oldest brand is GLEN GHOIL, and in addition it produces CLAN ARDOCH, GLEN CARREN, and HIGHLAND PEARL.

HALLGARTEN LIQUEURS
Some of England's best-known liqueurs come from the London firm of Peter Hallgarten, among them 2 with a whisky base: GLEN MIST and

CAN-Y-DELYN. For a long time the subsidiary firm Savermo also made a whisky liqueur called Redalevn; it was produced exclusively for the Manchester United football club, which apparently has no interest in it any longer. Hallgarten's blended Scotch brands have also been discontinued.

HAMASHKEH
Blended Scotch, KOSHER WHISK(E)Y, 80 proof, from EMA Kosher Foods, London.

HANCOCK'S RESERVE
Kentucky straight bourbon, 88.9 proof, from the LEESTOWN DISTILLING COMPANY, part of SAZERAC.

A well-balanced SINGLE-BARREL BOURBON (selected by master distiller Gary Gayheart) that has been on the market since 1991.

HANKEY BANNISTER
Blended Scotch, standard and 12-year-old de luxe, from INVER HOUSE DISTILLERS.

Since the end of the last century the London wine and spirit firm Hankey Bannister has

supplied its mainly aristocratic clientele with its own Scotch and Irish whisk(e)y. The firm has changed ownership several times since it was founded in 1757, and since 1988 the brand has belonged to Inver House, which is especially successful with it on the export market and in the duty-free sector.

HARROD'S
Needless to say, the elegant London department store has its own label. The blended whisky behind it probably comes from WHYTE & MACKAY.

HARTLEY PARKERS
Blended Scotch produced for the U.S. market by STAR LIQUOR.

HART'S
Blended Scotch, 8 years old, from the firm Donald Hart & Co., Glasgow, which also has the blends OLD CURLERS, OLD FOX, OLD GLASGOW, OLD KEG, SCOTS LION, and SPEAKERS.

HARVEY'S SPECIAL
Blended Scotch from J. & R. Harvey, Glasgow, a subsidiary of UD.

The brand has been in existence since roughly 1870; today it is mainly exported to the United States.

HARWOOD
Canadian blend from HEAVEN HILL DISTILLERS.

The Kentucky firm Heaven Hill imports this whisky in bulk and bottles it for the U.S. market.

HEATHER CREAM LIQUEUR
Scottish whisky cream liqueur, 34 proof, from Carmichael & Sons, a subsidiary of INVER HOUSE DISTILLERS.

Supposedly this was the first liqueur based on malt whisky, specifically BLADNOCH.

HEATHERDALE
Blended Scotch from CWS.

HEATHWOOD
Blended Scotch from C. & J. McDonald (UD).

HEAVEN HILL DISTILLERS
U.S. producer in Bardstown, Kentucky.

The distillery was founded in 1935 by the Shapira family, which still owns a majority share. Thus Heaven Hill is the last independent whiskey producer in the United States. The distillery's name comes from a Heavenhill family that is said to have operated a distillery on this spot in the 18th century.

The Shapiras, after first earning their money in real estate, recognized that there was more to be done with whiskey than simply bottling it. They developed a wholesaling concept that is now accepted worldwide. In this system the producer sells his newly distilled whisk(e)y to a broker, who assumes the cost of further warehousing and can thus do with the product whatever he wishes. The producer is thus assured of a small profit, but a quick one, and avoids the cost of transportation. The broker then resells the whiskey—usually to bottlers who do not have their own distilleries—at the full market price. This is the story, for example, behind the Heaven Hill bourbons MEDLEY and PENNYPACKER, which are even marketed in Germany.

At the same time, the Shapiras acquired a number of labels, some of them small, regional brands (but well known and with a long tradition), whose owners had gone under during Prohibition. They now produce these themselves:

Heaven Hill, Kentucky straight bourbon, 4 years old, 80 proof, and 6 years old, 90 proof, both of them

light to medium-heavy, everyday whiskeys that are appropriate for mixed drinks. For the Japanese market there is also a 28-year-old version—a tremendous age for a bourbon, and one that doubtless capitalizes more on the prestige factor than on its superior flavor.

Other ages of the same product are presented under different labels: EVAN WILLIAMS, ELIJAH CRAIG, HENRY MCKENNA, and OLD 1889.

Additional Heaven Hill brands are:

Bourbon: CABIN STILL, ECHO SPRING, J. T. S. BROWN, J. W. DANT, MATTINGLY & MOORE, T. W. SAMUELS, W. W. BEAM.

Blend: PAUL JONES, PHILADELPHIA, WILSON.

Rye: PIKESVILLE SUPREME, RITTENHOUSE RYE.

Corn: GEORGIA MOON, J. W. CORN.

Canadian: HARWOOD, Heaven Hill Canadian Blend (bottled solely for the U.S. market).

Scotch: Heaven Hill Blended Scotch (bottled solely for the U.S. market).

In addition to the United States, the firm supplies

mainly southern Europe, Scandinavia, and Japan.

(See also MEDLEY, OLD KENTUCKY RIFLE, PENNYPACKER).

Heaven Hill's production methods are altogether traditional: for 3 generations its stillmen have come from the Beam family (see JIM BEAM), one of their chief responsibilities being to carefully watch over the health of the yeast culture (with hops added).

For their own whiskeys they use a grain mixture consisting of 78 percent corn, 10 percent rye, and 12 percent barley malt; the sour mash component, at roughly 30 percent, is unusually high. The distillery draws on 6 wells, and with 44 warehouses, each containing 20,000 barrels, controls one of the largest stocks of whiskey in the United States.

(Tel. 502 348-3921)

HEDGES & BUTLER
Blended Scotch from Hedges & Butler, a subsidiary of Bass Charrington.

This wine merchant, established in Glasgow in 1667, once supplied the princely and royal courts of all of Europe. After World War I it went into the business of blending and exporting Scotch. Today the operation belongs to the British brewing giant Bass Charrington, and of the 6 different Hedges & Butler brands only 2 are left: a standard blend and a 12-year-old de luxe, both solely for export.

HENRY MCKENNA
Kentucky straight bourbon from HEAVEN HILL DISTILLERS.

A decent, everyday bourbon, which is offered as a 4-year-old at 80 proof, as a 100-proof bottled in bond, and recently also as a 10-year-old single-barrel.

This bourbon, which the Irish immigrant Henry McKenna began distilling in Fairfield (Nelson County) in 1855, was one of the most popular U.S. brands in the 19th century and was famous for its quality. Part of its success may have been owing to the fact that McKenna was probably the first distiller who did not sell his whiskey before it was 3 years old. All of the other producers sold their product as soon as it had been distilled and paid no attention to how it was ultimately marketed.

During Prohibition the distillery was closed, and the STITZEL-WELLER

distillery sold off its stores as "medicinal whiskey." McKenna's successor later reopened the old distillery and, together with the old stillmen and their apprentices, started producing a bourbon meant to duplicate as closely as possible the one that Henry had begun distilling in 1855. This amazing continuity lasted until 1941, when SEAGRAM took over the distillery—but not the old recipe—and promptly retired the brand. The distillery was torn down in 1976, and the brand name was acquired by HEAVEN HILL DISTILLERS.

HEUBLEIN INC.

One of the largest spirit producers in the United States, and since 1987 part of IDV/Grand Metropolitan.

Gilbert and Louis Heublein established a wine dealership in Connecticut in 1875. Beginning in 1892 they made a great deal of money from an invention that is today considered, with some justification, the beginning of the end of America's bar culture—namely, bottled premixes for cocktails.

After Prohibition Heublein started producing the brand that is still its most successful one today: Smirnoff vodka (currently the 9th-best-selling liquor in the world).

For a time the firm belonged to the U.S. tobacco giant Reynolds, but since 1987 it has been with IDV, for which it produces the following brands: AMERICAN CREAM, BLACK VELVET, BRETON'S HAND & SEAL, and MCMASTERS. (See also ROCK AND RYE.)

HEWITTS

Blended Irish whiskey, premium, 80 proof, from the IDG (PERNOD RICARD) MIDLETON distillery.

A very strong whiskey by Irish standards, consisting of 2 malts (6 and 10 years old) and a grain. It was introduced in the 1960s and conceived as a competitor for the Scottish blends that were making increasing inroads into Ireland at the time. To that end, it then contained peated malt whiskey as well.

Hewitts is a relatively small brand and is found only rarely outside of Ireland. This is not only a pity, but it also makes no sense, for the whiskey is superior to many of the other Midleton products and ould only help the embattled reputation of Irish whiskey.

It is named after an Irish family that opened the Watercourse distillery in Cork in 1793. That operation was shut down in 1975.

NI
Japanese blend, de luxe, 78 proof, from NIKKA.

HIELANMAN
Blended Scotch, 80 proof, from CADENHEAD.

An old brand that is not being bottled at the moment but is supposed to be revived in the near future.

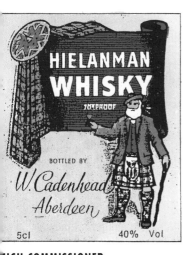

HIELANMAN WHISKY
70° PROOF
BOTTLED BY
W. Cadenhead
Aberdeen
5cl   40% Vol

HIGH COMMISSIONER
Blended Scotch, 8 years old, 86 proof, from GLEN CATRINE Bonded Warehouse Ltd.

HIGHLAND ABBEY
Blended Scotch from CWS.

HIGHLAND BIRD
Blended Scotch from William GRANT & SONS.

HIGHLAND BLEND
Blended Scotch, 15-year-old premium, from AVERY'S OF BRISTOL LTD.

Although Avery's no longer produces this brand itself, but rather buys it from an unidentified producer, Highland Blend has the same quality as always—superior to that of all the light-bodied, fashionable blends. Most of it is sold in Japan.

HIGHLAND CATTLE
Scottish vatted malt from J. & G. Grant (see GLENFARCLAS, GLEN DOWAN).

It is likely that the most important components of this brand come from the Glenfarclas distillery.

HIGHLAND CLAN
Blended Scotch from Highland Bonding, a subsidiary of SEAGRAM.

HIGHLAND CLUB
Blended Scotch from UD.

HIGHLAND DEW
Blended Scotch from UD.

HIGHLAND DISTILLERIES CO.
One of the few malt whisky producers still in Scottish hands. The firm was created in 1887 with the merger of the distilleries BUNNAHABHAIN and

Glenrothes; these were later joined by Glenglassaugh (1892), Tamdhu (1898), Highland Park (1935), Glenturret (1990), and The Macallan (1996).

In addition, since 1988 the firm has used the warehouses of the Parkmore distillery, which has long since ceased operation. It owns a part of one of its oldest and best customers, the blending house Robertson & Baxter (which in turn owns a share of Highland Distilleries). In 1970 Highland Distilleries took over Matthew Gloag & Son and thus became the owners of the blended Scotch brand The Famous Grouse. Additional labels are Black Bottle and Lang's.

HIGHLANDER

Blended Scotch from H. Stenham Ltd.

Like all Stenham Scotches, also available as a 3-, 5-, 8-, 10-, and 12-year-old and also like the others, designated primarily for the Latin American and Southeast Asian markets.

There is also a vatted Highlander: Highland Straight Malt.

HIGHLAND FUSILIER

Scottish vatted malt, 5, 8, 15, 21, and 25 years old, from Gordon and MacPhail.

A mild, fruity whisky that has won international awards. It was introduced in 1959 to mark the founding of the regiment of the same name.

HIGHLAND GATHERING

Blended Scotch from Lombard Scotch Whisky Ltd. (see Lombard's).

On the market since 1992 as a standard bottling and as an 8-, 12-, 15-, 18-, 21-, and 25-year-old.

HIGHLAND LEGEND

Blended Scotch from Angus Dundee.

HIGHLAND MIST

Blended Scotch from Glen Catrine Bonded Warehouse Ltd.

HIGHLAND NECTAR

Blended Scotch from UD.

HIGHLAND PARK

Scottish single malt (Orkney Islands) from James Grant & Co., a subsidiary of Highland Distilleries Co.

A very complex whisky—smoky, malty, and dry. Highland Park is a medium-weight with a distinguished reputation; it is considered the finest all-round whisky in the world of malts (according to the British whisky pundit Michael Jackson) and is also highly popular in blends, since it is thought to function as a catalyst.

Original bottling: 12 years old, 80 proof.

Gordon & MacPhail: 8 years old, 80 and 114 proof; vintage 1982, 113.6 proof; 15 years old (distilled 1970, Centenary Reserve), 80 proof.

Cadenhead: 17 years old (distilled 1977), 113.2 proof; 18 years old (distilled 1977), 104.6 proof.

Signatory: 20 years old, 107 proof.

The northernmost distillery in Scotland was probably built as early as 1795, at precisely the spot where the legendary preacher Magnus Eunson had run a moonshine operation. Eunson is considered to have been the first to use the method, now known from gangster films, of hiding his illegal wares in coffins to confuse the tax collectors; even his pulpit usually held a few casks. Now, of course, everything is done on the up-and-up, even in Orkney, and traditional methods are employed. The malting floors are still being used and the firm's own peat is scented with heather. The distillery has 4 stills and gets its water from the spring called Cattie Maggie's. It has belonged to Highland Distilleries since 1935 and is still operated by the Grants, who bought Highland Park in 1895.

(Tel. 1856 87 31 07)

HIGHLAND PEARL
Blended Scotch, 12 years old, from HALL & BRAMLEY.

HIGHLAND QUEEN
Blended Scotch from Macdonald & Muir, a subsidiary of MACDONALD MARTIN DISTILLERS.

In addition to the standard bottling, Highland Queen is offered as Grand Reserve, 15 years old, and Supreme, 21 years old.

HIGHLAND RESERVE
Blended Scotch from William GRANT & SONS.

HIGHLAND ROSE
Blended Scotch from BURN STEWART DISTILLERS, available as a standard blend and as a 12-year-old.

HIGHLANDS
Scottish whisky region. The concept of the Highlands is primarily one of historical, geographical, and cultural significance. To the north of the industrialized LOWLANDS lies the part of Scotland laden with all of the clichés that were exploited early on

by whisky advertising (see Dewar's): raw natural beauty, rebellious clans, and husky kilt-wearers who spend most of their time playing bagpipes and drinking whisky.

As relates to whisky production, "Highlands" is in fact only a catch-all term used for every area not otherwise covered by the regional designations Campbeltown, Islay, or Lowlands. The subdivisions Northern, Eastern, Southern, and Western relate solely to geography; the products of Highlands distilleries are much too diverse to permit one to make any valid assumptions about the character of their whiskies.

To confuse things even further, the malts from the islands of Arran, Jura, Mull, Orkney, and Skye are also ascribed to the Highlands.

HIGHLAND STAG
Blended Scotch from Red Lion Blending.

Highland Stag was introduced in the 1970s by a great-grandson of the great Long John Macdonald and is now marketed in Great Britain exclusively by Aldi.

HIGHLAND STAR
Blended Scotch from H. Stenham Ltd.

Like all Stenham Scotches, available as a 3-, 5-, 8-, 10-, and 12-year-old and, like the others, intended mainly for the Latin American and Southeast Asian markets.

HIGHLAND WOODCOCK
Blended Scotch from J. T. Davies Croydon.

This brand is sold mainly in the pubs of the Davies firm, founded in 1875, which also owns the Davison wineshop chain and is active primarily in the Greater London area.

HILL, THOMSON & CO.
Scottish blending firm, founded in Edinburgh in 1857. The house produces such well-known blends as Queen Anne and Something Special, as well as the brands Black Watch, St. Leger Light Dry, and Treasury. Since 1971 the firm has been a part of Seagram.

HILL & HILL
Blended American from Jim Beam Brands (American Brands).

Up until the 1980s this brand was a Kentucky straight bourbon, one that had only a local following.

HILLSIDE See GLENESK.

HIRAM WALKER & SONS

Canadian beverage concern with headquarters in Walkerville, Ontario, and a branch in Detroit, part of the spirit empire ALLIED DOMECQ.

The story of the development of this firm is presented in the article CANADIAN WHISKY. Hiram Walker first appeared on the international scene during Prohibition, when it supplied the thirst- and rotgut-plagued Americans with quality Canadian. There Walker also made contact with the notorious whisky smuggler Jimmy Barclay (see STODART), from whom it purchased in 1936 the Scotch brand BALLANTINE'S, among others. It was this connection that helped to establish the Scottish branch of the concern. In 1968, together with the Spanish wine and brandy producer Pedro Domecq, the firm of Hiram Walker Europa was founded, one of whose products is the Spanish whisky brand DYC. Domecq and Walker have meanwhile been absorbed into Allied Domecq. Within the group, Hiram Walker is responsible for the U.S. distribution of Allied products and, naturally, the production of its own brands, CANADIAN CLUB, MAKER'S MARK, ROCK AND RYE, and WALKER'S DELUXE, and of the CORBY blends McGUINNESS, MEAGHERS 1878, ROYAL RESERVE, SILK TASSEL, and WISER'S.

In addition to the Hiram Walker distillery in Windsor, Ontario, the firm has 2 other distilleries in Canada, one in Illinois, and one in Buenos Aires. (See also LOMOND STILL.)

HORSE'S NECK

A variant of the BOURBON HIGHBALL. Pour 1¾ oz. bourbon over ice in a tall glass, add a few dashes of Angostura, top with ginger ale, and garnish with a spiral of lemon peel.

HOT BUTTERED WHISKY

A whisky cocktail that helps Canadian loggers survive the bitter cold.

Crush a sugar cube in a fire-resistant glass, then add 1¾ oz. whisky, and heat. Pour boiling water on top and grate ice-cold butter into it. This may sound odd, and it certainly isn't much to look at, but it tastes wonderful.

HOT WHISKEY

An Irish specialty in cold weather (and much of the rest of the time). To ¾ or 1 oz. whiskey (if possible, POWER'S GOLD LABEL), add a little sugar syrup, cloves, and a slice of lemon. Top with hot water and serve in a wineglass.

HOUSE OF CAMPBELL

Blended Scotch from CAMPBELL DIS-TILLERS (PERNOD RICARD).

HOUSE OF LORDS

Blended Scotch, standard and 8- and 12-year-old de luxe, from CAMPBELL DISTILLERS (PERNOD RICARD).

This brand was originally bottled solely for the upper house of the Parliament but later, during Prohibition, for the American market as well.

House of Lords was at that time placed in extra durable bottles that could withstand the smugglers' highly unconventional methods of transport: the whisky was loaded into torpedos that were fired from former navy boats onto the beaches of Long Island at night. From there it found its way into New York City on garbage scows.

House of Lords is based on the malts from ABERLOUR, GLENALLACHIE, and EDRADOUR.

HOUSE OF PEERS

Blended Scotch from Douglas LAING & Co.

The standard versions are House of Peers and Gold Label, the DE LUXE X.O Extra Old, and 12 Years Old. In addition there is a 22-year-old vatted malt

House of Peers was first introduced in 1947. All bottlings are aged in barrels once again after blending. The vatted malt contains Islay, Speyside, and Lowland malts.

HOUSE OF STUART

Blended Scotch from GLEN CATRINE Bonded Warehouse Ltd.

HOWARD MACLAREN DE LUXE

Blended Scotch from GLEN CATRINE Bonded Warehouse Ltd.

HUDSON'S BAY

Blended Scotch, bottled for the U.S market by the New York firm SIDNEY FRANK.

HUNTLY

Blended Scotch from Huntly Blending, a subsidiary of UD.

The brand is sold in Hungary Lebanon, and what is left of Yugoslavia.

HYNARD'S FINEST

Blended Scotch from Hynard Hughes & Co. (see GAMEFAIR).

The light music of whisky falling into glasses
made an agreeable interlude.

James Joyce,
Dubliners

IDG (IRISH DISTILLERS GROUP)

The largest producer of Irish whiskey was created in 1966 through the merger of the JAMESON, POWER'S, and CORK distilleries. A few years later, in 1972, the Northern Ireland distillery BUSHMILLS was added, so that IDG had the monopoly in Ireland. In 1975 the group concentrated its efforts on the new MIDLETON distillery and closed all of its other operations except for Bushmills. But this attempt to cut costs failed to help them cope with falling demand, and the concern grew visibly weaker. In the late 1980s there began a takeover battle like nothing Ireland had ever seen before. All of the international spirit giants were involved, and finally the French concern PERNOD RICARD prevailed over its competitors ALLIED DISTILLERS, Guinness, and Grand Metropolitan. The purchase price was $525 million. Since that time IDG has focused on the international marketing of Bushmills and Jameson, paying far less attention to its other brands, which include COLERAINE, CRESTED TEN, DUNPHYS, HEWITTS, Midleton, PADDY, POWER'S GOLD LABEL, and THREE STILLS (see also Buena Vista, TULLAMORE DEW).

The IDG's monopoly continued until the founding of the COOLEY firm in 1991.

IDV (INTERNATIONAL DISTILLERS & VINTNERS)

This British wine and spirit concern, with headquarters in London, was created in 1962 by the merger of the firms W. & A. Gilbey (see GILBEY'S) and United Wine Traders. It was then taken over in 1972 by Grand Metropolitan. For the international beverage and grocery giant IDV oversees the entire spirit division, operating the distilleries Auchroisk (see THE SINGLETON OF AUCHROISK), GLEN SPEY, KNOCKANDO, and STRATHMILL as well as a related warehousing complex with its own cooperage in Blythswood, Renfrew, and a bottling plant in Dumbarton. Also part of IDV are the firms Gilbey, HEUBLEIN INC., Justerini & Brooks (see J & B), and NORTH BRITISH (50 percent).

Malt: Glen Spey, Knockando, Singleton, Strathmill.

Blended Scotch: J & B (see DUNHILL).

Liqueur: BAILEYS, DUBLINER, EMMETS, O'DARBY.

Canadian: BLACK VELVET, BRETON'S HAND & SEAL.

Australian: BOND 7.

IDV has now begun investing heavily in the so-called emerging countries, which it sees as the spirit markets of the future, unlike the saturated markets of Europe and North America.

It is placing great hopes on India, where in addition to its own production sites (SPEY ROYAL, GILBEY'S) it undertook a joint venture with the local whiskey producer Polychem in 1994. In addition, IDV owns several brands in Brazil (DRURY'S, GREGSON'S, OLD EIGHT). Among the other IDV spirits are Smirnoff vodka, Gilbey's gin, Malibu, Metaxa, and Veterano.

IMMORTAL MEMORY

Blended Scotch, 8 years old, 80 proof, from GORDON & MACPHAIL.

The "immortal memory" is that attached to the Scottish national poet Robert Burns (1759–96), whose birthday on January 25 occasions a thirst among committed  Scotsmen that compares with that experienced by their Irish neighbors on St. Patrick's Day. For the bicentennial of Burns's death, Gordon & MacPhail issued a special limited bottling of this high-class brand (see JOHN BARLEYCORN, ROBBIE BURNS).

IMPERIAL

1) Blended American, 80 proof, from BARTON DISTILLING (Canandaigua).

2) Scottish single malt (Speyside) from ALLIED DISTILLERS (ALLIED DOMECQ).

A malt full of character and with a nice balance between malt and peat.

Gordon & MacPhail: Vintage 1979, 80 proof.

Cadenhead: 16 years old (distilled 1976), 128.6 proof.

James MacArthur: 15 years old, 86 proof.

The distillery was opened in 1897 and closed again 2 years later. It continued to be idle for most of its life, aside from the years in which it belonged to the DCL, which operated it from 1955 to 1985. In 1989 it was acquired by Allied and again reopened.

Admirers are eager to see whether the malt will still have its delightful, old-fashioned character under the new owners and will finally be bottled as a single.

Imperial has 4 stills, and it takes its water from the Ballintomb Burn.

(Tel. 1340 81 02 76)

IMPERIAL GOLD MEDAL

Blended Scotch from COCKBURN'S OF LEITH.

INCHGOWER

Scottish single malt (Northern Speyside) from ARTHUR BELL & SONS (UD).

A slightly salty malt with a mild body.

Original bottling: 14 years old, 86 proof ("Flora & Fauna" series); the 12-year-old bottling from the previous owner, Bell & Sons, is no longer on the market.

The distillery was built in 1872 and taken over by Arthur Bell & Sons in 1938, which in turn became a part of UD but still owns the license.

Inchgower has 4 stills; its water comes from the Menduff Hills.

(Tel. 1542 83 11 61)

INCHGOWER

INCHMURRIN

Scottish single malt (Southern Highlands) from the Loch Lomond distillery, property of Glen Catrine Bonded Warehouse Ltd.

A mild, dry malt with a somewhat confusing history.

Original bottling: 10 years old, 80 proof.

Cadenhead: Most recently a 9-year-old from 1985 at 128 proof.

Inchmurrin is one of two malts from the Loch Lomond distillery; the other is called Old Rhosdhu. The distillery was built in 1965–66, and beginning in 1971 belonged to Barton Distilling, which closed it in 1984 and a year later sold it to Inver House Distillers. It remained closed until it was acquired by its present owner in

1986, which promptly started it up again.

The whole situation is complicated by the fact that the name "Lomond" pops up in various contexts. For one thing, it designates this distillery and the lake next to which it stands. There is also a malt whisky called Lomond that comes from another distillery (see Inverleven). Finally, there is the Lomond Still. Neither Inchmurrin nor Old Rhosdhu is produced from such stills, even though it is often claimed that they are. (For the differences between the 2 malts, see Old Rhosdhu).

Inchmurrin was for a time also available as a pure malt (without age designation), which usually means a vatted malt. This version comes from the period when there was not enough aged malt available to permit its being bottled as a single.

(Tel. 1389 75 27 81)

INDEPENDENT BOTTLERS

Many Scottish malt whiskies are bottled not only by their respective producers but also by independent bottlers. A whole raft of malts are available ONLY from these firms specializing in especially rare whiskies. These are brands that are either no longer produced at all or used only in blending, as well as special vintages that were never officially marketed.

One needs to distinguish among licensed bottlings, owner bottlings, and brand bottlings.

Licensed bottlings are those in which the producer leaves the bottling and marketing of its whiskies as single malts up to the independent firms (for example, SCAPA from GORDON & MACPHAIL, or Smith's GLENLIVET).

Owner bottlings are those that have not been authorized by the producer. These are legal only if the bottler's name appears on the label in larger type than that used for the name of the distillery.

Brand bottlings can be of either type. In a licensed brand bottling, for example, a firm buys the whisky from the producer and bottles it under its own name (for example, El Vino Islay Malt is actually BUNNAHABHAIN). In unofficial brand bottlings the whisky is bottled under an imaginary name (for example, GLEN GORDON from Gordon & MacPhail) and the producer is unnamed (there are a huge number of such imaginary brands, and only a few are listed here).

The most important independent bottlers are Wm CADENHEAD, Gordon & MacPhail, the SCOTCH MALT WHISKY SOCIETY, and SIGNATORY.

The increasing popularity of SINGLE-BARREL BOTTLINGS has recently led to the establishment of a large number of new firms of this sort. Although it was formerly necessary to have at one's disposal huge stocks of whiskies, so as to be able to offer a consistent repertoire over a longer period of time, it is now possible to do business if you own only a few barrels. The market is thus becoming more and more complex, and it is possible to mention only a few of the smaller new firms here: ADELPHI DISTILLERY LTD., THE CASTLE COLLECTION, James MACARTHUR & Co.

INDIAN WHISKEY

The West has scarcely noticed, but India has developed over the past few years into one of the largest whiskey producers in the world, even outstripping the Japanese. The rate of growth in the years 1990–94 was some 75 percent.

The country produces various types of whiskey: Indian blends, blends of Indian malts and Scottish blends (!), and even single malts (see McDOWELL'S).

The most important producers are the UB Group (United Brewers of India), Shaw Wallace, Jagatjit, Khoday, Mohan Meakins, and Polychem. The most prominent brands are BAGPIPER, DIRECTOR'S SPECIAL, JAGATJIT ARISTOCRAT, McDowell's, and Diplomat.

The chief consumers are the members of the middle class, whose number roughly corresponds to the population of the United States. Such a powerful market has naturally attracted the large international concerns, who have been scrambling to collaborate with native firms since the early 1990s. UD has invested in a joint venture with the UB Group, IDV is linked to Polychem (see also GILBEY'S), and HIRAM WALKER & SONS has teamed up with Jagatjit. Even the rather small firm DOUGLAS LAING & Co. is now represented in India.

INISHOWEN

Blended Irish whiskey, standard, 80 proof, from COOLEY DISTILLERY.

A mild, almost too pure whiskey that recently came on the market. It bears the name of a region in northwestern Ireland that was formerly known for the quality of its whiskey and as a moonshiner's paradise.

INTERNATIONAL DISTILLERS & VINTNERS

See IDV.

INVERARITY

A new Scottish company based in Edinburgh, bottling 2 brands: The Inverarity Single Malt (an unidentified Speyside malt) and The Inverarity Blend.

THE INVERGORDON

Scottish single grain (Northern Highlands) from INVERGORDON DISTILLERS (WHYTE & MACKAY, AMERICAN BRANDS).

This whisky has been on the market since 1990 and is one of the few grains available as a single. Moreover, it is the only one distilled in the Highlands. Normally it is bottled as a 10-year-old and at 86 proof, but one also encounters it in an older version in the "Stillman's Dram" series from Invergordon (see also BEN WYVIS). The producers describe its aroma as "distilled sunlight," and though that may strike you as overly poetic, you should be aware that Invergordon is by nature very mild, but by no means flavorless.

INVERGORDON DISTILLERS

Scottish whisky producer, Edinburgh, subsidiary of WHYTE & MACKAY (AMERICAN BRANDS).

In the late 1950s, when the Royal Navy abandoned its base in the northern Scottish port city of Invergordon, the construction of a huge distillery

mit, and Whyte & Mackay snapped it up. Since that time the malts have been issued by the new owner, and Invergordon itself is responsible for only the distillery and the blended Scotches and liqueurs: CLUNY, FINDLATER'S FINEST, GLAYVA, GLEN CLOVA, GLENDROSTAN, GLENFAIRN, GLEN LYON, GLEN SLOY, INVERNESS CREAM, JOCK SCOTT, LEGACY, MACKINLAY'S, NORTHERN SCOTT, PIG'S NOSE, SCOTS CLUB, SCOTS GREY, SCOTS POET, and SHEEP DIP. (See also BENEAGLES, CWS, SCOTTISH & NEWCASTLE BREWERIES.)

INVER HOUSE DISTILLERS
This Scottish production firm was created in 1965 by the U.S. spirit concern

complex was begun, in part as a way of creating jobs. It produces mainly GRAIN WHISKY, but since 1965 it has also distilled a malt called BEN WYVIS. Carlton Industries, the owners at the time, became more and more committed to malts. In 1966 they built the TAMNAVULIN distillery, and in the following years they acquired the distilleries BRUICHLADDICH, TULLIBARDINE, and DEANSTON. The Hawker Siddely Group took over the business in 1978 and added GLENALLACHIE and ISLE OF JURA. In a management buyout in 1988 Invergordon became independent, but not for long: it was able to ward off a takeover bid by Whyte & Mackay in 1991, but in 1994 it was forced to sub-

Publicker when it built the GAR-NHEATH distillery. The same firm also owned the distilleries BLADNOCH and LOCH LOMOND for a time—the former from 1973 to 1983; the latter from 1985 to 1986. When Publicker fell on hard times in 1988, Inver House was taken over by its management and established as an independent company.

In the following years Inver House acquired the distilleries KNOCKDHU and SPEYBURN as well as the Scotch labels CATTO's and HANKEY BANNISTER. Since 1995 the firm has also owned the malt OLD PULTENEY, and in 1996 it acquired BALBLAIR.

Additional brands: BLAIRMHOR, GLEN FLAGLER, Glengalwan, HEATHER CREAM LIQUEUR, INVER HOUSE GREEN PLAID, MacARTHUR's, and PINWINNIE ROYAL. (See also Erin's Isle.)

In addition, Inver House also produces gin and vodka, and since 1994 it has cooperated with the Chinese distillery Tuo Pai Distillers.

INVER HOUSE GREEN PLAID

Blended Scotch, standard, 12 and 17 years old, from INVER HOUSE DISTILLERS.

A typical LIGHT WHISKY, solely for export, especially to southern Europe, Holland, and Mexico.

INVERLEVEN

Scottish single malt (Lowlands, Dumbarton) from BALLANTINE & Son (ALLIED DISTILLERS, ALLIED DOMECQ).

A mild, rather sweet malt that has never been bottled officially.

Gordon & MacPhail: Vintages 1979, 1984, 80 proof.

Inverleven was built in 1938 as part of Ballantine's huge distillery complex in Dumbarton, which produces primarily GRAIN WHISKY. For malt production it had one POT STILL and a LOMOND STILL. Both were put in mothballs in 1991, so this whisky will not be available much longer.

(Tel. 1389 76 51 11)

INVERNESS CREAM

Blended Scotch from Longman, a subsidiary of INVERGORDON DISTILLERS (WHYTE & MACKAY, AMERICAN BRANDS.)

IRISH COFFEE

One of the few drinks whose inventor is known by name: Joe Sheridan, bartender at Shannon, the Irish airport, where at one time a large number of transatlantic flights touched down. The firm

IDG has even put up a plaque there in gratitude for Sheridan's contribution to the Irish whiskey industry.

In the 1950s and 1960s Irish coffee experienced such a boom in the United States that whiskey brands were created especially to meet the demand. (See BUENA VISTA, DUNPHYS.) Heat 1½ oz. Irish whiskey in a heat-proof Irish coffee glass (do not boil), stir in brown sugar, and fill with strong hot coffee. Stir again and top with slightly whipped cream (the cream must not be too liquid or too stiff, or it will sink; the same thing happens if you go too easy on the whiskey).

IRISH MIST
Irish whiskey herb liqueur, 70 proof, from CANTRELL & COCHRANE (ALLIED DOMECQ).

IRISH WHISKEY
First the clichés: The Irish invented whiskey. They don't do anything but drink and sing all day. Irish whiskey is oily-tasting and fragrant.

Now the realities: It cannot be proved that Irish monks were the first to distill whiskey or that it was they who introduced the art of distillation to Scotland in the Middle Ages. There

may be references to *aqua vitae* from the 14th century, but clearly this was distilled wine. The first written mention of a drink distilled from grain, as the British writer Jim Murray relates in his thorough study of the subject, is from the 16th century—or some years later than the first reference to Scottish whisky (1494). It is true that Irish whiskey was more important in the early years. By 1800 Ireland had more than 2,000 distilleries, and up until the 19th century—in the United States, even until the time of Prohibition—Irish played a far more important role than Scotch. A hundred years ago there were still more than 400 Irish whiskey brands in the United States alone, and in Portugal at that time it was customary to add Irish to port wine. Today the only surviving great names from that time are POWER'S and JAMESON, and the number of distilleries only recently rose again from 2 to 3.

There are various reasons for the collapse of the Irish whiskey industry. Perhaps the most important was the arrival of BLENDED WHISK(E)Y. It was an Irishman, Aeneas Coffey, who invented continuous distillation, which opened the way for this development, in about 1830 (see PATENT STILL). With the new technique it became possible to produce cheaper and milder grain distillates (see GRAIN WHISKY), but whereas the Irish stuck to their undiluted and powerful PURE POT STILL WHISKEY, in Scotland more and more producers changed over to diluting their heavy malt with grain. The result was not only less expensive, it was much more appealing to the taste of the new whisk(e)y consumers, the inhabitants of the growing industrial centers. The next blow came with the Irish struggle for independence against England (1916) and the subsequent civil war (1919–21). Aside from the misery that the war unleashed over the country, the loss of the British market, including that of the Commonwealth—Canada, Australia, South Africa, etc.—proved ruinous for the entire Irish economy. The only foreign market left was the United States, and in 1920 that country began its "noble experiment" with PROHIBITION. Suddenly the most important export market for Irish whiskey was lost. In those years the Irish not only lacked the criminal enterprise with which the Scots got around the American laws (see, for example, CUTTY SARK, STODART), but they also failed to build up sufficient stores for the period after Prohibition and the lifting of the trade embargo.

The period of the great distillery closings lasted until the 1950s, and it was only the merger of the large firms Power's, Jameson, BUSHMILLS, and CORK DISTILLERIES into the IDG that saved the last of them. Even the IDG was unable to recover the ground that had been lost, and only since its takeover by the French spirit concern PERNOD RICARD in 1988 has it begun a slow recovery. With Jameson and Bushmills, there are once again 2 internationally successful Irish whiskey brands. (In Ireland itself, the number 1 is still POWER's.) The success of the COOLEY DISTILLERY, established only in 1987, suggests that the gloomiest period for Irish whiskey may be coming to an end.

The Irish quench their thirst mainly with beer, for Irish whiskey is not only expensive, but it continues to lose its market share to Scotch and (Irish) vodka. One now encounters older Irish workingmen quaffing their Guinness with Power's only in the pubs of the Dublin suburbs and in the countryside. Young people, if they drink hard liquor at all, prefer vodka; the business world drinks Scotch.

The increasing consumption of Scotch may be the reason why the Cooley Distillery has adopted Scottish production methods rather than traditional Irish ones. All Cooley products are distilled only twice and are based at least in part on peated grains. This gives the whiskey a stronger body and a slightly smoky flavor, and the oiliness once so characteristic of Irish whiskey is avoided. But even the IDG brands from the MIDLETON distillery have overcome

that quality recently, even though they continue to distill 3 times and do not use peat at all, following the Irish tradition. In Irish whiskey's great years so-called pure pot still whiskey was all that was produced. This is a mixture of malted and unmalted barley to which at one time (until the 1960s) oats were added as well as small quantities of wheat and rye. It was then distilled in copper alembics (see POT STILL). This grain mixture gave Irish its character and gave pure pot still a higher alcohol content than that of Irish malt whiskey, which as a rule lacks the smoky flavor that is so valued in its Scottish counterpart. Pure pot still is still produced, to be sure, but without the barley; in addition, it is almost never bottled as such (see GREEN SPOT, REDBREAST) but rather incorporated into blends.

Since the middle of this century the Irish have bowed to international tastes and produced mainly blended whiskey. This can consist of malt, pot still, and grain, or of only any 2 of these types.

Most brands come from Midleton, the huge distilling complex belonging to the IDG, which produces as needed malt whiskeys, pot still whiskeys, and grains, combining them on the spot. The second IDG distillery, Bushmills, produces mal-

hiskey exclusively. Its production is
ither bottled as a single or diluted
ith grain from Midleton.

For aging the Irish use previously
sed sherry and bourbon barrels,
nd the minimum period is 3 years.
onger merging of the individual
omponents is extremely rare.

SLAND PRINCE
lended Scotch, 12-, 15-, and 21-
ear-old de luxe, from ISLE OF ARRAN
ISTILLERS.

Detail from map on page 301

99 Ardbeg   **96** Caol Ila

98 Bowmore   **100** Lagavulin

97 Bruichladdich   **101** Laphroaig

85 Bunnhabhain

ISLAY
Scottish whisky region. The island of
Islay in the west of Scotland is not only
home to a number of great malts, but
it is also the region whose whiskies are
most likely to have a distinctive, recognizable taste. Islay malts are extremely
strong, as a rule. They have an intense
flavor of peat (almost the entire island
is covered with a layer of it that turns
the groundwater yellow) and a hint of
the proximity of the sea (all Islay distilleries are situated on the coast). They
are also highly desired for blends, for
even a small quantity of Islay malt
lends them the typical peat-smoke
aroma. (A listing of brands is given in
the appendix.)

ISLAY LEGEND
Blended Scotch from MORRISON
BOWMORE DISTILLERS (SUNTORY).

The base malt is BOWMORE, and
the brand is sold mainly in France.

ISLAY MIST
Blended Scotch, de luxe and 17 years
old, from MACDUFF INTERNATIONAL.

The few who know this whisky
value it highly for its strength and elegance. Islay Mist was introduced in
1928 by D. Johnston & Co., which then
operated the distillery LAPHROAIG. In
addition to that malt the blend contains
THE GLENLIVET and GLEN GRANT.

The former owner, ALLIED DIS-
TILLERS, surrendered the brand to
MacDuff in 1992.

ISLE OF ARRAN DISTILLERS

Scottish producer. In 1991, the former manager at CHIVAS and HOUSE OF CAMPBELL, Harold Currie, began construction of the Lochranza Distillery, the first legal distillery on the island of Arran in 150 years. It has 5 stills and takes its water from a spring called Eason Biorach.

The first single-malt bottlings are expected in the year 2001.

Aside from these, the firm produces the vatted malt EILEANDOUR and the blends GLEN ROSA, ISLAND PRINCE, and LOCH RANZA.

ISLE OF JURA

Scottish SINGLE MALT (Isle of Jura) from INVERGORDON DISTILLERS (WHYTE & MACKAY, AMERICAN BRANDS).

A mild, somewhat sweet whisky whose slight flavor of salt betrays its island origins.

Original bottling: 10 years old, 80 and 86 proof; 26 years old, 90 proof ("Stillman's Dram").

Cadenhead: Markets under the name Jura a 12-year-old (distilled 1983), 126 proof.

The distillery, established in 1810, formerly produced a much stronger and peatier malt than it does today, one more similar to those of the neighboring island Islay. But in the early 1960s it was renovated by its then

owners SCOTTISH & NEWCASTLE BREWERIES and furnished with larger stills (today it has 4), so that the whisky is now more reminiscent of a Highland malt. The water comes from Loch a'Bhaile Mhargaidh.

(Tel. 1496 82 02 40)

No report on the island of Jura is complete without mention of the fact that it was here that George Orwell wrote *1984*, or that there are more deer here (roughly 5,000) than people (roughly 200).

I. W. HARPER

Kentucky straight bourbon from the BERNHEIM DISTILLERY of UD.

A somewhat dry whiskey, full of character. First introduced in 1875, it is one of the oldest bourbon brands. The standard version is called I. W. Harper Gold Medal and is 86 proof; the 15-year-old Gold Medal bottling is 80 proof. In addition there are the bottled in bond called I. W. Harper 101, at 101 proof, and a 12-year-old at 86 proof. The latter is the most elegant version; it is sold in a traditional carafe bottle and is the best-selling bourbon in Japan, for which reason it is hard to find in the United States. The recently introduced President's Reserve, at 86 proof, is designated exclusively for export.

J

Do you want a glass or a funnel?

Paul Cain,
Fast One

JACK & JILL

Slovenian blended whisky from the firm Dana, in Mirna.

A blend of imported Scotch malt and local grain brandy.

JACK DANIEL'S OLD NO. 7

Tennessee sour mash from the Jack Daniel Distillery, Lynchburg, from BROWN-FORMAN.

One of the very great brands in the world of spirits and truly a very good whiskey.

Jack Daniel's Old No. 7 Black Label is 86 proof and, as a rule, from 4 to 5 years old. It offers a perfect balance between smoothness and strength and is very versatile, which is to say one can drink it straight with ice, or in mixed drinks. The brand, one of the 30 best-selling spirits in the world, has been popular in the United States since the 1950s, in part because it became known at that time as Frank Sinatra's favorite whiskey. When asked whether he believed in God, the singer once replied: "I'm for anything that helps you get through the night, whether it's a prayer, a tranquilizer, or a bottle of Jack Daniel's."

Jack Daniel's Old No. 7 Green Label is an unpretentious, no-nonsense whiskey. It is identical in age and strength to Black Label but is blended from barrels that are less well developed and is therefore somewhat harsher. It is mainly found in the South, where the population is poorer and whiskey more expensive than in most regions of the United States. People who don't have enough money for Black Label buy Green Label instead. Every few years the distillery issues special editions; at the moment there is one at 96 proof bottled to celebrate the bicentennial of the state of Tennessee. The same distillery produces the brands GENTLE-MAN JACK and LEM MOTLOW'S.

In a lot of duty-free shops you can find a One-Day-Old Whiskey from

JACK DANIEL'S OLD DISTILLERY
LYNCHBURG, TENN.

Lynchburg that bears the legend "For Taste-Testing Only" (90 proof).

Jack Daniel (1846–1911), the legendary figure for which the brand was named, was already an independent distiller by the time he was 13 years old. He founded the present distillery in 1866, and his first brand was called Belle of Lincoln. His Old No. 7 was registered in 1887. Descended from Welsh immigrants, he was a thoroughgoing dandy, despite his short stature, and doubtless knew as much about marketing as his present-day successors. In around 1890 he began bottling his whiskey in the square bottle that is still typical of the brand today, and as early as the beginning of this century one could buy Jack Daniel's even in Europe. After Daniel's death, his nephew Lem Motlow took over the concern, and he managed to keep it going against almost impossible odds. Prohibition was repealed in the United States in 1933, but many counties continued the ban on alcohol—among them Moore County, in which the distillery operates. Motlow nevertheless succeeded in getting a distiller's license, with the proviso that he not serve his whiskey. Moore County is dry to this day, and visitors to the distillery are offered homemade lemonade.

Motlow's descendants sold the firm to Brown-Forman in 1956, but Lem Motlow is still listed as the distillery's owner. There is also a brand named after him, which is produced here for the regional market. Jack Daniel's gets its special character from an unusual type of FILTRATION (see also TENNESSEE WHISKEY). It is distilled from a mixture of 80 percent corn, 12 percent rye, and 8 percent barley malt; the sour mash component is 20 percent.

Since 1994, Jack Daniel's has been brewing a very decent beer for the regional market in Cincinnati, Ohio, and is also responsible for a number of the terrible pre-mixes that are so popular in the United States.

(Tel. 615 759-6180)

THE JACOBITE
Blended Scotch produced since 1983 by INVERGORDON DISTILLERS for Nurdin & Peacock, a British supermarket chain. It is available mainly in the chain's stores.

JACOB'S WELL
Kentucky straight bourbon, 84 proof, from JIM BEAM BRANDS (AMERICAN BRANDS).

A new brand from the house of Beam, which is produced by a special process related to the Spanish Solera system. This bourbon does not spend all 7 years of its aging period in the original barrels, but is mixed at certain intervals with other, specially aged whiskeys and then returned to the original barrels.

The name refers to the first spring that Jacob Beam, the founder of the Beam dynasty, tapped for the production of whiskey in 1795.

JAGATJIT ARISTOCRAT
Indian blend from Jagatjit Industries, the third-largest whiskey producer in the country.

JAMES E. PEPPER
Kentucky straight bourbon, 80 proof, from the BERNHEIM DISTILLERY of UD.

A light, medium-grade whiskey produced solely for export. The Pep-

per family was already involved in distilling in 1776, which is why it later advertised its bourbon as having been "Born with the Republic." (When Prohibition was declared, one wag added the line: "Died with Democracy.") The Peppers established several distilleries, including the famous Old Oscar Pepper Distillery in which E. H. Taylor learned his trade (see OLD TAYLOR) and James Crow distilled his first OLD CROW. Pepper whiskeys were very popular up until Prohibition, but then the name was acquired by Schenley, which ceased production in the 1960s. The present brand has been produced since the end of the 1980s by the new owner, UD.

JAMES FOXE
Canadian blend from SAZERAC.

One of the many brands that are produced in Canada but bottled and sold only in the United States. As is usual in such cases, the name of the distillery is not disclosed.

JAMES GORDON'S
Blended Scotch, premium, 8 years old, 80 proof, from James Gordon & Co., a subsidiary of GORDON & MACPHAIL.

This outstanding whisky was named after one of the founders of the firm of Gordon & MacPhail.

JAMES MARTIN'S

Blended Scotch from James Martin & Co., a subsidiary of MACDONALD MARTIN DISTILLERS.

Available as an 8-year-old V.V.O. and as a 12-, 17-, and 20-year-old DE LUXE.

James Martin, also known on account of his boxing skills as "Sparry" Martin, set himself up as an independent whisky dealer in Edinburgh in 1878. He was mainly engaged in export, and Macdonald & Muir, which has run his business since 1912, has continued that specialty. Martin's whisky became one of the leading Scotch brands in the United States after Prohibition. (Macdonald & Muir has operated under the name Macdonald Martin since 1953; in 1996 it was renamed Glenmorangie.) The brand achieved literary fame owing to a shipwreck: in February 1941, the British ship SS *Politician* sank off the Outer Hebrides with a cargo of roughly 50,000 cases of whisky, a large part of it Martin's. This incident inspired the Scotsman Sir Compton Mackenzie to write his best-selling novel *Whisky Galore*, which was later filmed. The wreck

was raised in 1990, and the rescued whisky is currently being sold under the name SS POLITICIAN.

JAMESON

Blended Irish whiskey, premium, 80 proof, from the MIDLETON distillery of the IDG (PERNOD RICARD).

This brand, the most popular Irish whiskey brand worldwide, has been available only since the 1960s. At that time the firm John Jameson & Son decided to market its whiskey itself instead of selling it by the barrel to other bottlers. Its first brand was CRESTED TEN; then in 1968 it brought out Jameson, which now meets almost 75 percent of the demand for Irish whiskey. It is light and gentle and consists of roughly equal parts pot still and grain whiskeys, 10 percent of which are aged in sherry casks.

In addition to the premium version, there is the elegant 12-year-old De Luxe Jameson 1780, which was introduced in the late 1980s and has a very high component of pot still whiskey. It contains roughly 33 percent sherry-cask-aged distillates and is rightly considered one of the finest of Irish whiskeys.

The most exclusive brand from the Jameson series is the 12-year-old Distillery Reserve, which is available only at the Midleton distillery.

Because of its high percentage of whiskeys aged in sherry casks, Distillery Reserve has been referred to as "the Macallan of Ireland," but in this case that is not necessarily a compliment, for unlike the strong Scottish malts, their unpeated Irish cousins easily run the danger of being dominated by the flavor of sherry.

Other brands from the house of Jameson are GREEN SPOT and RED-BREAST. Until a few years ago, Cadenhead bottled a 27-year-old whiskey from the old Jameson Distillery (distilled 1963, 136.2 proof), calling it simply Bow Street, after the firm's street address.

This distillery was closed in 1971 and now houses a whiskey museum.

Up until that time it was the center of the Irish whiskey industry. It was probably established or taken over in 1780 by John Jameson (1740–1823)—it is no longer possible to reconstruct its early history.

It is certain, however, that Jameson came from Scotland and was related to the legendary HAIG whisky dynasty. One of his sons married a daughter of Robert Stein, the co-inventor of continuous distilling, and ran the distillery during the period of its greatest expansion, up to the end of the 19th century. The Jamesons were known for their careful craftsmanship and the value they placed on aging at a time when whiskey was still being sold very young. They are considered the pioneers of aging in sherry casks. In 1966 the Jameson firm merged with John Power (see POWER'S) and Cork Distilleries (see MIDLETON, PADDY) to form the IDG, which now belongs to Pernod Ricard.

JAMIE STUART

Blended Scotch from WHYTE & MACKAY (AMERICAN BRANDS).

This brand formerly belonged to J. & G. Stewart (see STEWART'S FINEST OLD).

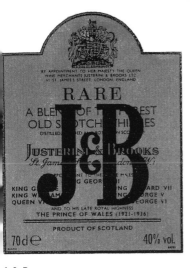

J & B

Blended Scotch from Justerini & Brooks, a subsidiary of IDV/Grand Metropolitan.

A clean, light-bodied whisky and one of the most successful spirit brands in the world.

Versions: Rare 8-year-old premium, Edwardian premium, Jet 12-year-old de luxe, Reserve 15-year-old de luxe, Victorian de luxe; for the official 500th birthday celebration of the Scottish whisky industry the firm produced a unique blend called Ultima, which consists of all of the various malt and grain whiskies available, a total of 128 (116 malts and 12 grains), many of them from distilleries that have long since closed.

J & B Rare is the number-2 brand on the international whisk(e)y market and is number 17 on the list of best-selling spirits. The brand's first success was in the United States in the 1930s, and it was from there that it went on to conquer the world market. One of the reasons for its success is the so-called light character, with which J & B and other brands supplanted the more intense blends of the old school (see LIGHT WHISK(E)Y).

The story of the house of Justerini & Brooks begins much earlier. Giaccomo Justerini, from Bologna, arrived in London in 1749, having followed an opera singer with whom he was in love. In order to earn a living, he

started mixing his father's liqueur recipe and in that same year opened, with George Johnson—the nephew of an opera producer—a spirits shop. What became of the love affair is unknown, but his business flourished, and 11 years later Justerini went back to Italy a wealthy man. The Johnsons continued to run the business and sold it in 1831 to Alfred Brooks, who gave it its present name.

When the whisky boom began in England in the 1880s, Justerini & Brooks was one of the first firms to buy up stocks of old whiskies with which to create its own blend (see CLUB).

In the 1950s, Justerini & Brooks merged with another concern to form United Wine Traders Ltd., and 10 years later that entity merged with W. A. Gilbey (see GILBEY'S) to form IDV. Both mergers were entered into in an effort to expand the international marketing network.

The base malts of all J & B bottlings come from the distilleries KNOCKANDO, AUCHROISK, GLEN SPEY, and STRATHMILL. The final blending of the more than 40 single whiskies takes place in the warehouses at Auchroisk.

JAPANESE WHISKY

Japan first started making whisky patterned after Scotch, but since the early 1980s it has also been producing bourbon. To Western palates accustomed to Scotch or bourbon, Japan's whiskies nevertheless seem too delicate. Some of them are blended extremely carefully but lack individual character. This is not to say that these are merely poor copies of Western originals; the difference is probably that Japanese palates are simply not attuned to stronger spirits. Accordingly, whisky is always diluted there with plenty of water. (Even the enormous quantities of the most expensive cognacs that Japan imports are served—*horribile dictu*—in tall glasses with ice and water.)

The Japanese whisky market is dominated by SUNTORY (roughly 70 percent market share), one of the largest spirit producers in the world.

The founder of the firm, Shinjiro Torii, built the first whisky distillery in Japan in 1923. His production manager was Masataka Taketsuru, who had studied chemistry in Scotland and later created the firm NIKKA, now number 2 in Japan. The first native whisky was introduced to the market in 1929. It was not especially successful; Japan's cosmopolitan, British-oriented upper class in the 1920s drank Scotch. Only when the Western lifestyle became more widespread after World War II did locally produced whisky become popular, for until import duties were lifted in 1989 the imports amounted to luxury articles. The only Western firm to have exploited the Japanese whisky boom as yet is SEAGRAM (who else?), which, together with the brewing concern Kirin (see KIRIN-SEAGRAM), opened a distillery south of Tokyo in the 1970s.

Despite a downward trend since the beginning of the 1990s, the Japanese whisky market is today one of the most profitable in the world. All of the major brands are produced by Suntory (for example, Kakubin, Reserve, Old, and Royal).

Production: There are only a few distilleries in Japan, but many of them are huge, highly automated, and very efficient. Whole batteries of stills produce various malts within a single distillery. That is essential in order to obtain enough different components for blends. Even so, Japanese blends do not contain anywhere near as many single malts as Scottish ones do (see SUNTORY).

In strict adherence to the Scottish formula, Japanese whiskies are composed of a blend of malt distilled twice in pot stills and continuously distilled grain whisky. Naysayers claim, to be sure, that the less expensive types are distilled from anything—molasses, for example—but not barley. That would be difficult to determine, and to my knowledge there are no legal restrictions that would offer assurance. What is certain is that Japan is the world's largest importer of Scottish malt whisky, shipped in tanks. This is then diluted with local whiskies; in the higher alcohol-content Japanese whiskies it amounts to 15 to 20 percent. Some Japanese firms have also invested in Scotland: Suntory has owned the MORRISON-BOWMORE group since 1994; Nikka owns the BEN NEVIS distillery; and TAKARA, SHUZO & OKURA, the TOMATIN distillery.

The Japanese also import some of their barley malt and peat from Scotland. It must be noted, however, that they use peat very sparingly; the flavor is predominantly malt. The minimum age is 3 years, and more expensive brands age for 12, 15, or 20 years. They use charred oak barrels they produce themselves, as well as sherry and bourbon barrels.

The generally accepted classifications STANDARD, PREMIUM, and DE LUXE also apply in Japan, but the designation SPECIAL is far more common. It is used for brands with a malt component of 30 percent or more.

The Japanese have been bottling pure malt whisky only since the 1980s, and only in relatively small quantities (for example, Suntory Yamazaki, NIKKA HOKKAIDO, KARUIZAWA), for they prefer importing Scottish brands.

JIM BEAM

Kentucky straight bourbon from Jim Beam Brands, a subsidiary of the conglomerate AMERICAN BRANDS.

The name Beam is extremely important in the world of bourbon,

both historically and economically. The brand Jim Beam has been around since 1942 and is currently available in several different versions.

Jim Beam White Label, 4 years old, 80 proof, the best-selling bourbon and one of the 20 top-selling spirits in the world; medium heavy and well balanced, a true mainstream whiskey that is good for mixing. In the United States there is also a 7 year-old version. As one might expect in America, the whiskey is also sold in a can as Jim Beam & Cola. Production of the 5-year-old Beam's Choice Green Label, at 86 proof, was recently stopped—unfortunately, for it had the most pronounced bourbon character. Beam's Black Label is the 8-year-old noble variant, at 90 proof, 80 proof for export.

In addition there is the 6-year-old Jim Beam Rye (Yellow Label), at 80 proof, which is rather sweet for a rye.

Finally, Beam's 8 Star is a blend with a high percentage of bourbon.

The firm was founded in 1935, as the James B. Beam Distilling Company, by H. Homel, O. Jacobson, H. Blum, and Jeremiah Beam. The latter was a descendant of Jacob Beam (1770–1834), who was in turn descended from a German immigrant by the name of Böhm and had begun distilling whiskey as early as 1795. The Beams have probably influenced the development of bourbon more than anyone else. They operate a whole string of distilleries (including the Early Times Distillery) and have produced talented stillmen, who have passed on the family's experience to other distilleries. Parker and Craig Beam, for example, are now responsible for production at Heaven Hill Distillers. It was Booker Noe (1864–1947)—a grandson of the Jim Beam for whom the brand is named and for a long time stillman at Ancient Age—who had the idea of bottling small-batch bourbons, and thereby

prepared the way for the Beams' rise into the bourbon aristocracy.

Although the firm was taken over by American Brands in 1967, it retained control over production and has meanwhile become responsible for the conglomerate's entire liquor production. This includes, since 1987, such famous brands as OLD CROW and OLD GRAND-DAD, as well as a number of Canadians. The whiskeys are produced in the Beam distilleries in Clermont and Boston, Kentucky, and in the Alberta Distillery in Calgary, Alberta; an additional bottling plant is in Cincinnati, Ohio.

Jim Beam whiskeys include the following brands:

Bourbon: BELLOW'S CLUB, BOURBON DELUXE, HILL & HILL, JACOB'S WELL, Jim Beam, Old Crow, Old Grand-Dad, OLD TAYLOR, SUNNY BROOK, as well as the small-batch bourbons BAKER'S, BASIL HAYDEN'S, BOOKER'S, KNOB CREEK.

Rye: Jim Beam, OLD OVERHOLT.

Blends: Beam's, BELLOW'S PARTNER'S CHOICE, CALVERT, Hill & Hill, KESSLER, P.M., Sunny Brook.

Canadian: ALBERTA, AUTUMN GOLD, CANADA HOUSE, LORD CALVERT, WINDSOR.

Liqueur: ROCK AND RYE.

Production: The Beams keep their grain mixture a secret, but it is assumed that they have 3 different mixtures and accordingly 3 different whiskey styles: one for the ryes, one for Old Grand-Dad and Basil Hayden's (here they claim to add more rye than in any other brand on the market), and one for the remaining brands.

The yeast culture has been cultivated since the end of Prohibition. It is the same for all brands and is mixed before fermentation with hops.

(Tel. 502 543-9877)

JIM GRANT
Kentucky straight bourbon from Gaetano, a firm established in California in 1954, which has its brands produced by various distilleries (see BARRISTER'S).

J. M. & CO. SUPERIOR MOUNTAIN DEW
Blended Scotch from Malpas Stallard, a trading house in Worcester that was first mentioned in 1642 but is possibly even older.

JOCK
Blended Scotch, 5 years old, 80 proof, from BENNACHIE.

Until only recently, this brand was called Black Jock. It is intended mainly for the Scottish market.

OCK SCOTT

Blended Scotch from Findlater, Mackie Todd & Co. (see FINDLATER'S FINEST), a subsidiary of INVERGORDON DISTILLERS (WHYTE & MACKAY, AMERICAN BRANDS). On the market since the 1930s and currently available as a 3- or 5-year-old standard and a 12-year-old DE LUXE.

OHN BARLEYCORN

The Scottish national poet Robert Burns (1759–96) published a number of works under this pseudonym, including an open letter to the British prime minister William Pitt in which he protested the high tax on whisky. Since his time John Barleycorn has also been used as an eponym for

whisky. Jack London published under this title a novel about his personal experience with whisk(e)y and other drinks (subtitled "Alcoholic Memoirs").

(See also IMMORTAL MEMORY, ROBBIE BURNS.)

JOHN BARR

Blended Scotch from WHYTE & MACKAY (AMERICAN BRANDS).

This brand was originally produced by J. Walker & Co. (see JOHNNIE WALKER); it was intended solely for the British market, was not exactly a hit, and was sold in the early 1990s by Walker's new owner, UD.

JOHN BEGG BLUE CAP

Blended Scotch from J. Begg, a subsidiary of UD.

John Begg, who was already very successful with the malt from his ROYAL LOCHNAGAR distillery, established in 1845, staked his money on the market potential of blended Scotch and soon built up a worldwide marketing network for his Blue Cap. His son made the brand into a best-seller with the help of the long-popular advertising slogan "Take a peg of John Begg" (which, in view of the large Jewish population of Glasgow, was also presented in Yiddish: *"Nem a schmeck fun Dzon Bek"*). He sold the business, which for a time also operated the distillery BEN WYVIS, to DCL in 1916. It now belongs to UD,

DEWAR

for which it holds the license for Royal Lochnagar.

One of the base malts for the rather old-fashioned Blue Cap comes, as it always has, from this distillery. The de luxe version, John Begg Gold Cap, has been discontinued.

JOHN FINCH
Blended American from KENTUCKY BOURBON DISTILLERS.

JOHN HANDY
Blended Scotch produced for the U.S. market by SAZERAC.

JOHNNIE WALKER
Blended Scotch, 86 proof, from John Walker & Sons, a subsidiary of UD.

Johnnie Walker is considered virtually synonymous with Scotch whisky, and the simple but strong standard version Red Label has been one of the best-selling whiskies of any kind for decades. The same can be said of the somewhat milder Black Label in the premium blended Scotch category. In addition, there is a sinfully expensive Blue Label, which is mainly offered in duty-free shops and contains up to 60 percent malts. Finally, there is a Johnnie Walker Swing, also called Celebrity in a number of countries; its bottle has a rounded bottom that allows it to swing back and forth when you touch it. This shape was created in the 1920s for use on large ocean steamers and is supposed to ensure that the bottle won' tip over, even on high seas. Additiona de luxe versions are sold in variou: Asian markets: Johnnie Walker Gol in Japan, Johnnie Walker Superior i Taiwan, and the brands Johnni Walker Premium and Honour. A new 18-year-old Gold Label has been o the market since 1996. It is reportedly based on an old recipe of Alexande Walker's and is produced only in limited quantities. In the same year, the company launched a 15-year-old Pur Malt, a VATTED MALT of 86 proof.

The base malts are TALISKER CARDHU, and DAILUAINE.

The success of this brand rests i large part on clever marketing: sinc 1908 Johnnie Walker has been pre sented in the same square bottle witl a red or black label, and its red-coatec

andy is one of the best-known symbols in the history of advertising. It also didn't hurt that Winston Churchill was devoted to the brand.

The firm John Walker & Sons started in 1820 as a small delicatessen business in Kilmanrock; beginning in 1856 it experimented with the production of blended whiskies, and by the end of the century it had become so successful that it bought the Cardhu distillery so as to ensure sufficient supply. In 1925 the firm joined the DCL, for which it operated the Talisker distillery for a time.

JOHNNY DRUM
Kentucky straight bourbon, 15 years old, 101 proof, from KENTUCKY BOURBON DISTILLERS.

JOHN PLAYER SPECIAL (JPS)
Blended Scotch from Douglas LAING & Co.

JPS whiskies appear in only relatively small quantities and are destined mainly for the Far East. The well-known cigarette firm permits Laing to use the name

on a franchise basis. It appears in the following versions: Standard Fine Old, premium Special Rare and 15 Years Old, de luxe 12 Years Old.

JOHN'S LANE See POWER'S GOLD LABEL.

JONES ROAD
Irish PURE POT STILL WHISKEY from the Dublin Whiskey Distillery.

This distillery was founded in 1873 and shut down in the early 1940s. It is thanks to the Cadenhead bottling firm that a few bottles of this whiskey became available several years ago. It was distilled in 1942, bottled in 1991 at 130 proof, and named after the address of the distillery (originally the brand was called DWD). After so many years in the barrel, the whiskey is of course no longer representative of the former products of the distillery and is now more of a collectors' item. The British author Jim Murray judged it, fairly enough, "not altogether undrinkable."

195

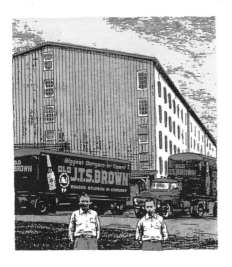

JPS See JOHN PLAYER SPECIAL.

J. T. S. BROWN

Kentucky straight bourbon, 80 proof, from HEAVEN HILL DISTILLERS.

A light, rather dry, everyday bourbon with a historic name. John Thompson Street Brown was a well-known personality in the whiskey industry at the end of the 19th century. He was one of the founders of the BROWN-FORMAN concern but left it, while it was still small, when it began to forsake quick profits for longer aging. He disappeared from the scene for a time but later founded at least 2 other distilleries, neither of which remained in operation for long. His descendants developed a similar talent for short-lived businesses, but one way or another the name J. T. S. Brown & Sons survived until the 1980s. Then Heaven Hill—always on the lookout for old names and new stocks—took over what was left of the firm and created from it this small brand for the local market.

J. T. S. Brown is also available as a blended American.

JUSTERINI & BROOKS See J & B.

J. W. CORN

Straight corn whiskey from HEAVEN HILL DISTILLERS.

J. W. DANT

Kentucky straight bourbon, 100 proof, from HEAVEN HILL DISTILLERS.

A simple, everyday bourbon that bears the name of an old distilling family. The Dants got into the whiskey business in 1836. They built a number of distilleries and made a lot of money with their brand YELLOWSTONE. They survived Prohibition by producing medicinal alcohol, but then the firm changed hands a number of times, finally landing at UD. The latter sold the remaining stocks to Heaven Hill, which is currently bottling them under the name J. W. Dant. Once the old barrels are exhausted, Heaven Hill intends to produce the whiskey itself but only for the local market.

K

I like it: I always did,
and that is the reason I never use it.

Robert E. Lee,
on being ordered whiskey
by his physician, c. 1850

KARUIZAWA
Japanese single malt, 86 proof, from Sanraku Ocean.

KASSER LAIRD
A firm founded in Horsham, Pennsylvania, in 1989, a subsidiary of LAIRD & Co., that has a number of brands in its program: BANKER'S CLUB, BARRISTER'S, CANADIAN GOLD, COUNTRY CLUB, DUNHEATH, KASSER'S 51, MONOGRAM, PRESS CLUB, YOUNG'S SPECIAL BLEND.

KASSER'S 51
Blended American from KASSER LAIRD.

KELT "TOUR DU MONDE"
Scottish vatted malt, 80 proof, from INVERGORDON DISTILLERS (WHYTE & MACKAY, AMERICAN BRANDS).

The producers of this brand, available only since 1995, made use of centuries of experience. In the days when whisky and other spirits were still sold by the barrel and not in bottles, it was discovered that long sea voyages were beneficial to the aging process. Accordingly, after the regular aging period barrels of Kelt whisky are sent on a 3-month voyage around the world. The various ports of call are listed on the label.

KENNEDY'S
Kentucky straight bourbon and blended American from M. S. WALKER.

KENTUCKY BOURBON DISTILLERS
Independent bottler near Bardstown, Kentucky.

The distillery was formerly called the Willet Distillery. It was shut down during Prohibition and reopened only in the 1980s by a descendant of the Willet family. Production is supposed to begin again in the near future. At the moment the firm is still relying on whiskeys from other producers. Its main supplier is the distillery HEAVEN HILL, which is only a stone's throw away.

Here the whiskey is bottled under brand names, some of which date back to the time of the old Willet distillery. (The distillery names given on the various labels are fictitious, as is so often the case with U.S. whiskeys.)

A large part of the firm's production is exported; its chief European market is Great Britain.

Brands: BOURBONTOWN CLUB, JOHN FITCH, JOHNNY DRUM, KENTUCKY VINTAGE, NOAH'S MILL, OLD BARDSTOWN, OLD DISTILLER, PURE KENTUCKY, Rowan's Creek.

KENTUCKY DALE
Kentucky straight bourbon from the LEESTOWN DISTILLING COMPANY, property of SAZERAC.

KENTUCKY GENTLEMAN
Kentucky straight bourbon from BARTON DISTILLING (Canandaigua).

K

A number of medium-heavy, everyday bourbons have been presented under this name since the 1940s, one at 80 proof and one at 100 proof (bottled in bond), as well as a 6-year-old at 86 proof.

Kentucky Gentleman is also available as a blend (80 proof).

KENTUCKY LEGEND
Kentucky straight bourbon, single barrel, from the Boulevard distillery, property of AUSTIN NICHOLS DISTILLING COMPANY (PERNOD RICARD).

This powerful bourbon is simply KENTUCKY SPIRIT bottled at barrel strength. It is available only in duty free shops.

KENTUCKY SPIRIT
Kentucky straight bourbon, 101 proof single barrel, from the Boulevard distillery, property of AUSTIN NICHOLS DISTILLING COMPANY (PERNOD RICARD).

One writer recommended that one drink this bourbon only in a dimly li room, next to a wood fire, while looking at old engravings of hunting scenes

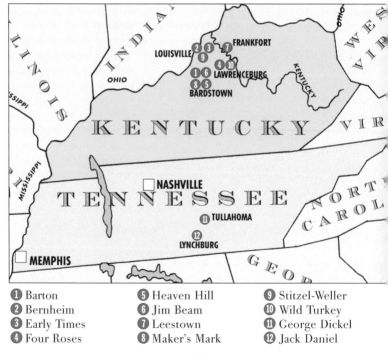

1 Barton
2 Bernheim
3 Early Times
4 Four Roses
5 Heaven Hill
6 Jim Beam
7 Leestown
8 Maker's Mark
9 Stitzel-Weller
10 Wild Turkey
11 George Dickel
12 Jack Daniel

You don't have to follow his advice, but be aware that this is a connoisseur's whiskey and should never be touched by ice.

KENTUCKY TAVERN

Kentucky straight bourbon, 80 and 100 proof (bottled in bond), from BARTON DISTILLING (Canandaigua).

This brand was created around the turn of the century. Beginning in 1917 it was served in government-owned hospitals and veterans' homes and produced for that purpose even during Prohibition—"medicinal whiskey," it was called. For that reason there were considerable stocks of Kentucky Tavern available at the end of the great drought, and the brand became a best-seller. Today it is consumed mainly in Kentucky itself. It is also available as a blend (80 proof).

KENTUCKY VINTAGE

Kentucky straight bourbon from KENTUCKY BOURBON DISTILLERS.

KESSLER

Blended American from JIM BEAM Brands (AMERICAN BRANDS).

A best-seller in the United States, but not available in Europe.

KHODAY

Indian producer with headquarters in Bangalore, South India.

The 4th-largest whiskey producer on the subcontinent began as a brewer and producer of malt extract before entering the expanding spirit business. Brands: PETER SCOT, RED KNIGHT.

KILBEGGAN

[Gaelic for "small church"]

Blended Irish whiskey, 80 proof, from COOLEY DISTILLERY.

A standard blend containing roughly 30 percent malt, on the market since 1994. Kilbeggan was created by the great blend-master Jimmy Lang, who previously worked for CHIVAS, where he was responsible, for example, for the brand PASSPORT. He also created the premium version of Kilbeggan, the somewhat stronger blend called Locke's. In both cases he had only a few relatively young malt and grain whiskeys to work with. With longer aging and a greater variety of single whiskeys, the flavor of this brand could improve greatly in the next few years. Only recently, for example, the percentage of peated malt was increased.

Both brands are distilled in Cooley's Riverstown Distillery. Their names come from the historic Locke distillery in Kilbeggan. That facility experienced the great years of Irish whiskey but now serves only as a warehouse for Cooley whiskeys (see LOCKE'S).

KILLYLOCH
Scottish Lowland single malt from the GARNHEATH distillery, property of INVER HOUSE DISTILLERS.

This whisky has never been bottled officially as a single, but rather used exclusively for blending. Now and

Vintage 1972
Single Lowland Malt Scotch Whisky
Matured in sherry casks for 22 years
Distilled at the Killyloch Distillery
on 21.3.72
Cask no. 2064/3
70cl

again there has also been a Killyloch vatted malt. Since the distillery has been closed since 1985, the bottling that Signatory issued in 1994 (22 years old, 105.2 proof, aged in sherry casks) caused something of a stir in interested circles—it is now available only at collectors' prices. The name goes back to a misprint: the whisky was actually named for the Lillyloch, the source of its water, but the first batch of barrels bore the present name, and since the malt was not intended to reach the public, it was never changed.

KINCLAITH
Scottish single malt (Lowlands, Glasgow).

A light malt, on the sweetish side, the aroma of which reminded Michael Jackson of "melons dusted with ginger."

Gordon & MacPhail: Vintages 1966, 1967, 1968, all 80 proof.

Cadenhead: Most recently the firm had a 24-year-old (distilled 1965) at 92 proof.

Kinclaith was built in 1957–58 as part of the STRATHCLYDE complex, in which the firm LONG JOHN produced mainly GRAIN WHISKY. When the British brewing concern Whitbread took control there in 1975, Kinclaith was torn down. Supplies are therefore surely limited.

K

KING ARTHUR
Blended Scotch from Bulloch Lade & Co. (UD).

KING BARLEY
Czech single malt, 86 proof, from Seiko's Tesetice Distillery. This whiskey is produced in the Scottish manner (distilled twice in pot stills), and the peat is even imported from Scotland. King Barley is aged for at least 6 years in oak barrels. They have been distilling whisky in Tesetice for 20 years now.

KING CHARLES
Blended Scotch from William Grant & Sons.

KING EDWARD I
Blended Scotch from William Lawson, a subsidiary of Bacardi.

KING GEORGE IV
Blended Scotch from Distillers Agency, a subsidiary of UD.

This brand was introduced at the end of the 19th century and was at that time, as now, intended primarily for export. Just now King George IV is the number-1 Scotch in Denmark.

The visit of George IV to Scotland in 1822 was the first of an English monarch for 200 years. Much of what now passes for typical Scottish folklore was simply invented for that occasion (see Dewar's).

KING HENRY VIII
Blended Scotch from H. Stenham Ltd.

Like all Stenham Scotches, also available as a 3-, 5-, 8-, 10-, and 12-year-old and intended mainly for the Latin American and Southeast Asian markets. In a number of European countries one can also find King Henry VIII in supermarkets among the lower-priced whiskies.

KING JAMES VI
Blended Scotch from Forth Wines, a trading firm founded in Kinross-shire in 1963. In addition to this brand, the firm also produces a blend called Strathfillan. Both are intended mainly for the British market.

KING JOHN

Blended Scotch from H. STENHAM LTD.

Like all Stenham Scotches, also available as a 3-, 5-, 8-, 10-, and 12-year-old and intended mainly for the Latin American and Southeast Asian markets.

KING OF KINGS

Blended Scotch from James Munro & Son, a subsidiary of UD.

KING OF SCOTS

Blended Scotch from Douglas LAING & Co.

There are a number of DE LUXE blends under this name, all of them in fancy ceramic or crystal carafes and sold mainly in Latin America and the Far East. In addition to a 12-, a 17-, and a 25-year-old, there are: Rare Extra Old, Proclamation, Flagship, and the standard blends Gold Label and Numbered Edition.

The brand has been in existence since 1880. It was acquired by Laing in the 1950s.

KING ROBERT II

Blended Scotch, standard and 12-year-old de luxe, from Wm Maxwell, a subsidiary of Peter J. RUSSELL.

The Robert after whom the brand was named was the first Scottish king from the tragic house of Stuart.

KING'S CROWN

Blended Scotch from MONTEBELLO.

KING'S PRIDE

Blended Scotch from MORRISON BOWMORE DISTILLERS (SUNTORY).

KING'S RANSOM

Blended Scotch, de luxe, from Wm WHITELEY, a subsidiary of CAMPBELL DISTILLERS (PERNOD RICARD).

It is said of this brand that it always contains some whisky that has been on a sea voyage—a custom from the time when barrels of whisky and other spirits that improve with age were loaded onto ships as ballast, which proved beneficial to them. It is also said that Truman, Stalin, and Churchill toasted the signing of the Potsdam Agreement with King's Ransom in 1945.

KING'S WHISKY

Blended Scotch from Northern Blending, a subsidiary of BURN STEWART DISTILLERS.

K

This brand is still on the market but is no longer being produced.

KING WILLIAM IV

Blended Scotch from J. Gillon (UD).

KININVIE

Scottish malt distillery in Duffstown, Speyside. The distillery was opened only in 1990 by William Grant & Sons, and it will be some time before the malt is ready to be bottled.

KINROSS WHISKY CO.

Scotch producer in Sussex. This family operation was founded in 1970 by John Stoppani and produces mainly for export, notably to Europe and the Far East. Its brands are: Albion's Finest Old, Derby Special, Glen Baren, and Gold Blend.

KIRIN-SEAGRAM

Japanese producer with its own distillery near Tokyo.

Since the early 1970s, Kirin, Japan's largest brewer and part of the Mitsubishi industrial empire, has also been engaged in the whisky-making business. Together with the Canadian spirit giant Seagram, Kirin built a distillery at the foot of Mount Fuji, in which it produces both malt and grain whiskies. The blends created there also contain Scottish malts (presumably from Seagram distilleries). Kirin whiskies are considered the driest in Japan and are available only there: Crescent, Emblem, Robert Brown.

KNOB CREEK

Kentucky straight bourbon, 9 years old, 100 proof, from Jim Beam Brands (American Brands).

A sweet but powerful small-batch bourbon that was introduced to the market in 1992 and carries an unusual, highly attractive label. Knob Creek is named after a stream near Abraham Lincoln's birthplace in Hodgeville, Kentucky. The distillery in which Abe's father worked from time to time once stood there.

KNOCKANDO

[Gaelic for "black hillock"]

Scottish single (Speyside) from Justerini & Brooks (see J & B), a subsidiary of IDV/Grand Metropolitan.

A mild, not inelegant malt for every occasion and a major international brand.

Original bottling: Knockando is bottled only as a vintage, as a rule at 10–15 years and 20–25 years. The label gives the date it was distilled and the date of bottling. Currently, for example, there is a 1980 that was bottled in 1995, as well as a 1969 bottled in 1993.

This practice is based on the recognition that whiskies do not develop evenly, that the desired degree of aging is not always attained in the same period of time. The different vintages therefore may not have the same age, but they have the same taste. In this sense, the term *vintage* does not have the same connotation as it does in the case of port wine or champagne.

The distillery was founded in 1898 and taken over in 1904 by GILBEY, the firm that created the IDV in 1962 with Justerini & Brooks (see J & B). Within that concern, Justerini is responsible for whisky production, and it uses Knockando as an important base malt for the J & B blend.

The distillery has 4 stills and gets its water from the Cardnach spring. The whisky ages for a time in sherry casks.

(Tel. 1340 81 02 05)

KNOCKDHU

Scottish single malt (Speyside, Banff shire) from INVER HOUSE DISTILLERS. The official version of this malt is called AN CNOC. Only the independent bottlers use the name of the distillery.

Gordon & MacPhail: Vintage 1974, 80 proof.

Adelphi: 11 years old (distilled 1982), 125 proof.

KOSHER WHISK(E)Y

Whisk(e)y produced under the supervision of a rabbi and therefore in accordance with Jewish dietary rules (See HAMASHKEH, OLD WILLIAMSBURG NO. 20.)

L

He'd go to mass every mornin'
if holy water were whiskey.

Irish proverb

LADYBURN

Scottish single malt (Lowlands) from William GRANT & SONS.

The distillery is a small part of the grain distillery GIRVAN. Malt was distilled here only between 1966 and 1976. Bottlings were available only from Cadenhead.

LAGAVULIN

[Gaelic for "the small cave with the mill"]

Scottish single malt (Islay) from WHITE HORSE (UD).

One of Scotland's most celebrated whiskies, of overwhelming complexity, sovereign, masculine, and uniquely smoky.

Original bottling: 16 years old, 86 proof (from the series "Classic Malts").

Cadenhead: Most recently a 15-year-old from 1978 at 128.8 proof.

The origins of the distillery are unclear, for in the middle of the 18th century there were roughly 10 distilleries in this vicinity. The first legal founding was in 1816, and it is possible that the present-day Lagavulin goes back to that one.

In 1867 the operation of the distillery was taken over by the firm James L. Mackie (see LOGAN), which became White Horse Distillers in 1924. White Horse still holds the license. Lagavulin is also one of the base malts for the WHITE HORSE blend.

The distillery operates with 4 stills and gets its water from the Solan Lochs.

(Tel. 1496 30 24 00)

AING, DOUGLAS & CO.

independent blending firm, founded in Glasgow in 1950, with the following brands:

EATON'S SPECIAL RESERVE, GLEN DRUMM, HOUSE OF PEERS, JPS (see JOHN PLAYER SPECIAL), KING OF SCOTS, LANGSIDE, McGIBBON'S, 77, SIR WALTER RALEIGH. (See also SS POLITICIAN.)

Since 1994 the firm has had a joint-venture relationship with the Indian spirit firm Kedir.

AIRD & CO.

U.S. firm in Scobeyvilley, New Jersey, that has been in the distilling business since the 18th century. It still produces applejack in its distillery in Virginia. It buys its whiskey brands in Kentucky: FIVE STAR BLEND, PRIVATE STOCK, SENATOR'S CLUB, SEVEN STAR, WILLIAM PENN. (See also KASSER LAIRD.)

AIRD'S PREMIUM CANADIAN

Canadian blend from LAIRD & CO.

AMMERLAW

New Zealand single malt, 10 years old, 86 proof, from WILSON Distillers (SEAGRAM).

Lammerlaw has been on the market since 1984 and is produced in Dunedin, the first settlement of Scottish immigrants in New Zealand. Dunedin is the Gaelic name for Edinburgh.) Good barley, peaty ground, and soft water are richly abundant on New Zealand's South Island. They make it possible to use traditional

SINGLE MALT

Lammerlaw

WHISKY

A ten year old malt whisky distilled in the time honoured traditions of the ancient distillers and carefully matured in fine oak casks. The distinctive flavour is born in the snow capped Lammerlaw mountains in the south of New Zealand and the mountain water found there used to create this unique malt whisky.

AGED 10 YEARS

DISTILLED & BOTTLED · Wilson Distillers · IN NEW ZEALAND

SINGLE MALT Whisky

43% VOL   WILSON DISTILLERS, DUNEDIN, NEW ZEALAND   70 cl

Scottish methods and give this malt its taste.

The distillery has only one still (steel instead of the usual copper) and gets its water from Deep Creek. It ages its product in American oak barrels.

Lammerlaw is now available all over the Pacific and also in Great Britain.

LANG'S

Blended Scotch from Lang Bros., a subsidiary of ROBERTSON & BAXTER.

A very refined Scotch, said to be the Queen Mum's favorite brand.

Lang's standard version is called Supreme, and the DE LUXE editions are Supreme De Luxe and Select 12 Years Old.

The Lang brothers began blending whisky in the cellar of a Glasgow

whisky: disinfectants, diesel fuel, tar, seaweed, and Lord knows what else. In vain, I'm afraid, for you simply have to taste it for yourself. You will either be blown away or you'll never want to touch it again.

Original bottling: 10 years old, 80 and 86 proof; 15 years old, 86 proof. One occasionally also finds a 1977 at 86 proof in duty-free shops.

On its label, which is certainly convincing in its simplicity, 1815 is given as the date of the distillery's founding, but it was first documented in 1826. The founder, Donald Johnston, died a distiller's death: he drowned in a barrel of half-finished whisky. The Johnston family continues to run the distillery today, although it has belonged to LONG JOHN since the 1960s. Laphroaig is one of the few distilleries whose malting floors are still in operation. They even

church in 1861, and in 1875 they acquired the GLENGOYNE distillery.

Since 1965 they have been a part of Robertson & Baxter and are responsible for the CUTTY SARK blend from BERRY BROS. & RUDD. Lang's whiskies are based on Glengoyne and age for at least 9 months in oak barrels after blending.

LANGSIDE
Blended Scotch from Douglas LAING & CO.

LAPHROAIG
Scottish single malt (Islay) from D. Johnston & Co., a subsidiary of AL-LIED DISTILLERS (ALLIED DOMECQ).

The most ridiculous substances have been invoked in attempts to describe the taste of this overpowering

continue to cut their own peat here. The 7 stills process water from Kilbride Dam, and the distillates are aged in bourbon barrels. Laphroaig is one of the base malts in the blends ISLAY MIST and LONG JOHN.

(Tel. 1496 30 24 18)

LAPHROAIG®

LAUDER'S

Blended Scotch from MACDUFF INTERNATIONAL.

An old brand, already successful in the 19th century, which is now especially popular in Latin America. It originally belonged to the firm Archibald Lauder & Co., which was later bought by HIRAM WALKER & SONS and has belonged to the present owner since 1991.

LAWSON, WILLIAM

Scottish producers established in 1972 in Coatbridge, Lanarkshire, who oversee the whisky interests of the Italian Martini & Rossi group. Martini, in turn, has long been part of the world's largest spirit producer, Bacardi Ltd., of Bermuda.

For this group Lawson runs the distillery MacDuff (see GLEN DEVERON), a blending and bottling complex in Coatbridge, and a warehouse and bottling works in Glasgow. Lawson also cooperates with the firm Wm LUNDIE & Co. and has 3 blends in its program: WILLIAM LAWSON'S, CLAN MUNRO, and KING EDWARD I.

The Lawson name derives from that of a Scottish whisky dealer who at the end of the 19th century produced a "Lawson's Liqueur Whisky" for the Dublin firm E. & J. Burke. Lawson was fired in 1903, but his name was retained by the Burkes, who delivered the brand in large quantities to the Bahamas during Prohibition (see LIGHT WHISK(E)Y). The label was acquired by Martini & Rossi in 1963 and marketed all over Europe. Later Martini & Rossi consolidated its whisky activities under the name William Lawson Distilleries. In 1980 the entire group was taken over by the Luxembourg concern General Beverage, which has been allied with Bacardi since 1995.

LEDAIG See TOBERMORY.
LEESTOWN DISTILLING COMPANY
U.S. distillery in Frankfort, Kentucky, owned by TAKARA SHUZO & OKURA and SAZERAC. A water tower with the

legend "The Home of Ancient Age" marks this spot just outside Frankfort, Kentucky's capital, where whiskey has been distilled since roughly 1860. The distillery has changed its name as often as it has changed owners: under E. H. Taylor (see OLD TAYLOR) it was called O.F.C (1870–1886), under G. T. Stagg it was G. T. Stagg, and when it was taken over by Schenley in 1929 it soon became known as Schenley. In the 1970s it bore the name of its best-known product: Ancient Age Distilling Co. (see ANCIENT AGE). Since 1982 it has been run by the Sazerac firm, which gave it its present name in 1992 and in the same year sold it to the Japanese concern TAKARA, SHUZO & OKURA. That firms owns the distillery itself, but the brands still belong to Sazerac.

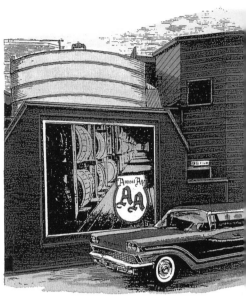

The Leestown company was the first firm to market a SINGLE-BARREL BOURBON, in 1984, called BLANTON'S. Its other brands are: Ancient Age, BENCHMARK, BULLEIT, CANADIAN AGE, EAGLE RARE, ELMER T. LEE, HANCOCK'S RESERVE, and ROCK HILL FARMS.

The distillery no longer operates in the traditional manner, for the mash is heated under pressure and cooled in vacuum tanks. In addition the warehouses are heated in winter. The grain mixture ("mash bill"), with its high percentage of corn, results in rather sweet whiskeys. It consists of 80 percent corn, 10 percent barley malt, and 10 percent rye; the sour mash component is 33 percent, and the yeast culture dates back to the Schenley years.

(Tel. 502 223-7641)

L

LEGACY

Blended Scotch, premium, from In-
tergordon Distillers (Whyte &
Mackay, American Brands); see also
Mackinlay's.

LEM MOTLOW'S

Tennessee sour mash from the Jack
Daniel Distillery (see Jack Daniel's
Old No. 7), owned by Brown-Forman.

A 1-year-old whiskey, 90 proof,
which is difficult to find outside Tennessee and Georgia.

LIGHT WHISK(E)Y

This concept means one thing in
Scotland, another in America.

In Scotland: light, milder Scotches,
with a high percentage of Lowland
malt and little (if any) caramel coloring, which are mainly exported to the
United States (Cutty Sark, J & B,
Passport, William Lawson's). There
is reason to suspect that the Americans' preference for light Scotches
goes back to Prohibition, for the
whiskies sold during that time were
generally considerably diluted. Canadian whiskies, which also enjoyed a
boom in the United States in those
years, are also lighter in flavor (see
also Cutty Sark, Sanderson's Gold,
Inver House Green Plaid).

In the United States: American
light whiskey is distilled with a very
high alcohol content, which means
that at first it does not taste like anything at all. It is then aged in used or
untreated new barrels, which doesn't
help any, and is finally mixed with
aromatic substances and sweet coloring, so that it at least looks and tastes
remotely like whiskey. This travesty
came into fashion in the 1970s, more
among producers, to be sure, than
consumers. While the former doubtless thought they could respond in
this way to the trend toward clear, less
intense spirits such as vodka, buyers
assumed the opposite—that one could
drink it as one would vodka if you
weren't fond of more powerful taste
sensations. Light whiskey has been
largely abandoned. Today only the
Barton Distilling firm continues to
produce a few brands of this sort:
Barton's QT, Colonel Lee, Kentucky Gentleman, Tom Moore.

LINKWOOD

Scottish single malt (Speyside, Elgin)
from UD.

A medium-weight malt with a
highly praised elegance.

Original bottling: 12 years old, 86
proof ("Flora and Fauna" series).

L

Gordon & MacPhail: 15 and 21 years old, 80 proof; vintages 1961 and 1968, both 80 proof; 14 years old (distilled 1979), 117 proof.

Cadenhead: 17 years old (distilled 1978, sherry cask), 111 proof.

James MacArthur: 11 years old, 121 proof.

Linkwood was founded in 1820 and repeatedly renovated, but without altering the structure's Victorian exterior. The sense of tradition was so strong that at times they didn't even remove the cobwebs, so as not to risk any change in the quality of the whisky. In 1933 Linkwood was taken over by the DCL, which until recently had the distillery run by John McEwan & Co. (see Abbot's Choice). Between 1985 and 1990 it was closed, but it is now operating again with 6 stills, drawing its water from springs near Milbuies Loch.

(Tel. 1343 54 70 04)

LINLITHGOW See St. Magdalene.

LIQUEURS, WHISK(E)Y

The production of liqueurs, like the art of distillation originated in the Orient. It is possible that both techniques arrived in Europe at about the same time, for it is relatively certain that even in its earliest days whisk(e)y was often drunk mixed with herbs, honey, milk, or other substances.

Today it is necessary to distinguish between herb, cream, and citrus liqueurs.

Herb liqueurs are the oldest category. They were already being produced by monks in the Middle Ages and were thought of primarily as medicines. The base alcohol—in this case, whisk(e)y—is flavored with herbal essences, either natural or identical to natural ones. The mixture is generally aged for several months in wooden barrels, so that the various flavors can merge. As a rule, herb liqueurs are stronger than other types. In addition to the market leader, DRAMBUIE, there are a number of very good products. For example: DUNKELD ATHOLL BROSE, GLAYVA, GLEN MIST, IRISH MIST, LOCHAN ORA, Mulligan's, ÒRAN MÓR, STAG'S BREATH.

Cream liqueurs are a relatively recent invention. When the R & A Bailey firm first introduced its BAILEY'S ORIGINAL IRISH CREAM in 1975, it was immediately highly successful, and other firms set out to imitate it. The market for these light digestifs (30 proof is the minimum, and they are rarely more than 34 proof), which are essentially simply cream (with a minimum fat content of 10 percent) and whisk(e)y, continues to expand, and it is now almost impossible to count the number of brands. In addition to Bailey's there are CAROLANS, COLUMBA CREAM, DUBLINER, EMMETS CLASSIC CREAM, HEATHER CREAM, MEADOW CREAM, and many others.

Citrus liqueurs: The technique of flavoring alcohol with citrus peel was already used in the Orient. In the United States a liqueur type called ROCK AND RYE was developed, and in addition there is a citrus liqueur from

WILD TURKEY. The world-famous SOUTHERN COMFORT is not a whiskey liqueur at all, although it is generally considered one.

LISMORE

Blended Scotch from Wm LUNDIE & CO.

Available in a whole series of bottlings: Finest, Signature, Select 8 Years (standard); Special Reserve 12 Years (premium); Special Reserve 15 Years, 18 Years (de luxe); and Highland Malt, Pure Malt 8 Years (vatted). In addition there is a Lismore Single Malt, 21 and 25 years old, the producer of which is not revealed. The brand is exported mainly to Europe and the Far East.

LITTLEMILL

Scottish single malt (Lowlands, Dumbarton) from GLEN CATRINE Bonded Warehouse Ltd.

A typical Lowland: light, soft, and round.

Original bottling: 8 years old, 80 and 86 proof. Occasionally one still finds the 8-year-old of the previous owner, Gibson, in a squat bottle.

Cadenhead and Signatory issue bottlings from time to time.

Founded in 1772, this distillery lays claim to the coveted title of "Oldest Distillery in Scotland." It has frequently changed hands, most recently in 1994, when GLEN CATRINE took it

over when Gibson (see BARTON DIS-TILLING) went bankrupt. That firm had reopened Littlemill only in 1989, after a rest period of 5 years, and closed it again in 1992. It is still closed, but it is hoped that it will again be put into operation.

Up until the 1930s they distilled at Littlemill 3 times, and up until the 1970s there were also 2 additional malts produced here: Dumbuck and Dunglass, the latter a vatted malt. The distillery has 2 stills and gets its water from the Kilpatrick Hills; that is, from the HIGHLANDS.

(Tel. 1389 87 41 54)

LOCHAN ORA
[Gaelic for "golden sea"]

Scottish whisky herb liqueur from the CHIVAS & GLENLIVET GROUP (SEA-GRAM).

LOCH DHU See MANNOCHMORE.
LOCH KINDIE
Scottish vatted malt from William GRANT & SONS.

LOCH LOMOND
Scottish distillery (Highlands) be-longing to GLEN CATRINE Bonded Warehouse Ltd. Two single malts are produced here: INCHMURRIN and OLD RHOSDHU (see also GLENSHIEL). The distillery has 4 stills and draws its water from Loch Lomond.

LOCHRANZA DISTILLERY See ISLE OF ARRAN DISTILLERS.
LOCH RANZA
Blended Scotch from ISLE OF ARRAN DISTILLERS.

LOCHSIDE
Scottish single malt (Eastern High-lands) from Macnab Distilleries, a subsidiary of Distilerias y Crianza (see DYC), which belongs in turn to HIRAM WALKER & SONS and with it to ALLIED DOMECQ.

A medium-heavy malt with a dis-tinct note of sherry, rarely found any-more.

Original bottling: 10 years old, 80 proof.

Gordon & MacPhail: The firm most recently had a 1966 at 80 proof.

James MacArthur: 27 years old, 121 proof (grain).

The distillery was created in 1957 out of a former brewery and was originally set up for the production of malt and grain whisky. Both were blended and bottled on the spot. In 1970 grain production was discontinued; then in 1973 Lochside came into the possession of the Spanish spirit concern DYC. This occasioned some raised eyebrows in Scotland: purchases within the Scottish whisky industry by Canadians and Americans could be accepted under the premise that at least these were distant relations who understood something about whisk(e)y themselves, but just what the "Continentals" thought they were doing in Scotland was a mystery. It ceased to be one when it became known that the new owners were shipping the majority of the malt home to turn it into Spanish whisky. Possibly the whole uproar could have been avoided if people had known at that time that the well-known Hiram Walker firm is behind Distilerias y Crianza. In any case, the outpouring of patriotism was in vain, for since 1992 the 4 stills have stood idle, and Lochside is up for sale.

(Tel. 1674 67 27 37)

LOCKE'S

Blended Irish whiskey, 80 proof, from COOLEY DISTILLERY.

The premium version of the brand KILBEGGAN, on the market since 1994.

Both brands are distilled (since 1989) in Cooley's Riverstown Distillery, but they were named for the historic Locke Distillery in Kilbeggan.

Kilbeggan has long been a part of the changing history of Irish whiskey. In 1757 Gustavus Lambert founded the Brusna Distillery here in a former monastery. It was taken over in the middle of the 19th century by John Locke, renamed, and expanded into a flourishing operation. But even "Locke's Liquor" suffered in the great Irish whiskey crisis of our own century (see IRISH WHISKEY). Black marketing and a political affair of the then owner did the rest, and the Locke distillery was shut down in 1953. (Remaining stores of the whiskey were sold in Germany in the 1960s under the name Old Galleon.)

After the pot stills had been sold and the distillery had been used for a time as a pig farm, Cooley took over what was left of the complex in 1987, and it now serves as the warehouse for all of the Cooley whiskeys. There are plans to start producing malt here again on a small scale in the future; for that purpose the old pot stills of the idle Tullamore distillery (see TULLAMORE DEW) were recently acquired.

LOGAN

Blended Scotch (12-year-old de luxe) from WHITE HORSE (UD).

This expressive, old-school Scotch was named after James Logan Mackie, who founded the firm Mackie & Co. in 1856. His nephew and successor, Peter Mackie, created the brand White Horse, whose name the firm has carried since 1924. Logan —formerly Laird of Logan's—is a de luxe version of White Horse and unfortunately very difficult to find. The base malts are probably CRAIGELLACHIE and LAGAVULIN.

LOMBARD'S

Scottish whisky from Lombard Scotch Whisky Ltd., a small blending and trading firm with headquarters on the Isle of Man.

The standard blend is called Gold Label; in addition there are a 5-year-old and 12-year-old de luxe blend and a 12-year-old Pure Malt (vatted).

The firm has other blends as well: AGE OF SAIL, GOLDEN PIPER, and HIGHLAND GATHERING. It is also responsible for the BENEAGLES series "Birds of Prey."

LOMOND

Scottish single malt (Lowlands, Dumbarton) from BALLANTINE & SON (ALLIED DISTILLERS, ALLIED DOMECQ)

This whisky came from INVERLEVEN, the malt distillery—shut down in 1991—that was part of Ballantine's huge grain operation in Dumbarton. It was intended exclusively for blends. It was produced in LOMOND STILLS and was issued only once (1992) as a single malt, in a bottling by the SCOTCH MALT WHISKY SOCIETY, 19 years old (distilled 1972), 116.6 proof.

LOMOND STILL

A distilling apparatus; a variant of the POT STILL, which makes it possible to produce stronger, oilier whiskies. This form of alembic was developed by HIRAM WALKER & SONS and installed in the distilleries GLENBURGIE, INVERLEVEN, MILTONDUFF, and SCAPA. In the first 3, Lomond stills were used in combination with pot stills, producing second-rate whiskies used exclusively in blends (see GLENCRAIG, LOMOND, MOSSTOWIE). During the 1980s the Lomond stills were removed from these distilleries. At Scapa the entire production had been revised; up until it was shut down in 1993, the first distillation there was done in Lomond stills.

LONG JOHN

Blended Scotch from ALLIED DIS-
TILLERS (ALLIED DOMECQ).

An international best-
seller, currently available as a
standard and as a 12-year-old
de luxe.

"Long" John Macdonald
founded the distillery BEN
NEVIS in 1825. The firm
Long John International
now operates the distil-
leries LAPHROAIG and TOR-
MORE. (See also GLENUGIE,
HIGHLAND STAG, KIN-
CLAITH, THE REAL MACKAY,
Schenley, SCORESBY RARE.)

LONGMORN

Scottish single malt (Speyside, Elgin)
from the CHIVAS & GLENLIVET GROUP
(SEAGRAM).

An outstanding, lush, and complex
malt that has too long been overshadowed by its great (Chivas) brothers,
GLEN GRANT and THE GLENLIVET,
and has only recently begun to be
marketed more aggressively.

Original bottling: 15 years old, 90
proof.

Gordon & MacPhail: 12 years old,
80 proof; vintages 1963, 1964, 80
proof; 1969, 122.4 proof.

Cadenhead: 11 years old (distilled 1984, sherry cask), 121.4 proof.

Blackadder: 12 years old, 117.2
proof.

The distillery was built in 1894–95
and is one of the few to have been in
continuous operation ever since. It
has 8 stills and gets its water from
local springs.

(Tel. 1542 78 34 00)

LONGROW

Scottish single malt (Campbeltown)
from the SPRINGBANK distillery, property of J. A. MITCHELL & CO.

A peaty malt, full of character,
and unfortunately very scarce. It is
more reminiscent of ISLAY malts
than of those of Campbeltown. The
British wine magazine *Decanter* once
wrote of it that it had the smell of
wet sheep and the aggressiveness of
a tiger.

Original bottling: 16 and 18 years
old (distilled 1974), 92 proof; both
versions are no longer available, but
for 1997 a new 10-year-old bottling
has been announced.

Cadenhead: The firm recently
had an 18-year-old (distilled 1974) at
104.4 proof.

Signatory: 8 years old (distilled
1987), 86 proof.

Unlike its big brother Springbank,
Longrow is smoked over a generous
amount of peat and always distilled
twice. The malt bears the name of a
distillery that stood close to Springbank up until the end of the 19th
century, the remains of which are
now used as a bottling plant.

LORD BALTIMORE
Blended American from MAJESTIC.

LORD CALVERT
Canadian blend from JIM BEAM Brands (AMERICAN BRANDS).

An international best-seller and one of the many Canadian brands that belong to a U.S. firm.

LOWLANDS
Scottish whisky region. The Lowland distilleries are clustered south of an old district border between Greenock in the west and Dundee in the East. Currently only 2 of them are in operation: AUCHENTOSHAN and GLEN-KINCHIE.

Lowland malts are unspectacular whiskies—light, dry, and comparatively lacking in the aroma of peat. Their image has always suffered because of their—purely geographic—proximity to the industrial grain distilleries that are also situated in the Lowlands.

These malts are especially valued for blends, however, since they serve to balance the stronger HIGHLAND and ISLAY malts and the more neutral grains.

LOWRIE'S
Blended Scotch from UD.

A very old and now scarce brand.

William P. Lowrie had already gained experience as the manager of the PORT ELLEN distillery before he set himself up as an independent whisky dealer in 1869. He is considered one of the first producers of BLENDED SCOTCH WHISKY and for a time owned the distilleries GLEN-TAUCHERS and CONVALMORE. The latter was run by the firm William P. Lowrie & Co. until 1985.

LUNDIE, WM & CO.
Scottish producers with headquarters in Glasgow.

The Lundies have been in the whisky business for 3 generations. They were involved in Chivas for a time, but they were known mainly as skilled brokers, negotiating among distillers, blending firms, and bottlers. Since these activities generally take place inside the larger concerns, Lundie & Co. has gone into blending and cooperates in this business with William LAWSON.

Blends: AWARD, LISMORE, PRESTIGE D'ECOSSE, ROYAL HERITAGE, TRIBUTE.

M

I was born below par
to th' extent of two whiskies.

C. E. Montague,
Fiery Particles

M

THE MACALLAN

Scottish single malt (Speyside) from HIGHLAND DISTILLERIES CO.

The rave reviews of this whisky have become so numerous that aficionados who wish to be known for their exclusive taste have begun to regard it with suspicion.

But no matter. Macallan was and is a masterwork of impressive fullness and complexity. Even though it is aged exclusively in sherry casks, the taste of sherry does not overpower the other elements. The balance is perfect.

Original bottling: 7 years old, 80 proof, for the Italian market; 8 years old, 80 proof, for the French market; 10 years old, 80 and 114 proof; 12 years old, 86 proof; 18 years old (with date, currently 1976; many Macallan lovers are convinced that 18 is the best age for this whisky), 86 proof; 25 years old (distilled 1968), 86 proof. Older vintages are treasured like the noble products of the châteaux of Bordeaux: 1950, 1963, and 1964 are considered to be some of the finest malts of the century, and a 60-year-old Macallan from 1926 fetched about $23,000 at an auction

in 1993. Two years before, a bottle of the same age went for less than half that.

Cadenhead: 19 years old (distilled 1976, sherry cask), 111.6 proof.

The distillery was founded in 1824, and since 1892 it has been operated by the Kemp family. They still own a share in Macallan, but the majority share is now held by Highland Distilleries. The former shareholders Rémy Martin and SUNTORY surrendered their holdings in 1994 and 1996, respectively. Those interests dated back to the 1970s, when the distillery experienced financial difficulties owing to the fact that SEAGRAM, at that time one of its main ustomers, changed the formula for its CHIVAS REGAL brand. Previously, Macallan had been an important component in that blend, and at that time it was appreciated only locally as a single. All of this changed in the 1980s, when Macallan was skillfully placed on the market. The driving force behind this was Allan Shiach, the head of the firm and author of such successful filmscripts as "When the Gondolas Wear Mourning."

The main emphasis in the production of this whisky is on its aging in sherry casks (chiefly oloroso). In fact, Macallan is the only malt that is aged exclusively in such barrels (although the whisky intended for blends has to make do with bourbon barrels). That is a considerable factor in its cost, for now that sherry can be exported only in bottles the barrels have become very scarce in Scotland. Macallan buys them in Spain and has them reconditioned there at its own expense. By the time such a barrel arrives in the Highlands, some 3 or 4 years later, it has cost roughly 10 times as much as a bourbon barrel.

The distillery has 21 unusually small stills and draws its water from its own drilled wells.

(Tel. 1340 87 14 71)

MACANDREWS
Blended Scotch from MACDONALD MARTIN DISTILLERS.

MacAndrew's

MACARTHUR, JAMES & CO.
Independent bottler in Glasgow. A relatively small house that bottles only malts, generally 12 years old, increasingly at barrel strength.

MACARTHUR'S
Blended Scotch, standard and 12-year-old DE LUXE, from INVER HOUSE DISTILLERS.

This brand has been in existence since 1877. Since the 1970s it has been popular in Great Britain as an inexpensive supermarket Scotch.

MCCALLS
Canadian, Scotch, and bourbon from MONTEBELLO.

MCCALLUM'S PERFECTION
Blended Scotch from UD.

An outstanding blend based on CRAGGANMORE, the majority of which is exported to the Far East. The brand

M

McCALLUM'S

has been in existence since 1911.

The brothers Duncan and John McCallum were already respected pub owners and wine and spirit dealers in Edinburgh at the beginning of the 19th century. They operated several distilleries and were for a time the licensees for the distilleries BENROMACH and Cragganmore.

MCCAULEY'S
Canadian blend from SAZERAC.

One of the many brands that are produced in Canada but bottled and sold only in the United States. The name of the distillery, as is usual in such cases, is not disclosed.

MCCLELLAND LTD., T. & A.
A blending and trading firm that was founded in Glasgow in 1818 and opened the distillery BLADNOCH in that same year. McClelland was run for a time by Jimmy Barclay (see STODART). It now belongs to MORRISON BOWMORE DISTILLERS and thus to SUNTORY, for which it produces the blend CLAN ROY and a number of Morrison malts: McClelland's Highland (5-year-old GLEN GARIOCH) McClelland's Islay (5-year-old BOWMORE), McClelland's Lowland (5-year-old AUCHENTOSHAN).

MCCOLLS
Blended Scotch produced for the U.S. market by STAR LIQUOR.

MCCORMICK
The McCormick distillery in Wetson Missouri, founded in 1856, was long considered one of the oldest continuously operated distilleries in the United States. It has been shut down since the mid-1980s. McCormick now buys its whiskey in Kentucky and bottles it under its own name.

The firm puts out a straight bourbon, a blended American, an (imported) Scotch, and a Canadian (also gin, vodka, brandy, rum, and tequila).

Other McCormick brands are: B. J. HOLLADAY, PLATTE VALLEY Straight Corn, STILLBROOK.

MACDONALD GREENLEES LTD.
Subsidiary of UD, for which it produces a number of blends and operates the distilleries CRAGGANMORE and GLENDULLAN.

M

The firm was founded in about 1900 by James Calder and owns such well-known blended Scotch brands as OLD PARR, GILLON'S, and SANDY MACDONALD.

MACDONALD MARTIN DISTILLERS

Scottish producer, created by the firm Macdonald & Muir in 1953. Macdonald Martin owns the distilleries GLEN-MORANGIE (since 1918) and GLEN MORAY (1923) and produces a number of blends: BAILIE NICOL JARVIE, CLAN MURDOCK, CRABBIE'S, GLEN NIVEN, Highland Queen, JAMES MARTIN'S, MAJOR GUNN'S, MILORD'S, and MUIR-HEAD'S BLUE SEAL. Since 1996 the company has been called GLENMORANGIE.

MCDONALD'S SPECIAL BLEND

Blended Scotch from C. & J. McDON-ALD, a subsidiary of UD.

This brand is sold mainly in the Republic of South Africa.

MCDOWALL

Blended Scotch from Brodie Crawford & Co. (see BRODIE'S SUPREME).

MCDOWELL'S

Indian whiskey from the UB group.

One of the great Indian brands. McDowell's is available as No. 1, Travel, and Premium. McDowell also produces India's only single malt (from native malt, distilled in pot stills, and aged in bourbon barrels).

MACDUFF See GLEN DEVERON.

MACDUFF INTERNATIONAL

Scottish producer with headquarters in Glasgow, which was founded in 1992 by Stewart MacDuff, Charles Murray, and Ted Thomson—3 old hands in the Scottish whisky industry—and owns the following blends: CUMBRAE CASTLE, GRAND MACNISH, ISLAY MIST, LAUDER'S, THE STEWART MACDUFF, STRATHBEG.

MCEWAN, JOHN & CO.

Scottish producer with headquarters in Leith. The Scottish farmer John McEwan got into the whisky business in 1863 and was soon very successful with his brand ABBOT'S CHOICE. His firm was taken over in 1933 by the DCL, and now belongs to UD. Since 1945 McEwan has been the licensee for LINKWOOD. It also bottles the blend CHEQUER'S.

MCGAVIN'S

Blended Scotch from SPEYSIDE DIS-TILLERY.

MCGIBBON'S

Blended Scotch from Douglas McGibbon & Co., a subsidiary of Douglas LAING & Co.

Two standard versions are available: Premium Reserve and Special Reserve. There are also 3 DE LUXE blends: 12 Years Old, Golf Bag, and Golf Club. All are offered in ceramic containers in the shape of golfing equipment (balls, clubs, bags, etc.). They are very popular with collectors and are available mainly in duty-free shops.

MCGUINNESS

Canadian blend from CORBY, a subsidiary of HIRAM WALKER & SONS (ALLIED DOMECQ).

A rather simple blend available in 2 versions: Old Canada and Silk Tassel.

MACKINLAY'S

Blended Scotch from INVERGORDON DISTILLERS (WHYTE & MACKAY, AMERICAN BRANDS).

One of the oldest names in the blended Scotch business. The first Mackinlay's was already around in the middle of the 19th century. In 1985 the brand was again presented as The Original Mackinlay. It is now one of the most successful blends in Great Britain.

Charles Mackinlay began as a wine dealer in Leith in 1815. For a time his descendants controlled the distilleries MORTLACH, GLEN MHOR, GLEN ALBYN, LITTLEMILL, ISLE OF JURA, and GLENALLACHIE.

After losing its independence, Mackinlay was merged with John E. McPherson & Co. (see CLUNY) in 1961, and since 1985 Mackinlay McPherson has been a part of INVERGORDON. In addition to the above-mentioned Original Mackinlay, there are also the 12-year-old Legacy and Mackinlay's Reserve.

Base malts: BRUICHLADDICH, Glenallachie, Isle of Jura, TAMNAVULIN and TULLIBARDINE.

MACLEAY DUFF

Blended Scotch from UD.

The name of this blend goes back to that of a firm founded in Glasgow in 1863, which operated the MILLBURN distillery for a long time (see also GLEN LYON).

MACLEOD'S ISLE OF SKYE

Blended Scotch, standard, 12 years old premium, 18 years old de luxe, from Ian MacLeod & Co., a subsidiary of Peter J. RUSSELL. This brand has been around for more than 100 years. The name suggests that TALISKER, from the Isle of Skye, is one of the base malts. The standard bottling contains 8-year-old malts and 4-year-old grains and, like the older bottlings, is left to age in the barrel another 6 months after blending.

MCMASTERS

Canadian blend from HEUBLEIN INC. (IDV/Grand Metropolitan).

One of the many brands that are produced in Canada but bottled and sold only in the United States. As is usual in such cases, the name of the distillery is not disclosed. The same can be said of the blended Scotch that Heublein markets under this name in the United States.

MAC NA MARA

Blended Scotch, 80 proof, from PRABAN NA LINNE.

The third brand from this small firm came on the market in 1995. The name is Gaelic and means "son of the sea," not a bad name for a whisky from the Isle of Skye. TALISKER must be one of the base malts.

MACNAUGHTON

Canadian blend from the VALLEYFIELD distillery, property of UD.

This whisky is produced in Canada but sold exclusively in the United States. The brand formerly belonged to GLENMORE DISTILLING, but when that operation was sold to BARTON DISTILLING, it was retained by UD.

MACPHAIL'S

Scottish single malt from GORDON & MACPHAIL.

This full-bodied and well-balanced malt is available at 10, 15, 21, 25, 30, and 40 years old, also from the years 1960 and 1973, all 80 proof. In addition, there is MacPhail's Gold "106," 10 years old and 121 proof. The producer of this malt is not revealed. For its centennial in 1995 the Gordon & MacPhail firm issued a vatted malt called MacPhail's Centenary, which was put together from 100 singles up to 50 years old.

MAJESTIC

A trading firm established in Baltimore in 1943 that produces a whole series of brands: CANADIAN LAKE, CANADIAN LEAF, CANADIAN PEAK, CHARRED KEG, CLASSIC CLUB, CLUB 400, LORD BALTIMORE, OLD SETTER, ROYAL MAJESTIC, SCOTCH ISLAND, TRAVELER'S CLUB.

MAJOR GUNN'S

Blended Scotch from MACDONALD MARTIN DISTILLERS.

MAJORITY

Blended Scotch from CWS.

MAKER'S MARK

Kentucky straight bourbon from HIRAM WALKER & SONS (ALLIED DOMECQ).

An outstanding whiskey, with depth despite its smoothness. Maker's Mark comes from one of Kentucky's smallest distilleries and is considered, owing to its relatively small production, as a model of the so-called SMALL-BATCH BOURBONS. It is one of the few bourbons in which wheat is used instead of rye, which contributes a great deal to the highly praised mildness of this brand.

Currently it is available in 4 versions (all using the Scottish spelling, without an "e"): Red Seal, 86 and 90 proof, at least 6 years old, the market leader in Kentucky and now a fixture in the "scene" bars of New York City; Gold Seal Limited Edition, 101 proof, unfortunately as limited as the name implies; Vintage, a single barrel at barrel strength (distilled 1983, 1984), on the market since 1996; Black Seal, 94 proof, a special edition for the Japanese market.

A maker's mark is a master's seal placed on silver or pewter. The labels of this whiskey have such a seal, consisting of a star, the letter "S", and the Roman numeral IV. The star stands for Star Hill Distillery, the "S" for the Samuels family, and the "IV" for the 4 generations of the family that have been involved in the business of distilling whiskey (by now it is 5).

The first of them was Taylor W Samuels (related to Daniel Boon and Jesse James), who opened distillery in Deatsville in 1844. Th present Star Hill Distillery was estab

Maker's Mark
WHISKY
KENTUCKY STRAIGHT BOURBON
OLD STYLE SOUR MASH

...ished in Loretto, Nelson County, Kentucky, in 1889. It had been inactive for a long time when Bill Samuels, Sr., acquired it in 1953. He renovated it with great care (such care that it is now a historic monument) and in 1959 brought out the first Maker's Mark. For a long time the family ran the distillery only as a sideline, as its major income came from the lumber business. Because of this, it was able to place more emphasis on the quality of the whiskey than on its quantity. The breakthrough from a small, provincial brand valued only by the initiated to a fashionable, metropolitan whiskey came in 1980, with a front-page article about the business in the *Wall Street Journal*. Suddenly everyone wanted to buy Maker's Mark—especially the Canadian concern Hiram Walker, which acquired the distillery in 1981 (and was subsequently absorbed into Allied Domecq).

Despite the increased demand, the Star Hill Distillery continues to adhere to a number of time-consuming practices, the most important of which is a low distilling intensity: instead of the 80 percent alcohol per volume allowed, they work here with only 60 or 65 percent, which produces a distillate that is not as pure but has more flavor. It is then filtered through ground charcoal, which takes out any impurities. The wood is air-dried for a year before it is worked, so as to reduce the astringent effect of the tannins. (The used

barrels are sent to GLENMORANGIE in Scotland.) Other unusual features are the grain mixture of 70 percent corn, 16 percent wheat, and 14 percent barley malt, as well as the sour mash component of 32 percent. The yeast culture is probably the oldest in Kentucky; it dates back to before Prohibition and is augmented with hops.

The output is 18 barrels a day—not a lot, compared to the 1,000 barrels that many other distilleries produce. I don't wish to exaggerate the noble conservatism of Maker's Mark; it also puts out a mint julep pre-mix.

(Tel. 502 865-2099)

MALT WHISKY

The distillate of fermented barley malt. Scotland's oldest whisky variety is now generally considered the most perfect and varied form of whisk(e)y in the world.

The taste of malt whisky is essentially determined by malt sugar and by the smoke employed in the malt's preparation. Traditionally, the entire production process takes place in a single distillery, and each distillery places particular emphasis on the use of its own spring water. The quality of the water greatly influences the taste and character of a whisk(e)y. Today a number of barley varieties are used, most of them from Scotland.

To turn the grain into fermentable malt sugars, the barley is dampened and allowed to sprout. As soon as this

occurs, the barley is dried over a peat fire and then milled. It is then made into a mash—that is, mixed with hot water to release the sugar. The resulting "wort" is then caused to ferment with the addition of yeast, producing a beer-like brew that can be distilled.

Only a very few Scottish distilleries continue to perform this whole process. Most of the so-called malting floors have been closed, and their pagoda-shaped roofs are now purely ornamental. Today the grain is treated in special malt houses by ma-

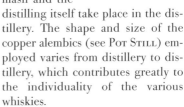

chine and dried with hot air, to which a given percentage of peat smoke is added as required.

Only the mixing of the mash and the distilling itself take place in the distillery. The shape and size of the copper alembics (see POT STILL) employed varies from distillery to distillery, which contributes greatly to the individuality of the various whiskies.

Few distilleries in Scotland distill their malt 3 times; twice is the rule. The first distillate is called "low wines" and has an alcohol content of roughly 25 percent by volume. The second distillation is accomplished in a pot still, and this time it is important

the alcohol content exceed 95 percent or the distillate will be too pure and flavorless. Before being stored in barrels it is diluted with spring water to roughly 63 percent alcohol, or 126 proof. This strength has proven to be optimal for the aging process.

It is now felt that the character of a whisk(e)y is determined most of all by the manner in which it is aged and the length of time it is given.

By far the majority of whiskies reach the market in the form of blended whisk(e)y (see BLENDED SCOTCH WHISKY); only a very small percentage are bottled as malt whisky. Of the latter, one must distinguish between SINGLE MALT and VATTED MALT. A single malt comes from one specific distillery; vatted malts combine singles from various distilleries. (See also BOTTLING, SINGLE-BARREL BOTTLING.)

to separate out the middle run, for it alone has the desired quality. The beginning of the run, called the "foreshot," contains fusel oil and must be diverted, as must the watery end of the run, called the "feints." The chief responsibility of the stillman is to determine which part of the distillate qualifies as the middle run, an art in itself.

The fresh "baby whisky" is colorless and contains about 70 percent alcohol; under no circumstances should

Scottish malts are classified according to their geographical origin, but only rarely do these designations indicate a whisky's character. The various regions are: HIGHLANDS (with the subregion SPEYSIDE), LOWLANDS, CAMPBELTOWN, and ISLAY.

MANHATTAN

One of the most famous cocktails in bar history. It exists in countless variations, and people will tell you any number of stories about who first created it. One of them has it that it was invented by Winston Churchill's mother at the Manhattan Club.

Manhattan Perfect: Pour 1½ oz. Canadian whisky, ½ oz. dry vermouth, ½ oz. sweet vermouth, and a few dashes of Angostura into a mixing glass filled with ice. Stir well and strain into a chilled cocktail glass. Garnish with a cherry.

Manhattan Dry: 1½ oz. Canadian, ¾ oz. dry vermouth, and a twist of lemon peel.

Manhattan Sweet: 1½ oz. Canadian, ¾ oz. sweet vermouth, dashes Angostura, and a cherry.

The fact that Canadian was the original base for a Manhattan suggests that this cocktail was devised during PROHIBITION, not only because it was especially common in those years to hide spirits in colorful mixtures, but also because Canadian was the one real whisky most readily available in the United States. Now Americans generally make their Manhattans with bourbon, which is perfectly logical, for its more intense flavor is not overshadowed by the vermouth and you don't have to use so much whisky. (A Manhattan is actually an aperitif cocktail and therefore shouldn't be too strong.)

For other versions of the Manhattan, see BLACKTHORN, BOBBIE BURNS, BROOKLYN, ROB ROY, RORY O'MOORE, SCOFF-LAW.

MANNOCHMORE

Scottish single malt (Speyside, Elgin) from John HAIG & Co. (UD).

A rather light malt, dry and well balanced.

Original bottling: 12 years old, 86 proof ("Flora & Fauna" series). A 10-year-old Mannochmore recently came on the market under the name Loch Dhu (Gaelic for "black lake"). It was aged in bourbon barrels that had been charred again and is therefore almost black.

Cadenhead: 18 years old (distilled 1977), 121.8 proof.

Signatory: The firm recently had a 12-year-old (distilled 1976) at 124.8 proof.

The distillery was built only in 1971 and most of the time produces malts for the Haig blends. After having been shut down for 4 years, it was again put into operation by UD in 1989, and a few years later began issuing its official version. Mannochmore has been shut down again, however, since 1995. It has 6 stills and the water comes from Bardon Burn.

(Tel. 1343 86 03 31)

MARIE BRIZARD
This traditional French firm, established in Bordeaux in 1889, has also been active on the American whiskey market for a number of years. From its Miami branch it markets the brands MOHAWK and NEWPORT.

MAR LODGE
Scottish vatted malt, 12 years old, from Findlater Mackie Todd & Co. (see FINDLATER'S FINEST), a subsidiary of INVERGORDON DISTILLERS (WHYTE & MACKAY, AMERICAN BRANDS).

MASON'S
Blended Scotch from Peter J. RUSSELL.

MASTER BLEND
Thai blended whiskey from SEAGRAM.

This blend consists of 5-year-old Scottish and New Zealand malts and local rice brandy. The brand was introduced in 1995 and is as yet the only blend of this type in Thailand, which is considered one of the growing Far East markets. Heretofore the country has consumed mainly native rice whiskeys (brands: Gunn, Singha, Chao Praya, Singharaj, VO Thai Whisky, Sang Thip), blended Scotch (JOHNNIE WALKER Black Label is the market leader), and Japanese blends.

MATTINGLY & MOORE
Kentucky straight bourbon, 80 proof from HEAVEN HILL DISTILLERS.

A passable everyday whiskey that is now produced only for the regional Kentucky market.

In 1876, Ben Mattingly and Tom Moore founded a distillery under this name in Nelson County, Kentucky. The brand was acquired by SEAGRAM after PROHIBITION, then by UD in the 1980s, and sold to Heaven Hill in 1992.

A second distillery that Moore and Mattingly founded in 1889 has been called since Prohibition the Barton Distillery (see BARTON DISTILLING), which in turn produces a brand called TOM MOORE.

MAYERSON & CO.

London whisky trading corporation. The firm was founded in 1953 and is one of the major British whisky brokers; that is, it buys whisky while it is still aging and then sells it to blending firms. In addition, Mayerson & Co. owns the brands GLENROB, SCOTTISH ENVOY, and STRATH-ROYE.

MEADOW CREAM

Irish whiskey cream liqueur, 29 proof, from PERNOD RICARD.

MEAGHERS 1878

Canadian blend from CORBY, a subsidiary of HIRAM WALKER & SONS (ALLIED DOMECQ).

MEDLEY

Kentucky straight bourbon produced by Dethleffsen, Flensburg, for the German market. It comes from the HEAVEN HILL DISTILLERS and is bottled in Germany.

This is all that survives of a proud name. The Medleys got into the bourbon business in 1812 and operated several distilleries. In the 1950s they had a certain amount of success with the brand EZRA BROOKS, which is now produced by SHERMAN.

After changing hands several times, the operation was finally acquired in 1995 by BARTON DISTILLING, which now uses the old Medley distillery in Owensboro, Kentucky, as a warehouse.

Several former Medley brands are now produced by different firms:

DAVIESS COUNTY, Ezra Brooks, RITTENHOUSE.

MELDRUM HOUSE

Michel Couvreur, a native of Burgundy, bottles various malt and grain whiskies under this name. Their sources are not named, even in the case of singles or vatteds. Despite this air of mystery and their rather high prices, Meldrum House whiskies have their admirers, especially among adventurous whisky lovers who like to stray off the well-trodden paths.

Old Meldrum is the former name of the malt distillery GLEN GARIOCH.

MEN'S CLUB

Indian blend from Polychem.

This brand, introduced in 1974, is available as Black Label and Red Label.

The producer, Polychem of Bombay, has been linked with the British firm IDV on a joint-venture basis since 1993 and also owns the brands WHITE HOUSE and ROYAL SECRET.

MERLYN CREAM LIQUEUR
Welsh whisky cream liqueur from THE WELSH WHISKY CO.

MICHTER'S See A. H. HIRSCH RESERVE.
MIDLETON
Irish distillery and brand belonging to IDG (PERNOD RICARD), founded in 1825 by the Murphy brothers in Midleton, County Cork. In 1867 the Murphys joined up with 4 other distilleries in the area to form the Cork Distilleries Company (CDC), which later became famous for the brand PADDY. Once the CDC had again merged with John Power (see POWER'S GOLD LABEL) and JAMESON to form the Irish Distillers Group (IDG), it was decided to consolidate all distilling activities in Midleton. The new Midleton distillery was opened in 1975 only a few hundred yards away from the old one. In this super-modern facility, which looks from the outside more like a power plant than a traditional distillery, there are 9 huge pot and patent stills. They produce the various whiskey varieties, including 3 malts, that serve as the base of all the IDG brands that do not come from BUSHMILLS (see also IRISH WHISKEY). They also make gin and vodka here, for in Ireland, as elsewhere, sales of clear spirits have outpaced

those of whiskey, especially among the young.

The old Midleton distillery is now a whiskey museum, virtually identical to the one that the IDG set up in the old Jameson distillery in Dublin.

Since 1984 the distillery has produced a super premium blend under the name Midleton Very Rare. It carries the year in which it was bottled

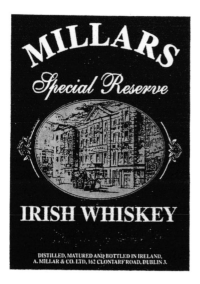

on the label and is issued in very small quantities. The blend is reformulated each year, and after modest beginnings a high-class brand is being developed here with an increasing percentage of pot still whiskeys. From the start, its price has been exorbitant.

MIKE COLLINS

A COLLINS based on Irish whiskey.

MILLARS SPECIAL RESERVE

Blended Irish whiskey, standard, 80 proof, from COOLEY DISTILLERY.

This brand was originally called Millars Black Label, but now that it is also being sold outside of Ireland it uses this name so as not to be confused with JOHNNIE WALKER Black Label.

There is also a Millars Gold, which cannot be called whiskey because it is only 60 proof and therefore bears the designation Specially Selected Spirits.

In the early 1990s, in its search for new brands with old names, the young Cooley firm discovered Adam Millar & Co. This firm, trading in wine, tea, and spirits, had been founded in Dublin in 1843 by a cousin of John Jameson's. For a time it had belonged to Peter Barry, a deputy of the Fin Gael (one of the 2 major political parties in Ireland), and it had once had a blended Scotch called Glenmillar in its program.

MILLBURN

Scottish single malt (Highlands, Inverness) from UD.

A mild malt with a full body.

Original bottling: 18 years old (distilled 1975), 117.8 proof ("Rare Malts Selection").

Gordon & MacPhail: Vintage 1972, 80 proof.

Cadenhead: 11 years old (distilled 1983), 116.8 proof.

James MacArthur: 12 years old, 86 proof.

This distillery was probably already in existence in 1807, but it was first documented in 1825. It was bought in 1943 by the DCL, which closed it in 1985. Today it houses the Beefeater Distillery Restaurant. Stores are therefore limited. The 12-year-old vatted malt that the licensee, MACLEAY DUFF, formerly issued under the name The Mill Burn is already impossible to find.

MILLIONAIRE
A variation of the WHISKEY SOUR: shake 1½ oz. bourbon, ¾ oz. lemon juice, 1 egg white, ½ oz. Triple Sec, and a few dashes of grenadine vigorously with ice.

MILLWOOD WHISKEY CREAM
Irish whiskey cream liqueur from Koninklijke Cooymans B.V., Tilburg, Holland, 29 proof, obviously an Irish-Dutch coproduction in which the cream does not come from Ireland.

MILNER'S BROWN LABEL
Blended Scotch produced by W. H. Milner for the brewery Marston, Thompson & Evershed, which serves it in its roughly 900 pubs in England and Wales.

MILORD'S
Blended Scotch, 12 years old, de luxe, from MACDONALD MARTIN DISTILLERS.

This brand was originally created for the Venezuelan market, but now it is sold mainly in Denmark.

MILROY'S
This London whisky shop is actually called the Soho Wine Market, but malt lovers around the world know it only under the name of the brothers John and Wallace Milroy. John, who opened it in 1964, continues to run it today, while Wallace has made a name for himself as the author of *The Malt Whisky Almanac,* now in its 6th edition. The Milroys plan to offer single-malt bottlings of their own in the near future; for example, TALISKER and GLENFARCLAS.

(3 Greek Street, London W1)

MILTONDUFF
Scottish single malt (Speyside, Elgin) from G. BALLANTINE & Son (ALLIED DISTILLERS, ALLIED DOMECQ).

A malty, medium-heavy malt that is especially valued for blends.

Original bottling: 12 years old, 80 proof.

Cadenhead: 30 years old (distilled 1964), 101.8 proof.

Miltonduff was founded in 1824 and was acquired by HIRAM WALKER & SONS (now part of Allied) in 1936. In the 1970s it was greatly expanded, and for a time 2 Lomond stills were installed, in which a malt called MOSSTOWIE was distilled.

Today Miltonduff operates with 6 stills and gets its water from the Black Burn. As early as the Middle Ages the monks of a Benedictine abbey were taking water from this small stream, at least for brewing beer. Miltonduff is one of the base malts for the Ballantine's blends.

(Tel. 1343 54 74 33)

MINT JULEP

One of the oldest and most popular American mixed drinks. The British traveler John Davis described it in 1803 as "an alcoholic drink with mint that is drunk in the morning in Virginia," and in 1806 *Webster's Dictionary* defined the mint julep as "a kind of liquid medicine."

At one time it was prepared with peach brandy, the earliest American liquor. Since the 19th century it has generally been made with bourbon. In the Old South, the homeland of the mint julep, the recipe varies from family to family. Essentially it is a combination of mint, sugar, and whiskey. It is important that the mint be very fresh.

Crush 2 sugar cubes in a heavy glass, add some mint leaves and lightly bruise them, fill with crushed ice, and add 1¾ oz. bourbon. Stir well and garnish with a sprig of mint. If you add ½ oz. peach brandy, you have a Georgia mint julep.

Mint juleps are the traditional drink at the Kentucky Derby, which takes place each May—the beginning of the mint season—in Louisville.

MITCHELL, J. A.

Scottish producer in Campbeltown.

The Mitchells have been operating the SPRINGBANK distillery in Campbeltown since 1837. It is the oldest

and, along with GLENFARCLAS, one of the last independent family businesses in the Scottish whisky industry. They also own the highly respected bottler CADENHEAD and the EAGLESOME firm.

MOFFAT See GARNHEATH.

MOHAWK
Kentucky straight bourbon from MARIE BRIZARD.

MOIDART
Scottish vatted malt, 10, 21, 25, and 30 years old, 92 proof, from CADENHEAD.

The name of this wonderfully balanced whisky refers to the small village on the west coast of Scotland on which Bonnie Prince Charles, from the house of Stuart, landed in 1745 to fight for the last time for his country's independence. It was also from Moidart that he sailed into exile a year later after his defeat.

(See also DRAMBUIE.)

THE MONARCH
Blended Scotch, 10-year-old premium, from Lambert Bros.

During World War I, The Monarch was a favorite in the Allied messes in France. Today it is sold mainly in the Far East.

MONOGRAM
Blended American from KASSER LAIRD.

MONSTER'S CHOICE
Blended Scotch, 80 proof, from Strathnairn Whisky, a subsidiary of GORDON & MACPHAIL.

This brand has been in existence since the turn of the century, and if it is not "Nessie's Favorite Drink," as the label maintains, it is certainly highly popular with tourists visiting Loch Ness.

MONTEBELLO
U.S. trading firm established in Baltimore in 1933. It markets the following brands in America: BRITANNIA BLENDED WHISKEY, KING'S CROWN, MCCALLS.

MONTROSE WHISKY
British trading firm with headquarters in London, founded in 1973. It exports its brands mainly to Asia and Latin America: GLEN KINDIE, GREAT MAC, OLD MONTROSE, PIPE MAJOR.

MONT ROYAL LIGHT
Canadian blend from SEAGRAM.

MOONSHINE
American term for alcohol that is distilled illegally. Illegal whisk(e)y is

probably still being distilled in Scotland and Ireland (see POITÍN) but by no means in quantities as large as in the United States, where in 1969 alone upward of 10,000 illegal production sites were discovered and destroyed. Moonshine is so popular not only because there are still parts of the country in which alcohol is forbidden (as, for example, in the county that is home to the JACK DANIEL distillery), but also because people like avoiding the high taxes on alcohol and they like making it for the heck of it. In some regions of the United States people openly confess to moonshining, and everyone has an uncle or a cousin who produces the stuff. Visitors to these regions are discouraged from doing any investigating, however, for every stranger could be a federal employee, and they live dangerous lives here.

Since moonshine is now distilled primarily for home use, it is usually fairly pure. One tests it before drinking it by pouring out a spoonful and putting a match to it: pure distillate burns evenly with a blue flame; rotgut with a yellow flame. But be warned about using fire around moonshine: with its high alcohol content it is highly combustible.

MOORLAND
Blended Scotch from GRIERSON'S.

MORNING GLORY FIZZ
A variation on the fizz based on Scotch: shake vigorously with ice 1½ oz. Scotch, ¾ to 1 oz. lemon juice, ½ to ¾ oz. sugar syrup, 1 egg white, 1 bar spoon of powdered sugar, and a dash of Pernod. Strain into a tall glass and fill with soda.

MORRISON BOWMORE DISTILLERS
Scottish producers, owned by the Japanese firm SUNTORY.

The business, founded in 1951 by Stanley P. Morrison, operates the distilleries AUCHENTOSHAN, BOWMORE, and GLEN GARIOCH. Morrison also owns the McCLELLAND blending house and the brands CLAN ROY, ISLAY LEGEND, KING'S PRIDE, PREMIER, ROB ROY, and SWORDS.

Before Suntory took over the firm in 1994, the Morrison family held the majority of stock.

MORTLACH
Scottish single malt (Speyside, Duff

town) from UD.

A complex malt with a great deal of character, especially impressive in its early years.

Original bottling: 16 years old, 86 proof ("Flora & Fauna" series).

Gordon & MacPhail: 15 and 21 years old, 80 proof; vintages 1960, 1966, 1984, each 80 proof; also a series of older vintages and—now only rarely—a 50-year-old (distilled 1942), 80 proof.

Cadenhead: 8 years old (distilled 1987), 125.4 proof.

James MacArthur: 10 years old, 86 proof.

Adelphi: 11 years old (distilled 1984), 119.4 proof.

Mortlach dates back to 1824 and is thus the oldest of the 7 distilleries in Dufftown. For a brief time it was owned by the Grants—more precisely the GLEN GRANT Grants—who exploited it and then shut it down. For a few years it belonged to a certain John Gordon, who sold the whisky, modest man that he was, as The Real John Gordon. George Cowie then took over the operation in 1854. He later became the mayor of Dufftown

and hired a young man by the name of WILLIAM GRANT. Grant worked for 20 years at Mortlach before he felt he knew enough about the business and set himself up on his own by founding GLENFIDDICH, one of the most successful whisky dynasties in Scotland. Mortlach itself was taken over in 1923 by John Walker & Sons (see JOHNNIE WALKER), which continued to run the distillery under the name Cowie and later, by way of the DCL, became part of UD.

Mortlach has 6 stills, and the water comes from the Conval Hills.

(Tel. 1340 82 03 18)

MOSSTOWIE

Scottish single malt (Speyside, Elgin) from the MILTONDUFF distillery, property of G. BALLANTINE & Son (ALLIED DISTILLERS, ALLIED DOMECQ).

A malty aperitif whisky that is now very difficult to find.

Gordon & MacPhail: Vintages 1975 and 1979, both at 80 proof.

Mosstowie was produced in the LOMOND STILLS that were used at Miltonduff between 1964 and 1981. At that time it was rarely marketed and for that reason is highly prized by collectors.

M. S. WALKER

U.S. trading firm established in Somerville, Massachusetts, in 1933 that markets in America the following brands: CALDWELL'S, KENNEDY'S, S. S. PIERCE.

A BLEND OF 100% SCOTCH WHISKIES

MUIRHEAD'S.

FAMOUS SINCE - 1824

TRADE MARK

BLENDED SCOTCH WHISKY

PRODUCT OF SCOTLAND
BLENDED AND BOTTLED IN SCOTLAND BY

Charles Muirhead & Son Ltd.

EDINBURGH   Est. 1824

MUIRHEAD'S BLUE SEAL

Blended Scotch from Charles Muirhead & Son, a subsidiary of MACDONALD MARTIN DISTILLERS.

This brand has been in existence since the 1920s and is now sold throughout the world.

MURDOCH'S PERFECTION

Blended Scotch from SPEYSIDE DISTILLERY.

When Murdoch's still belonged to Campbell & Clark, this blend was easier to find than it is now, but it is still worth looking.

THE MURRAYFIELD

Blended Scotch, de luxe, 10, 12, and 15 years old, 86 proof, from BENNACHIE

A new blend, chiefly intended for the Scottish market, that has already received a number of awards.

N·O

I'll buy my own whiskey,
I'll make my own stew;
If I get drunk, madam,
It's nothing to you.

CHORUS

Rye whisky rye whiskey
Rye whisky I cry,
If you don't give me rye whiskey
I surely will die.

American folk ballad

NATU NOBILIS

Brazilian blend from SEAGRAM.

This used to be a small Scotch brand, but now Natu Nobilis is put together out of Brazilian grain and Scottish malt and sold exclusively in Latin America.

NEWPORT

Kentucky straight bourbon and blended Scotch from MARIE BRIZARD.

NEW YORKER

A variation on the WHISKEY SOUR: Stir 1½ oz. bourbon, the juice of a quarter to a half of a lemon, and a dash of grenadine with ice in a tumbler.

NEW ZEALAND

Whisky came to New Zealand along with the first Scottish settlers in the middle of the 19th century. They settled at Dunedin (Gaelic for Edinburgh) on South Island. There was plenty of peat there, as well as soft water, and barley could be grown successfully, so nothing stood in the way of producing whisky in the Scottish way. The first distillery was established by Howden & Robertson. But extremely high taxes led to the decline of commercial whisky production beginning in 1875, so that buyers had to make do with imports or MOONSHINE. The latter became especially popular under the name Hokonui.

It was not until 1968 that the WILSON firm (see WILSON's) once again tried to get into the business. It was taken over by SEAGRAM in 1981 and now has 2 successful brands: a malt called LAMMERLAW and the blend Wilson's. Today New Zealand whiskies are exported increasingly to Australia, now that the whisky industry there has given up the ghost.

NICHOLS

American blend based on WILD TURKEY, 86 proof, from AUSTIN NICHOLS DISTILLING COMPANY (PERNOD RICARD).

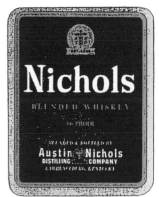

NIKKA

Japanese producer with headquarters in Yoichi, Hokkaido.

With a market share of around 20 percent, Nikka is the second-largest whisky producer in Japan, after SUNTORY.

The firm operates 2 malt distilleries and 1 for grain, the products of which are then processed in its own warehouse and blending complex. Since 1989 it has also owned the Scottish BEN NEVIS distillery.

Nikka was founded in 1952 by Masataka Taketsuru, who studied chemistry in Scotland in the 1920s and worked there for a time in a distillery. Back in Japan, he began at

Suntory as a stillman, then in 1934 went independent as a producer of apple juice. But he continued to experiment with various methods of producing whisky. His first brand was introduced in 1940, but it was only in the 1960s that Taketsuru got into the business in a big way (see JAPANESE WHISKY).

Today Nikka is a subsidiary of Asahi Brewing, one of the 3 major beer brewers in the country, and produces the following brands: ALL MALT, CORN BASE, FROM THE BARREL, GOLD & GOLD, GRAND AGE, HI, NIKKA HOKKAIDO, PURE MALT, RYE BASE, SUPER NIKKA, SUPER SESSION, THE BLEND, and TSURU.

NIKKA HOKKAIDO
Japanese vatted malt, 12 years old, from NIKKA, on the market since 1984.

NOAH'S MILL
Kentucky straight bourbon, 15 years old, 114.2 proof, from KENTUCKY BOURBON DISTILLERS.

NORTH BRITISH

Scottish grain distillery in Edinburgh, owned by Lothian Distillers, a consortium of the firms IDV and ROBERTSON & BAXTER.

The distillery was founded in 1886 by A. Usher (see USHER'S GREEN STRIPE) and other blending firms and was for a long time the only independent grain producer in Scotland. Since 1993 it has been controlled by the present owners, who supply the firm SEAGRAM, and others, with grain.

North British Grain is normally not bottled as a single, but at the moment there are 2 16-year-old bottlings from Signatory: one from 1979, aged in sherry casks, 86 proof, and one from 1964 at 92 proof.

NORTHERN LIGHT

Canadian blend from BARTON DISTILLING (Canandaigua).

The Barton firm, with headquarters in Kentucky, imports this whisky in bulk and bottles it for the U.S. market.

NORTHERN SCOT

Blended Scotch from INVERGORDON DISTILLERS (WHYTE & MACKAY, AMERICAN BRANDS).

NORTH PORT (BRECHIN)

Scottish single malt (Eastern Highlands) from UD.

A light, somewhat sharp whisky that has not become especially popular, owing to a low rating by the

whisky authority Michael Jackson. But this should not prevent anyone from trying one of the Cadenhead bottlings.

Original bottling: "Rare Malts Selection."

Gordon & MacPhail: Vintages 1970, 1974, both 80 proof.

Cadenhead: 18 years old (distilled 1976), 122.8 proof.

The distillery, also called Brechin, was founded in 1820. In 1922 it was acquired by the DCL, which sold it in 1983. North Port was at one point a component in a vatted malt called GLEN DEW.

498 AD was the fateful year when Fergus, Angus and Loarn, sons of King Erc of the Scotti mounted an eastern expedition from the Glens of Antrim to invade and colonise the Oban shores, naming their little kingdom 'Dalriada'. Fergus Mac Erc became the first monarch, his seat the great fortress of Dunaad. Angus and Loarn held the lands to the North and South in which the latter Loarn gave his name. The monarch moved North to the ancient Pictush fortress of Dun a' Mhonaidh near Oban. The Scotti brought with them the sacred block of time worn red sandstone known as 'Lia Fail' the symbolic 'STONE OF DESTINY'

O·B·A·N
'Little Bay of Caves'

ALONG THE SHORES OF LORN LIES A RECORD OF MAN FAR MORE ANCIENT THAN THAT OF ANY CITY IN THE LAND. THE FIRST SETTLERS ARRIVED ON THE MAINLAND IN 5,000 BC AND SHELTERED IN THE NATURAL CAVES OF THE LAND THEN KNOWN AS 'AN OB'. THE 'DISTILLERY CAVE' WAS ONE SUCH SHELTER HIDDEN IN THE 'CREAG A' BHARRAIN CLIFFS WHICH RISE DRAMATICALLY ABOVE THE 'OBAN DISTILLERY'

Producer of a Delicate
SINGLE MALT
WEST Highland MALT
SCOTCH WHISKY

The coastland of the gaelic people known as 'Garra Gael' fell to the dreaded Viking overlordship in the middle of the eighth century when their rule was at its harshest It was then that the warrior King Somerled mac Gillibride became foremost in Oban history. Part Viking, part Celt, he rallied his repressed and despairing countrymen leading them towards a new and lasting freedom from their oppressors. His spirit is said to live upon the precipitous crag of Dun Ollaugh which for centuries has been the home for the descendants of his son and heir Dougall mac Somhairlie, the founder of the great 'CLAN MACDOUGALL'

OBAN

Scottish single malt (Western Highlands) from UD.

A mild malt with a smoky charm and a wonderful balance.

Original bottling: 14 years old, 86 proof (from the "Classic Malts" series). With luck one can also still find the 12-year-old in the highly popular carafe (80 proof).

The distillery was probably established as early as 1794. It was acquired by DEWAR in 1923, and with that firm came to its present owner. It has 2 stills, and its water comes from Loch a' Bhearraidh. The licensee is the firm John Hopkins & Co., which uses Oban in its blends (see GLEN GARRY).

(Tel. 1631 56 21 10)

OCEAN
Japanese blend from Sᴀɴʀᴀᴋᴜ Oᴄᴇᴀɴ.

O'DARBY
Irish whiskey cream liqueur, 34 proof, from IDV/Grand Metropolitan.

ODDBINS
The British wine shop chain Oddbins offers a whole series of inexpensive single-malt vintage bottlings in its shops, the sources of which it does not reveal. At the moment it is selling a Single Lowland from 1985, a Single Highland (distilled 1984), a Single Islay (distilled 1984), a Single Island (distilled 1978), and 2 Single Speysides (distilled 1973 and 1984).

Oddbins is part of the spirit giant Sᴇᴀɢʀᴀᴍ.

OLD ANGUS
Blended Scotch from R. H. Tʜᴏᴍsᴏɴ & Co., a subsidiary of UD.

A very old brand, probably based on Tᴇᴀɴɪɴɪᴄʜ, and now marketed mainly outside of Europe.

OLD ARGYLL
Blended Scotch, premium, from Bᴜʀɴ Sᴛᴇᴡᴀʀᴛ Dɪsᴛɪʟʟᴇʀs.

OLD BARDSTOWN
Kentucky straight bourbon, 6 years old, 80 proof, and 10 years old, 101 proof, from Kᴇɴᴛᴜᴄᴋʏ Bᴏᴜʀʙᴏɴ Dɪs-ᴛɪʟʟᴇʀs.

A very well known brand up until the 1950s; at that time it came from

the house of Willet. One of the descendants of that family is bottling the whiskey today, although it is distilled by Hᴇᴀᴠᴇɴ Hɪʟʟ Dɪsᴛɪʟʟᴇʀs.

OLD CHARTER
Kentucky straight bourbon from the Bᴇʀɴʜᴇɪᴍ Dɪsᴛɪʟʟᴇʀʏ, owned by UD.

A robust whiskey that attains a luxurious fullness with increasing age.

Old Charter is available at 100 proof (ʙᴏᴛᴛʟᴇᴅ ɪɴ ʙᴏɴᴅ); as an 8-year-old at 80 proof; as a 10-year-old at 86 proof; as The Classic 90, 12 years old, 90 proof; and as Proprietor's Reserve, 13 years old, 90 proof.

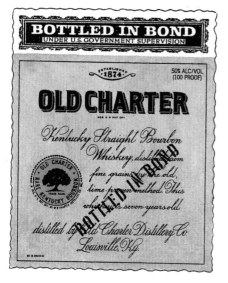

in the early 1980s that it was decided to bottle the whiskey, which can now boast the impressive legend "at least 30 years old" but is a perfect example of a whiskey that spent too much time in the barrel—solely a collectors' item.

OLD COURT

Blended Scotch from A. Gillies, a firm that formerly belonged to Gibson International. Gibson went bankrupt in 1994, and its assets were taken over by GLEN CATRINE, which therefore owns this brand today but is not currently producing it. One of the base malts was GLEN SCOTIA.

OLD CROW

Kentucky straight bourbon from JIM BEAM BRANDS (AMERICAN BRANDS).

A typical, everyday, old-school bourbon, which is to say sweet but not too mild and therefore very good for mixing. At one time it was known in America's black ghettos as "Dirty Bird."

In addition to the standard version at 80 proof, there is a 100-proof Bottled in Bond.

Old Crow is one of the oldest whiskey brands in the United States. It was created by the Scottish immigrant Dr. James Crow, a chemist who did not actually invent the SOUR MASH

This brand was first introduced in 1874. Since the end of Prohibition it has come from the Bernheim Distillery.

OLD COMBER

Irish pure pot still whiskey from the Old Comber distillery in Belfast.

Only a few bottles of this brand are still on the market. They are offered by the Northern Irish firm James E. McCabe, which in 1970 bought up the remaining stores of this distillery shut down in 1953. Unfortunately, it was only

process but perfected it using scientific methods. He worked in the Old Oscar Pepper Distillery (see JAMES E. PEPPER) and introduced to American distilling the saccharimeter and thermometer, used everywhere today, to keep the fermentation process under control. The Old Crow Distillery was opened in Frankfort, Kentucky, in 1872. Its bourbon was considered one

THE OLD CROW
DISTILLERY COMPANY

of the best in the 19th century and was able to maintain its popularity up into the 1950s.

But in the early 1960s the Old Crow made its last flight; the new owners, American Brands, closed it down. Old Crow has since been produced by the house of Beam.

OLD CURLERS
Blended Scotch from Donald Hart & Co. (see HART'S).

OLD DECANTER
Blended Scotch, 12 years old, de luxe, from COCKBURN'S OF LEITH.

OLD DISPENSARY
Kentucky straight corn whiskey, 100 proof, from BARTON DISTILLING (Canandaigua).

The name says it all. The whiskey is found only in the southern states.

OLD DISTILLER
Kentucky straight bourbon from KENTUCKY BOURBON DISTILLERS.

OLD DUBLIN
Blended Irish whiskey, 80 proof, from the MIDLETON distillery, property of IDG (PERNOD RICARD).

A lesser brand in the bottom price category.

OLD EIGHT
Brazilian blended whiskey from IDV/Grand Metropolitan.

OLD 1889
Kentucky straight bourbon, 4 years old, 80 proof, from HEAVEN HILL DISTILLERS.

OLD ELGIN
Scottish vatted malt from GORDON & MACPHAIL.

This whisky consists exclusively of SPEYSIDE malts and is available at 8, 15, and 21 years old, as well as in the vintages 1938, 1939, 1940, 1947, and 1949.

OLD EZRA See EZRA BROOKS.

OLD FASHIONED
A wonderful cocktail, said to have been prepared first in Louisville, Kentucky, and popularized in New York City by JAMES E. PEPPER. Crush

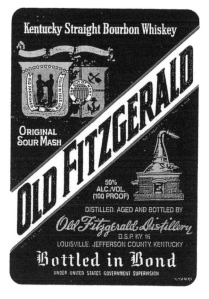

a sugar cube, a quarter of an orange, and a quarter of a lemon in a tumbler with a pestle; mix with 1¾ oz. rye or bourbon, add ice, and top with soda or tap water.

OLD FETTERCAIRN

Scottish single malt (Eastern Highlands) from the Fettercairn distillery, property of WHYTE & MACKAY (AMERICAN BRANDS).

A light, well-balanced malt, whose unique aroma has reminded many a tester of wet soil.

Original bottling: 10 years old, 80 and 86 proof.

Cadenhead: 13 years old (distilled 1980), 92 proof.

Signatory: 14 years old (distilled 1980), 86 proof.

Fettercairn was opened in 1824 and has been owned by Whyte & Mackay since the 1980s. The distillery has 4 stills, draws its water from the nearby Cairngorm mountains, and ages in bourbon and sherry barrels.

(Tel. 1561 34 02 44)

OLD FITZGERALD

Kentucky straight bourbon from the STITZEL-WELLER distillery of UD.

A very cultivated whiskey, masculine and luxurious. Currently there are 3 versions: Old Fitzgerald Prime Bourbon, 80 and 86 proof; Old Fitzgerald's 1849, 8 years old, 90 proof; Very Special Old Fitzgerald, 12 years old, 90 proof.

This bourbon had its genteel image from the beginning, for John E. Fitzgerald, who started a distillery in Frankfort, Kentucky, in 1870, originally supplied only private clubs and the major shipping lines whose sternwheeler plied the Mississippi and Ohio rivers. The brand became available to the broader public only in 1889 and also became a success in Europe beginning in 1904. The Fitzgerald distillery was the first to regularly use wheat instead of rye, and it is one of the last to distill its whiskey in POT STILLS (as one sees from the label).

Since the end of Prohibition, Old Fitzgerald has been produced in the Stitzel-Weller distillery, always with wheat instead of rye. (See also OLD RIP VAN WINKLE.)

OLD FORESTER

Kentucky straight bourbon from the EARLY TIMES DISTILLERY, property of BROWN-FORMAN.

A grand old name in Kentucky and still an outstanding whisky (they use the Scottish spelling) of the old school; very popular in Louisville and highly praised by Raymond Chandler, but virtually impossible to buy in Europe.

Old Forester is available at both 86 proof and 100 proof (bottled in bond). Both are distinguished by a relatively high percentage of rye (18 percent). Old Forester is therefore somewhat tart compared to the new-fangled bourbons with less rye, whose excessive corn makes them too smooth for many palates.

Introduced in 1874, Old Forester is the oldest brand from the house of

Brown-Forman and the first bourbon ever to be sold as an original bottling (that is, by its producer). At a time when there were no regulations against diluting a whiskey with all sorts of things, that was a real guarantee of quality.

OLD FOX
Blended Scotch from Donald Hart & Co. (see HART's).

OLD GLASGOW
Blended Scotch from Donald Hart & Co. (see HART's).

OLD GLOMORE
Blended Scotch from James Williams Ltd., a small firm in Wales that has been producing and bottling its own brand since 1830, but only for the regional market in Pembrokeshire.

OLD GRAND-DAD
Kentucky straight bourbon of the old style, strong and spicy. The great Fats Waller wrote a song about this whiskey, with the lines: "Who's the one that I adore, though he beats me to the floor—Old Grand-Dad."

The standard version is 86 proof, as is the Special Reserve. In addition there is a BOTTLED IN BOND at 100 proof and the powerful 114 Barrel Proof at 114 proof.

The old grandfather after whom this whiskey was named was Basil Hayden, who distilled whiskey in Marion County, Kentucky, back in the 18th century. In 1882, his descen-

dants built the R. B. Hayden & Co. Distillery, which produced the first bourbon under the name Old Grand-Dad.

Today the brand is produced by JIM BEAM, according to a formula that, like the yeast culture, is said to date from before Prohibition.

The recipe includes a relatively high percentage of rye and is similar to the one used in producing the brand BASIL HAYDEN's.

OLD HIGHLAND BLEND
Blended Scotch from ELDRIDGE, POPE & Co., one of the largest breweries in Dorset (founded in 1833). The brand has been on the market since 1908, and the malts (in generous quanti-

ties) from which it is blended are listed on the label: GLEN GRANT, THE GLENROTHES, GLENFARCLAS, GLENFIDDICH (see also CHAIRMAN'S).

OLD INVERNESS
Blended Scotch from J. G. THOMSON, a subsidiary of the British brewing concern Bass Charrington. This brand has been sold since 1961, mainly in Scotland.

OLD KEG
Blended Scotch from Donald Hart & Co. (see HART'S).

OLD KENTUCKY RIFLE
Kentucky straight bourbon, 80 proof.

This whiskey is distilled by HEAVEN HILL DISTILLERS and is then shipped by the tankful to Bremen, where the firm Eggers & Frank bottles it for the German market.

OLD MATURED
Blended Scotch from D. Crawford & Sons, a subsidiary of UD.

Old Matured is very popular in Greece and is one of the rising Scotch brands.

OLD MONTROSE
Blended Scotch, de luxe and vatted malt from MONTROSE WHISKY, chiefly for export.

OLDMOOR
Blended Scotch from William GRANT & SONS.

OLD MULL
Blended Scotch from WHYTE & MACKAY (AMERICAN BRANDS).

This brand was introduced by John Hopkins (see GLEN GARRY) in 1880. When Hopkins's later owner, UD, took over the firm Arthur Bell & Sons (see BELL'S) in 1985, it was forced to give up a number of brands to satisfy anti-monopoly laws. One of these was Old Mull, which has since been owned by Whyte & Mackay. It is probable that OBAN is one of the base malts.

OLD ORKNEY
Blended Scotch, premium, 8 years old, 80 proof, from GORDON & MACPHAIL. The Scots often refer to this whisky as Double O.

OLD OVERHOLT
Straight rye whiskey, 86 proof, from JIM BEAM BRANDS (AMERICAN BRANDS).

The smoothest of the few ryes still being distilled: tart, spicy, and very drinkable.

The farmer Abraham Overholt first started distilling whiskey in Pennsylvania, home of the most famous ryes of the 19th century, in 1810. Old Overholt is now produced in one of the Beam distilleries in Kentucky. The grain mixture includes 59 percent rye.

With luck one can still find Old Overholt 1810, a bottling at 93 proof distilled in Pennsylvania.

OLD PARR

Blended Scotch, de luxe, from MacDONALD GREENLEES LTD. (UD).

A very satisfying blend and one of the best-selling de luxe Scotches.

Old Parr was created in 1871, and after enjoying initial success in London was degraded into an export brand. Today it is especially successful in Japan. In addition to the regular 12-year-old, there are Old Parr Superior, Old Parr 500, Old Parr Tribute (in a decanter), and Old Parr Elizabethan.

One of the base malts is CRAGGANMORE.

OLD POTRERO

Single-malt rye whiskey from the Anchor Distillery, San Francisco.

A true rarity: the only rye made from 100 percent rye (51 to 65 percent is common), and the only one made entirely from malted rye. Old Potrero is double pot-still distilled and, of course, very hard to find. The first 1,448 bottles came out in 1996 as 1-year-old cask-strength whiskey (124 proof) and were available only in selected restaurants in California, Maryland, and Washington, D.C.

The whiskey is made by Fritz Maytag, the legendary microbrewer of Anchor Steam Beer, member of the cheese-making family (Maytag Blue), and successful vintner. As a passionate rye drinker, he tried to reproduce the old quality of this once-famous drink, experimenting with traditional methods of American whiskey production. Hence Maytag uses only malted rye, small copper pot stills, and no chill-filtering, and bottles his whiskey at a very young age.

Old Potrero is the name of the hill in San Francisco where the distillery and the famous Anchor Brewery are located.

OLD PULTENEY

Scottish single malt (Northern Highlands) from INVER HOUSE DISTILLERS.

A fresh, slightly salty aperitif whisky—the common nickname "Manzanilla of the North" is therefore fully justified.

PRODUCT OF SCOTLAND

70cl · 40 % vol

OLD PULTENEY
The Northernmost Distillery on the Mainland

aged **8** years

Rare SINGLE *Highland* MALT
SCOTCH WHISKY

Gordon & MacPhail: 8 and 15 years old, 80 proof; vintage 1961, 80 proof.

The distillery stands on the northernmost point of Scotland and was founded in 1826. For a time it belonged to the DEWAR firm, then in 1955 it passed to HIRAM WALKER & SONS, and with that concern later to ALLIED DISTILLERS, who had it run by James & George STODART. The greater part of this malt went into the BALLANTINE blends and was therefore never officially bottled. That is now supposed to change, for Inver House, which bought the distillery in 1995, is said to be planning an original bottling.

Pulteney has 2 stills; the water comes from Loch of Hempriggs.

(Tel. 1955 60 23 71)

OLD RHOSDHU
Scottish single malt (Southern Highlands) from the LOCH LOMOND distillery, owned by GLEN CATRINE Bonded Warehouse Ltd.

A light, malty whisky for every occasion.

Original bottling: 5 years old, 8 proof.

Cadenhead: As Rhosdhu, 9 year old (distilled 1985), 121 proof; 1 years old (distilled 1985), 119 proof

Old Rhosdhu was formerly sold only as vatted malt, and it is only recently that it has been available as single—and that only rarely. It come from the same distillery as Inchmurrin but is somewhat stronger than tha malt. This is because the middle run of the second distillation is cut off at a different point than that of Inchmurrin (see MALT WHISKY; for information about the distillery, see INCHMURRIN)

OLD RHOSDHU

OLD RIP VAN WINKLE
Kentucky straight bourbon from th Stitzel-Weller distillery, operated b Van Winkle.

Old **RIP** **VAN WINKLE** **Handmade** **Bourbon**
Kentucky Straight Bourbon Whiskey

Asleep Many Years in the Wood

A highly cultivated whiskey with a great deal of character, which is bottled only in small quantities in the following versions: 10 years old, 90 proof; 12 years old, 90 proof; 15 years old, 107 proof; and a 20-year-old called PAPPY VAN WINKLE'S FAMILY RESERVE.

Julian "Pappy" Van Winkle (1874–1965) started out as a salesman for the Weller whiskey concern in 1893. He is considered one of the most prominent figures in the history of bourbon. He was clever enough to sell his whiskey to moonshiners, so that they could improve their own product, and to later take over the Weller business himself. A few years later he bought the John E. Fitzgerald distillery (see OLD FITZGERALD) as well. After Prohibition he merged with the Stitzel distilling family from Louisville, forming Stitzel-Weller.

This concern now belongs to UD, but in addition to that firm's brands it also still distills bourbon following the old Van Winkle family recipe. "Pappy's" grandson Julian Van Winkle III personally sees to it that only the best whiskeys find their way into his bottles. In one instance his bottlings are identical to the Stitzel-Weller brands: the 12-year-old Old Rip Van Winkle is another label for their Very Special Old Fitzgerald. (See also DAVID NICHOLSON, 1843.)

OLD ROYAL
Blended Scotch, 21-year-old de luxe, from BURN STEWART DISTILLERS.

OLD ST. ANDREWS
Blended Scotch from Old St. Andrews Ltd., Kent.

This brand was created for the export market in 1970; its packaging—a 2.25-liter bottle in a miniature leather golf bag, and imitation golf balls filled with whisky—helped to make it a tremendous success in golf-crazed Japan.

OLD SETTER
Kentucky straight bourbon from MAJESTIC.

OLD SMUGGLER
Blended Scotch from James & George STODART (ALLIED DISTILLERS, ALLIED DOMECQ).

An old brand that was especially prized in the United States during Prohibition—the name helped—and is even today one of the best-selling Scotches there.

OLD SPENCER
Blended Scotch from EAGLESOME (J. A. MITCHELL).

OLD TAYLOR
Kentucky straight bourbon from JIM BEAM Brands (AMERICAN BRANDS).

A mild bourbon, 6 years old, at 86 and 100 proof (bottled in bond).

Colonel Edmund H. Taylor, Jr. (1832–1922) is considered one of the pioneers of the American whiskey industry. He worked all his life to improve the quality of bourbon and was one of the main forces behind the BOTTLED IN BOND act, which made possible a kind of guarantee of quality for whiskey for the first time.

Originally a banker in Versailles, Kentucky, Taylor learned the art of distilling in the Old Oscar Pepper Distillery (see JAMES E. PEPPER) and produced his first Old Taylor in 1887.

Today the brand is produced in one of the Beam distilleries; Taylor's old distillery is now only a warehouse.

OLD THOMPSON
Blended American from BARTON DISTILLING (Canandaigua).

OLD WELLER See W. L. WELLER.

OLD WILLIAMSBURG NO. 20
Kentucky straight bourbon, 3 years old, 101 proof.

A medium-heavy everyday bourbon and perhaps the only kosher bourbon (see KOSHER WHISK(E)Y on the U.S. market.

It has been produced since 1994 by the Royal Wine Corporation in Williamsburg, Brooklyn.

100 PIPERS
Blended Scotch from the house of SEAGRAM.

On the market since 1965, the brand is now particularly successful in Spain, Latin America, and the Far East. The base malts are THE GLENLIVET, GLEN GRANT, and LONGMORN (See also BLACK WATCH.)

ÒRAN MÓR
Scottish whisky herb liqueur based on a 12-year-old malt, 80 proof, from the Famous Glen Malt Whisky Co., Edinburgh.

ORDER OF MERIT
Canadian blend from UD.

P · Q

What butter or whiskey'll not cure,
there's no cure for.

Irish proverb

PADDY

Blended Irish whiskey, standard, 80 proof, from the MIDLETON distillery of the IDG (PERNOD RICARD).

A light and simple whiskey that has long enjoyed great popularity in Ireland. The brand was originally marketed under the somewhat sterile name Cork Distilleries Co. Whiskey; then in the 1930s it was renamed after Paddy O'Flaherty, the most successful salesman of the firm, founded in 1867. He had become so beloved for his generosity that people had simply begun ordering "Paddy O'Flaherty's Whiskey." A nickname for Patrick, Paddy is often used as an affectionate name for any Irishman.

PALMER

A variant of the WHISKEY SOUR: Stir 1¾ oz. bourbon with ice and a dash of lemon juice and a dash of Angostura.

PAPPY VAN WINKLE'S FAMILY RESERVE

Kentucky straight bourbon, 20 years old, 90.4 proof, from the Stitzel-Weller distillery, property of UD.

A very convincing and rare ver-

sion of OLD RIP VAN WINKLE. Only a very few bourbons can survive such long aging, but this one does so brilliantly.

PARAMOUNT

Blended American from Paramount, a firm established in Cleveland, Ohio, in 1934. It also bottles gin, vodka, and rum under the same name.

PARKER'S

Blended Scotch from ANGUS DUNDEE.

PASSPORT

Blended Scotch from SEAGRAM.

This brand is virtually unknown in Scotland, but it is one of the 10 best-selling blended Scotches worldwide.

Passport is a LIGHT WHISKY that has been produced since 1968. The base malts are THE GLENLIVET, GLEN GRANT, LONGMORN, and CAPERDONICH. Its most important markets are southern Europe, Latin America, the United States, and Korea.

PATENT STILL

Also called a Coffey still or continuous still. A distilling apparatus used in the production of GRAIN and STRAIGHT WHISKEY.

As a rule, patent stills are made up of 2 tall, connected copper columns in which the grain mash is distilled through steam forced in the opposite direction. A series of partitions and vents inside the stills ensure that a very pure and high-percentage alcohol can be collected in a relatively short time (rectification). The process is called continuous distillation because the desired result is achieved in a single operation, as opposed to the 2 distillations required with a POT STILL.

Although patent stills are also used in the United States, the whiskey produced there cannot be compared to the almost neutral grain whisk(e)y of Scotland, Ireland, and Canada. In Kentucky and Tennessee they distill twice, and only the first distillation takes place in a continuous still. This consists of only a single copper column, and one can therefore say that the similarities between Scottish and American patent stills are more a matter of form than of content (for details, see BOURBON).

The patent still was invented in Scotland by Robert Stein about 1830 and developed further by Aeneas Coffey. It was this invention that first made it possible to produce blended Scotch whisky and thus led to the worldwide popularity that whisk(e)y enjoys today.

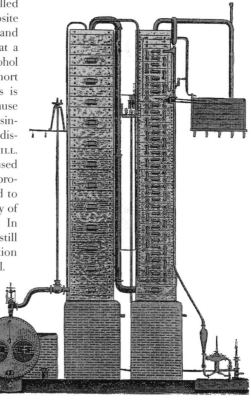

PAUL JONES
Blended American from HEAVEN HILL DISTILLERS.

PENNYPACKER
Kentucky straight bourbon from HEAVEN HILL DISTILLERS.

This whiskey is imported by the firm Borco, in Hamburg, and bottled in Germany.

PERNOD RICARD
As one of the largest spirit concerns in the world, the French *pastis* producer is naturally also involved in the whisk(e)y business.

Since acquiring the IDG in 1987, it controls virtually the entire Irish whiskey industry, and through its subsidiary AUSTIN NICHOLS DISTILLING COMPANY (since 1980) it is also represented on the American market.

The French concern's Scotch interests have been tended since 1974 by the subsidiary CAMPBELL DISTILLERS.

Malt: ABERLOUR, EDRADOUR, GLENALLACHIE.

Blends: CLAN CAMPBELL, GLENFORRES, HOUSE OF CAMPBELL, HOUSE OF LORDS, KING'S RANSOM, WHITE HEATHER.

Irish: BUSHMILLS, COLERAINE, CRESTED TEN, DUNPHYS, HEWITTS,

PERNOD

JAMESON, MIDLETON, PADDY, POWER'S GOLD LABEL, THREE STILLS.

American: KENTUCKY SPIRIT, NICHOLS, WILD TURKEY.

Canadian: ROYAL CANADIAN.

PETER DAWSON
Blended Scotch from the firm of the same name, which now belongs to UD.

P. Dawson began as a blender in Glasgow in 1882, owned several distilleries, including BALMENACH, and until 1982 was the licensee for GLEN ORD.

The brand was introduced at the end of the 19th century and was a bestseller in the 1920s. It is now mainly exported, primarily to Latin America.

PETER SCOT
Indian whiskey, premium, 85.6 proof, from KHODAY.

The label says "Malt Whisky" but then adds "Blended with the choicest whiskies," so that it is unclear what this really is. Judging from the taste, a certain amount of grain whiskey is added and there is no use of any kind of peat.

Peter Scot is one of India's great brands. In 1993 some 1.2 million bottles were sold.

PHILADELPHIA
Blended American from HEAVEN HILL DISTILLERS.

PHILLIPS
The firm Phillips, founded in Minneapolis in 1933, markets a Kentucky

straight bourbon under this name, a blended American, a Canadian, and a blended Scotch (not to mention vodka, gin, rum, and tequila). The producer is not named. (See also CALGARY TRAIL.)

PIG'S NOSE
Blended Scotch, 5 years old, from INVERGORDON DISTILLERS (WHYTE & MACKAY, AMERICAN BRANDS).

This is not bad stuff, even though the somewhat silly name would lead you to expect the worst. The label explains it by saying that the whisky is as soft as a pig's snout.

From its modest beginnings as a special bottling for a bar in Oldbury, near Bristol, Pig's Nose is now sold even in exclusive department stores like Fortnum & Mason. Since Invergordon acquired the brand it has also been exported (see SHEEP DIP).

PIKESVILLE SUPREME
Straight rye whiskey, 80 proof, from HEAVEN HILL DISTILLERS.

A rather light whiskey and at one time supposedly a great name.

The original home of this rye was Maryland, and that state is still its major market to this day, although it is now produced in Kentucky. The grain mixture is made up of 65 percent rye, 23 percent corn, and 12 percent barley malt.

PINCH
The name used in the United States for DIMPLE.

PINWINNIE ROYAL
Blended Scotch, 12 years old, de luxe, from INVER HOUSE DISTILLERS.

PIPE MAJOR
Blended Scotch, 5, 12, and 21 years old, from MONTROSE WHISKY.

PIPER'S CLAN
Blended Scotch from ANGUS DUNDEE.

PIRATEN WHISKY
German malt, 8 years old (distilled 1986), 80 proof, from Robert Fleischmann.

The Franconian brandy distiller Fleischmann, from Eggolsheim-Neuses, has been offering its own malt since 1995. The label says "Pur Malt," which suggests—even without the "e" on "pure"—some kind of vatted malt.

In any case, Piraten (Pirate's) Whisky is as yet the only German malt, and it is in fact perfectly drinkable.

PITTYVAICH
Scottish single malt (Speyside, Dufftown) from Arthur Bell & Sons (see BELL'S)/(UD).

A delicate, medium-heavy malt, smooth and round.

Original bottling: 12 years old, 86 proof ("Flora & Fauna" series).

Cadenhead: 16 years old (distilled 1977), 120 proof.

James MacArthur: 12 years old, 108 proof.

Pittyvaich was built in 1975 as an auxiliary distillery for Dufftown. It has been closed since 1995. It has 4 stills and draws its water from Jock's Well.

(Tel. 1340 82 05 61)

PLATTE VALLEY
Straight corn whiskey from McCORMICK.

P.M.
Blended American from JIM BEAM Brands (AMERICAN BRANDS).

In the 19th century there was a Scotch brand by this name from Wm SANDERSON & SON, as well as a morning version: A.M.

POIT DHUBH
[Gaelic for "black pot," or illegal still]

Scottish vatted malt from PRABAN NA LINNE, Isle of Skye, which is sold as Black Label at 80 proof and Green Label at 92 proof (both 12 years old), and as a 21-year-old (92 proof). The base malt is TALISKER.

Poit Dhubh was introduced in 1982. The brand enjoys a certain popularity in France, Canada, and Switzerland, in addition to the Western Hebrides.

POITÍN
[also poteen, or potcheen, Gaelic for "moonshine whisk(e)y"]

The risky and often bloody history of illegal distilling in defiance of the tax on spirits begins in Scotland in 1644 and in Ireland in 1760. For landless small farmers, distilling leftover grain was often the only way to raise the cash with which to pay the lease. The imposition of the tax forced many of them to choose between starving or breaking the law. Since illegal distilling was always considered an act of resistance against the English, in rural areas of Ireland and Scotland the government's tax collectors were bound to encounter hostility. For a time, the Scottish national poet Robert Burns and Aeneas Coffey, one of the inventors of the PATENT STILL, were among these hated excise officers. Even after a reduction of the tax in 1823 made it possible for many distillers to start operating legally, MOONSHINE continued to be produced in greater quantity than legal, so-called Parliament, whiskey for many years.

It was only the great famine that visited Ireland in 1845 and the general land reform in favor of the tenant farmers that forced poitín into the background. But illegal distilling was never fully stopped in either Ireland or Scotland, and even today there is more poitín in those countries than the many official bottlings would lead one to believe. It is not always made of barley, to be sure; it is just as likely to be produced from potatoes, corn, and sugar syrup.

In Ireland currently there is said to be a virtual moonshining renaissance, centered in the suburbs of the cities Dublin and Cork. From this it is only a step to the commercial production of poitín, as we see from the firm Bunratty Mead & Liqueur Co. and its BUNRATTY EXPORT POTCHEEN.

PORT DUNDAS

Scottish grain distillery in Glasgow, owned by UD.

The operation was opened as a malt distillery in 1827 and was one of the first to begin producing GRAIN WHISKY. Port Dundas is said to have once been bottled as a single.

PORT ELLEN

Scottish single malt (Islay) from UD.

A typical Islay malt, hearty and peaty, somewhat smoother than its famous neighbors—and unfortunately available in only limited supply.

Gordon & MacPhail: Vintages 1970, 1971, 1979, 1980, all 80 proof; 1977, 119.4 proof; 1978, 126.6 proof; 1980, 129.4 proof.

Cadenhead: The firm recently had a 12-year-old at 114.8 proof.

The distillery was established in 1825 and was taken over in 1836 by John Ramsay, a member of Parliament who did his part

for the whisky business. It was he, for example, who first exported whisky to the United States. In 1927 the distillery came by way of DEWAR to the DCL.

Although there has not been any distilling here since 1983, the large malt house is still in operation and supplies other Islay distilleries. Port Ellen has been of historical importance for the whisky industry in a number of ways. It was here in the 1820s that the first experiments with

continuous distillation were made (see PATENT STILL); also, the spirit safe, a device that helps the stillman to control the fresh distillate and is now installed in all of the world's distilleries, was first employed here.

Port Ellen had 4 stills and drew its water from the Leorin Lochs.

POT LID
Blended Scotch, standard, from BENNACHIE.

POT STILL
Distilling apparatus, the traditional alembic, which is used especially in the production of MALT WHISKY. Pot stills are onion-shaped copper vessels in which the grain mash is heated until the alcohol turns to steam and is again condensed by cooling. The first distillation produces a liquid containing roughly 28 percent alcohol, the so-called low wines. The second distillation is done in a smaller pot still and results in a distillate containing roughly 70 percent alcohol, so-called baby whisky. These are 2 separate processes, and one therefore speaks of this method as discontinuous distillation, in contrast to the continuous distillation accomplished in a PATENT STILL. As a rule, 2 pot stills are linked together, so that the second distillation follows directly upon the first. In Scotland it is rare to distill yet a third

time. The shapes and sizes of pot stills vary from one distillery to the next, and have much to do with the taste of the resulting product. The smaller and more compact the still, the stronger and oilier the distillate. (See also LOMOND STILL.)

When replacing their stills, many Scottish distilleries take particular care to see that the new apparatus is shaped exactly like the old, so that the style of their whisky will not be changed.

It is even said—jokingly, of course—that they go so far as to attack a new still with a hammer, putting dents in it to match those that its predecessor had suffered over the course of time.

POWER'S GOLD LABEL

Blended Irish whiskey, standard, 86 proof, from the MIDLETON distillery of IDG (PERNOD RICARD).

One of the great names in Irish whiskey, a complex blend with a great deal of character and Ireland's favorite brand. As Jim Murray put it, "a monster of a whiskey." It consists of roughly 70 percent pot still whiskey, the rest is grain; there is no malt at all.

In addition to the regular bottlings, there is a 34-year-old from 1956 at 146.4 proof. It was brought out in 1991 by Cadenhead under the name JOHN'S LANE.

The firm J. Power & Sons was founded in Dublin in 1791, and in the 19th century it became one of Ireland's major whiskey producers. It was known not only for quality but also for its clever marketing. It was one of the first to sell its whiskey in bottles, the advantages of which were twofold. First, it gave the firm control over the product that actually reached the hands of the consumer, whereas most whiskey was simply sold to dealers by the barrel. Second, the bottle with its label established a brand—in this case, the famous Gold Label with its 3 white swallows. (Because of these the whiskey was nicknamed "Three Swallows"—pun intended.) John Power & Son is also thought to have been the first firm to market its whiskey in a miniature bottle, the so-called Baby Power's.

Up into the 1950s the distillery in Dublin's John's Lane produced nothing but PURE POT STILL WHISKEY. Later it began adding continuously distilled whiskey to the blend. In 1966 the firm merged with the other surviving Irish producers to form IDG, and in 1976 the distillery was closed. Since that time Power's has been produced by the huge MIDLE-TON distillery, and since 1988 the IDG has been a part of the French spirit concern Pernod Ricard.

PRABAN NA LINNE

A firm founded on the Isle of Skye in 1976 by Ian Noble, who is dedicated to preserving Scotland's Gaelic heritage. This is evident from the names of his products—MAC NA MARA, POIT DHUBH, TÉ BHEAG NAN EILEAN. He has also established a college for the study of Gaelic.

PREMIER

Blended Scotch, 15-year-old premium, from MORRISON BOWMORE DISTILLERS (SUNTORY).

A refined Scotch found almost exclusively in the greater London area.

PREMIUM

The price category between STANDARD and DE LUXE. One now encounters "super premium" whiskies as well, which are priced even higher than de luxe bottlings. These price categories should not be assumed to reflect the quality of a given product.

PRESIDENT

Blended Scotch from UD.

PRESS CLUB

Blended American from KASSER LAIRD.

PRESTIGE D'ECOSSE

Blended Scotch, standard and 5-year-old premium, from Wm LUNDIE & Co.

PRIDE OF ISLAY
PRIDE OF ORKNEY
PRIDE OF STRATHSPEY
PRIDE OF THE LOWLANDS

Scottish vatted malts from GORDON & MACPHAIL.

To many Scotch lovers, this series of malts represents the ultimate in the art of vatting. They are based on a balanced blend of malts from the given region and are bottled at 12 years old and 80 proof. Pride of Strathspey is also available as a 25-year-old and in older vintages. It doubtless contains malts from the DALWHINNIE distillery, which was formerly called Strathspey.

PRINCE OF WALES
Welsh malt from THE WELSH WHISKY Co.

This whisky is something of a hybrid. It is a Scottish single malt (from the TOMATIN distillery), yet the 10-year-old bottling bears the designation "Single Vatted Malt Welsh Whisky." This makes sense only once you learn that the Scottish whisky, which is shipped in tanks to Brecon, Wales, is then filtered through a mixture of herbs and diluted with water to drinking strength (80 proof) before it is bottled. The firm Welsh Whisky has recently acquired its own distillery, but its first products will not be bottled until around the turn of the millennium.

In addition to the above-mentioned 10-year-old bottling, there are also the Prince of Wales at 12 years old and the 5-year-old called Airborne Forces, which was issued in 1994 on the occasion of the 50th anniversary of the Allied landing in Normandy.

PRIVATE STOCK
Kentucky straight bourbon from LAIRD & CO.

PROHIBITION
Alcohol was prohibited in the United States from 12:01 on the morning of January 17, 1920, to 5:32 in the afternoon of December 5, 1933. This was a hard time for thirsty Americans, who suddenly had to make do with black market products of doubtful origin and constantly risk being arrested or going blind.

This was also the time of speakeasies (in New York City alone there

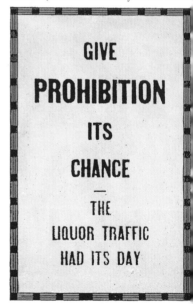

were more than 30,000 such establishments) and of organized crime: with black market spirits, unscrupulous petty gangsters like Al Capone were able to acquire huge fortunes and political influence in no time at all.

These 13 years changed the world of whisk(e)y in ways that are still felt today. Hardest hit, of course, were the Americans themselves. Only a very few distilleries managed to survive by producing medicinal alcohol; the vast majority were shut down, never to reopen.

The sudden drought in America was also one of the reasons for the decline of the Irish whiskey industry (see IRISH WHISKEY), which until that time had played a leading role worldwide. It never recovered from the loss of its most important foreign market.

By contrast, an enterprising few in Canada and Scotland managed to thrive. No law in the world could prevent HIRAM WALKER & SONS and SEAGRAM from coming to the aid of their needy brothers and sisters across the border and in the process conquering the world market. Even today more Canadian than domestic whisk(e)y is consumed in the United States (see CANADIAN WHISKY).

The popularity of Scotch in America goes back to the time of Prohibition as well. This is especially true of the Scottish LIGHT WHISKIES, which were created at that time specifically to satisfy American tastes accustomed to diluted spirits and fine Canadians (see CUTTY SARK, J & B). The stuff found its way into the country by way of the Caribbean. In the Bahamas alone, imports rose to the point that the natives would still be drinking them to this day if the whisky had not been smuggled into the country

States, this is twice the percentage of alcohol by volume; for example, 40 percent by volume is designated 80 proof. In Britain, needless to say, things are more complicated. There, to determine the amount of alcohol per volume it is necessary to multiply the given proof number by 4 and divide the result by 7: 70 proof equals 40 percent by volume.

Originally, alcohol content was determined by a simple but somewhat dangerous test: the fresh whisk(e)y was mixed with some gunpowder and set on fire. If the mixture burned with a steady flame the alcohol level was fine; if the level was too low, the flame guttered; if it was too high, it burned off your ears.

A similar method is still used in the United States to test illegally distilled whiskey (see MOONSHINE): pour some of it into a spoon and light

it was destined for (see also THE FAMOUS GROUSE, HOUSE OF LORDS, STODART).

Finally, Prohibition was the great era of cocktails and mixed drinks. Night clubs served ice and fruit juices, leaving it up to their patrons to add whatever liquor they brought in with them.

PROOF

The measure of ALCOHOL CONTENT. Although in most European countries the alcohol content is given as a percentage by volume, in English-speaking countries they still use the older designation "proof." In the United

; a steady, blue flame tells you that he whiskey is potable, a yellowish lame warns you to stay away from it.

PULTENEY See OLD PULTENEY.

PURE KENTUCKY

Kentucky straight bourbon from KENTUCKY BOURBON DISTILLERS.

PURE MALT

Japanese vatted malt, 86 proof, from NIKKA.

This brand is available in the versions Black, Red, and White. Whereas he first 2 are produced in Japanese distilleries, White consists exclusively of Scottish malts that are blended in Japan.

PURE POT STILL WHISKEY

The Irish designation for undiluted POT STILL whiskey; not to be confused with Scottish single MALT WHISKY, which is also produced by the pot still method but is made exclusively from malted barley.

Irish whiskey is distilled from malted and unmalted barley, a mixture that imparts a slight oiliness and gives Irish malt whiskey a pale appearance. Pure pot still was what established Irish whiskey's reputation, but today it is found only rarely (see GREEN SPOT, OLD COMBER, RED-BREAST).

To make things even more confusing, there is now a brand, THE TYRCONNELL, which calls itself pure pot still whiskey but is distilled solely from malted barley, making it a single malt of the Scottish stamp (see IRISH WHISKEY).

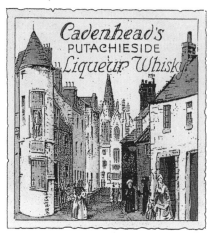

PUTACHIESIDE

Blended Scotch, de luxe, 12 and 25 years old, 86 proof, from Wm. CADENHEAD.

A gentle but full-bodied Scotch that has been on the market for more than a century. Putachieside contains no coloring agents and is now difficult to find, but a new bottling with a different label is planned for the near future. The whisky is named for a square that was formerly in the center of Aberdeen, Cadenhead's home town.

QUEEN ANNE

Blended Scotch from HILL, THOMSON & CO. (SEAGRAM).

Around the turn of the century this was one of the major brands, but now it has only a few dedicated admirers.

QUEEN ELEANOR
Blended Scotch from H. STENHAM LTD.

Like all Stenham Scotches, this one is available as a 3-, 5-, 8-, 10-, and 12-year-old and destined primarily for the Latin American and Southeast Asian markets.

QUEEN ELIZABETH
1) Blended Scotch from UD, STANDARD, for export.

2) De luxe blend from AVERY'S OF BRISTOL LTD.

In the United Kingdom it is no surprise that there should be 2 brands with such a name.

QUEEN MARY I
Blended Scotch from H. STENHAM LTD.

Like all Stenham Scotches, this one is available as a 3-, 5-, 8-, 10-, and 12-year-old and destined primarily for the Latin American and Southeast Asian markets. Queen Mary I is also available in various European supermarket chains.

QUEEN'S CHOICE
Blended Scotch from C. & J. MCDONALD (UD).

QUEEN'S SEAL
Blended Scotch from Peter J. RUSSELL.

Let me know what brand of whiskey Grant uses.
For if it makes fighting generals like Grant,
I should like to get some of it for distribution.

Abraham Lincoln

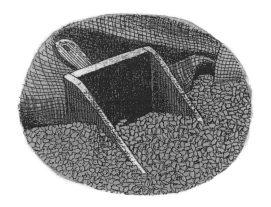

R

RACKE RAUCHZART

German blended whiskey, 80 proof, from A. Racke, Bingen.

One of the best-selling whisk(e)y brands in Germany.

The roughly 25 individual whiskies for this blend all come from Scotland now. Some years ago they stopped adding German corn spirits, but the blending is still done in Germany.

Racke Rauchzart was originally called Red Fox, but the name was changed in 1961 owing to protests from Scotland; the brand's success was unaffected by the change.

The Racke firm was founded in 1855 as a wine and vinegar house. It must be credited with having made whiskey popular in Germany (see GERMAN WHISKY). It also owns the successful brandies Dujardin and Scharlachberg and Pott rum.

RATTLESNAKE

A variant of the WHISKEY SOUR: mix in a shaker 1½ oz. bourbon, ¾ oz. lemon juice, 1 egg white, ½ oz. sugar syrup, 1 bar spoon powdered sugar, and a dash of anisette; shake vigorously and strain into a cocktail glass.

THE REAL MACKAY

Blended Scotch produced by LONG JOHN for the firm Mackay & Co.,

Guernsey. It is sold exclusively on the Channel Islands.

THE REAL MACKENZIE

Blended Scotch from Peter Mackenzie & Co., a subsidiary of UD.

The Mackenzies entered the distilling business in 1820, and at one time they owned the distilleries BLAIR ATHOL and DUFFTOWN. They were taken over by Arthur Bell & Sons (see BELL'S) in 1932. The chief markets for The Real Mackenzie are now Greece and South Africa.

REBEL YELL

Kentucky straight bourbon, 80 proof, from the STITZEL-WELLER distillery of UD.

A dry whiskey distilled with wheat instead of rye.

Rebel Yell was introduced to the market by W. L. Weller in 1936, and at that time its label read "Especially for the Deep South." For most of its life Rebel Yell has not, in fact, been sold north of the Mason-Dixon Line, and it soon acquired virtual cult status in the South. Since the distillery was taken over by the (British) United Distillers, it has been possible to buy this whiskey anywhere in the United States (and occasionally even in Europe), and it has lost its former stature in the South—at least in Kentucky.

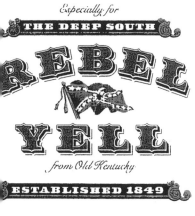

REDBREAST

Irish pure pot still whiskey, 12 years old, 80 proof, from the MIDLETON distillery of the IDG (PERNOD RICARD).

A devilishly good, perfectly balanced whiskey that has only recently come on the market again. Redbreast was first introduced in 1939; it was then produced in the JAMESON Dublin distillery and bottled by GILBEY. Even then it enjoyed an excellent reputation and was also known as "The Priest's

Bottle," an indication that Ireland's clergy are blessed with discerning palates. The distillery was closed in 1971, and the last Gilbey bottlings were distributed in 1985; they are considered to be past their prime.

Today Redbreast is marketed by Fitzgerald & Co.—remarkably poorly, one might add, for it is a shame that a whiskey of this quality is so little known.

RED DEVIL

Flavored blended Scotch from UD.

A new product, and a real waste: 8-year-old BELL'S flavored with herbs, spices, and chilis.

RED HACKLE

Blended Scotch from ROBERTSON & BAXTER.

This brand was originally produced by the Mssrs. Hepburn & Ross, who had served in a regiment whose hats were adorned with a cluster of red feathers, or hackle. It is therefore a very British label, as British as the Hepburn & Ross advertising slogan: "A handshake in every glass."

The firm has been a part of Robertson & Baxter since 1959.

RED KNIGHT

Indian blend, 85.6 proof, from KHODAY.

RED LION BLENDING

A London blending and trading firm that does most of its business as a brokerage and wholesaling operation. It also produces several of its own brands: CUSTODIAN, GLENCOE, GOLD LABEL, and HIGHLAND STAG (see also DINER'S).

RED ROOSTER

Blended Scotch from Peter J. RUSSELL.

RED ROSE

British blended whisky, de luxe, 80 proof, from Lancashire Whisky Producers.

This blend, available since 1991, is based on an almost forgotten tradition. At one time there was a thriving whisky industry in the county of Lancashire, south of the Scottish border. At the end of the 19th century there were 6 distilleries in Manchester alone, and in Liverpool as many as 9—among them the Bankhall Distillery, founded in 1710, which was at the time the largest distillery in the whole kingdom. The producers of Red Rose will tell you that the tradition of blending whisky is even older here than in Scotland. Production ceased at the beginning of World War I, and Lancashire whisky was forgotten until E. J. Hampson dug up the old histories. As brewmaster and head of the malt extract producers

Jeffreys Miller & Co. in Wigan, he first started selling small distilling equipment for home use, then finally got into the business of producing whisky himself. Just where he gets his whiskies is unclear, but it is virtually certain that they are produced in Lancashire. Hampson also stresses the quality of the local water, which he claims is especially pure and peaty.

In addition, much is made of the fact that Red Rose is not an English whisky but a Lancashire one—the rivalry between the 2 regions is at least as old as the red rose on the Lancashire coat of arms, after which both this whisky and the Wars of the Roses were named.

For all of its evocation of tradition, the operation is essentially only a hobby, and the output of Red Rose is extremely small: the best place to find it is at MILROY's in London.

RELIANCE
Blended Scotch from Forbes, Farquarson & Co., a subsidiary of UD.

The chief market for this brand is South Africa.

RIP VAN WINKLE See OLD RIP VAN WINKLE.

RITTENHOUSE RYE
Straight rye whiskey from HEAVEN HILL DISTILLERS.

When rye whiskey still amounted to something in the United States, this was one of the best-known brands.

R. J. HODGES
Kentucky straight bourbon and blended American from BLACK PRINCE.

ROBBIE BURNS
Blended Scotch from R. H. THOMSON & Co. (UD).

This whisky bears the name of Robert Burns (1759–96), who was, along with Walter Scott, one of the greatest Scottish writers and one of the precursors of English Romanticism. Burns praised the national drink of his homeland as a symbol of Scottish resistance to the English ("Freedom and whisky gang thegither"). He also wrote under the pseudonym JOHN BARLEYCORN and thereby created another name for whisky. (See also BOBBIE BURNS, IMMORTAL MEMORY.)

ROBERT BROWN
Japanese blend, standard, from KIRIN-SEAGRAM.

A dry and rather smoky blend of domestic and Scottish whiskies.

ROBERTSON & BAXTER
Scottish producer founded in Glasgow in 1855 and owned by the Robertson family.

Except for a brief period (1922–37) when it was under the control of the DCL, the business has always been independent. Takeover attempts by SEAGRAM and HIRAM WALKER & SONS were rebuffed in 1947 and 1980, respectively, but nevertheless had a major influence on the Scottish whisky industry.

Robertson & Baxter is involved in the firm HIGHLAND DISTILLERIES CO. and in NORTH BRITISH, and since taking over Long Bros. in 1965 controls the distillery GLENGOYNE, whose malts have since that time served as the base for the Robertson & Baxter brands ABERFOYLE, GAIRLOCH, and RED HACKLE (see also CUTTY SARK, DEFENDER).

ROB ROY
1) Blended Scotch from MORRISON BOWMORE DISTILLERS (SUNTORY).

This whiskey is named for a Scottish freedom fighter from the early 18th century who also served as the title hero of a novel by Walter Scott, a Berlioz opera, and two Hollywood potboilers.

2) A MANHATTAN made with Scotch: in a mixing glass stir 1 oz. Scotch, ½ oz. dry vermouth, ½ oz. sweet vermouth, and a dash of Angostura with ice. Strain into a cocktail glass.

ROCK AND RYE
A U.S. citrus liqueur with a whiskey base. Even before the Civil War it was customary to sweeten rye whiskey with rock candy. In time people started adding citrus juice as well. Once extremely popular, this drink is still produced by a number of firms, among

them Arrow, an IDV subsidiary, HIRAM WALKER & SONS, and Leroux, which belongs to JIM BEAM Brands.

ROCK HILL FARMS

Kentucky straight bourbon from the LEESTOWN DISTILLING CO., owned by SAZERAC.

A new, rather sweet SINGLE-BARREL BOURBON at 100 proof.

RODERICK DHU

Blended Scotch from Wright & Greig, a subsidiary of UD.

This brand has been around since the turn of the century. Since 1900 the firm that produces it has been the owner of DALLAS DHU. That distillery has now been turned into a museum, where it is still possible to buy Roderick Dhu.

RODGER'S OLD SCOTS BRAND

Blended Scotch from Slater, Rodger & Co., a subsidiary of UD.

The firm Slater, Rodger & Co., founded in Glasgow in 1873, was extremely export-oriented from the beginning, and its worldwide marketing network proved useful to other firms as well. In 1898 it began working with John Walker & Sons (see JOHNNIE WALKER), which ultimately took it over in 1911. Now, of course, they both belong to UD, for which Slater, Rodger & Co. operated the Banff distillery until 1983. Of the 14 blended Scotch brands the firm once produced, Rodger's is the only one to survive.

The brand sells well in the Near East and in Paraguay, where it is marketed under the name Rodger's Special.

RORY O'MOORE

A MANHATTAN made with Irish whiskey: stir 1½ oz. Irish, ¾ oz. sweet vermouth, and a dash of orange bitters in a mixing glass with ice, then strain into a cocktail glass.

ROSEBANK

Scottish single malt (Lowlands, Falkirk) from UD.

The most elegant of the Lowland malts, dry, gentle, and well balanced.

Original bottling: 12 years old, 86 proof ("Flora & Fauna" series); the

popular 8-year-old from the former owner, Distillers Agency (see DCL), has probably all been sold, as well as the 12-year-old.

Gordon & MacPhail: Vintage 1983, 80 proof.

Signatory: Vintage 1969, 103.4 proof.

There was a Rosebank distillery in 1817, but it is uncertain whether the present-day distillery with the same name has anything to do with it. The modern one started operating in 1840 at the earliest, 1864 at the latest. It was acquired by the DCL in 1914, then later by UD; it has been closed since 1993.

Rosebank was one of the few malts that were distilled 3 times. The water came from the Carron Valley Reservoir.

(Tel. 1324 62 33 25)

ROUTE
Japanese blend from SANRAKU OCEAN.

ROWAN'S CREEK
Kentucky straight bourbon from KENTUCKY BOURBON DISTILLERS.

A 10-year-old SMALL-BATCH BOURBON at 101 proof.

THE ROYAL AND ANCIENT
Blended Scotch, 10-year-old DE LUXE, from COCKBURN & CAMPBELL.

ROYAL BRACKLA
Scottish SINGLE MALT (Northern Highlands) from BISSET's (UD).

"Dangerously drinkable" is what Michael Jackson calls this smooth, somewhat sweetish malt.

Original bottling: No age designation, 80 proof; 10 years old, 86 proof.

Gordon & MacPhail: Vintages 1970, 1972, 1974, all 80 proof.

Cadenhead, Signatory, and James MacArthur also sometimes have it.

The distillery is called Brackla and was founded in 1812. It is situated very near Macbeth's Cawdor Castle and has borne the royal imprimatur ever since William IV declared it his favorite whisky in 1835. The Bisset firm took it over in 1926, and to this day Brackla is used in its blends. Along with Bisset, the whisky passed

in 1943 to the DCL and then to UD. The distillery was closed between 1985 and 1991.

It uses 4 stills and draws its water from the Cawdor Burn.

(Tel. 1667 40 42 80)

ROYAL CANADIAN

Canadian blend from Austin Nichols Distilling Company (Pernod Ricard).

One of the many brands produced in Canada but bottled and sold only in the United States.

As in most such cases, the name of the distillery is not disclosed.

ROYAL CITATION

Blended Scotch from the Chivas & Glenlivet Group (Seagram).

ROYAL COMMAND

Canadian blend from the Valleyfield distillery of UD.

ROYAL CULROSS

Scottish vatted malt, 8 years old, from A. Gillies, a firm that formerly belonged to Gibson International.

Gibson went bankrupt in 1994, and its assets, including the brand Royal Culross, were acquired by Glen Catrine, which is not currently producing it.

ROYAL FINDHORN

Blended Scotch, 5 years old, 80 proof, from Gordon & MacPhail.

ROYAL GAME

Blended Scotch from Winerite Ltd., Leeds, a wholesale and retail chain founded in 1973.

ROYAL HERITAGE

Blended Scotch, 21-year-old de luxe, from Wm Lundie & Co.

ROYAL HOUSEHOLD

Blended Scotch, premium, from James Buchanan & Co. (UD).

Aside from Japan, the only place you can find this brand today is in the little Rodel Hotel on the Isle of Harris, in the Outer Hebrides. In the 1920s, the owner of the hotel, Jock McCallum, had his own small blended Scotch

brand. Encouraged by James Buchanan, he entered his whisky in a competition to decide who would be the exclusive producer for the royal household in future. McCallum's whisky was declared the winner, and McCallum himself was granted permission to serve his blend, now called Royal Household, in his own hotel. The whisky has not been drunk at court for a long time, but McCallum's descendants continue to exercise their old rights.

ROYAL IRISH

Blended Irish whiskey from the distillery of the same name in Belfast. The distillery has long been closed, and the name is included here only because the Scottish firm of CADENHEAD bottled the sole remaining bar-rel of this whiskey (at 39 years old, 123.2 proof) in 1991, on the occasion of its 150th-year jubilee. The brand was formerly known under the name Dunville's and enjoyed a certain popularity—not only because of its acknowledged quality, but also because of the football club that was recruited from among the distillery workers. In 1963, the Distillery Football Club made it as far as the UEFA Cup finals.

ROYAL LOCHNAGAR

Scottish single malt (Eastern Highlands) from John Begg (UD).

A malty, uncomplicated whisky with a fine body.

Original bottling: 12 years old, 80 proof; Selected Reserve, without age designation, 86 proof (a luxury edi-

tion available mainly in duty-free shops).

The distillery was established in 1845 by John Begg, an uncommonly enterprising man who some years later sold the adjacent property to Queen Victoria. No sooner had the monarch arrived for her first visit than Begg invited her to come look at the distillery—warning her that she should come the following afternoon before 6, the end of the workday, or there would be nothing to see. The queen was not deterred by this discourteous pronouncement and was obviously impressed by the sample given her, for Begg was granted the right to add the highly marketable "Royal" to the firm's name. It is also reported that the Queen subsequently added zest to her tea and even to her Bordeaux in the form of a splash of Lochnagar.

Begg had another triumph with his blend JOHN BEGG BLUE CAP, based then as now on Royal Lochnagar. In 1916 the firm became part of the DCL, and it now belongs to UD.

The distillery has 2 stills and the water comes from the mountain Lochnagar.

(Tel. 1339 74 22 73)

ROYAL LORD CANADIAN RYE
Canadian blend from Brodie Crawford & Co. (see BRODIE'S SUPREME).

ROYAL MAJESTIC
Canadian blend from MAJESTIC.

ROYAL RESERVE
Canadian blend from CORBY, a subsidiary of HIRAM WALKER & SONS (ALLIED DOMECQ).

ROYAL SALUTE
Blended Scotch from the CHIVAS & GLENLIVET GROUP (SEAGRAM).

A 21-year-old de luxe blend aimed at the prestige market (note the ceramic decanter in a velvet pouch), introduced in 1953 for the coronation of the English queen. Its name and age refer to the 21-gun salute fired from the ships of the royal fleet.

Base malts: STRATHISLA, THE GLENLIVET, LONGMORN, and GLEN GRANT.

ROYAL SECRET
Indian blend from Polychem (see MEN'S CLUB).

RUSSELL, PETER J.
An influential family business founded in Edinburgh in 1936, one of the largest independent whisky firms and

one oriented especially toward export. Russell does the bottling for the firms CORNEY & BARROW and SAINSBURY'S, and produces the following blends: BLACK ROOSTER, BLACK SHIELD, CHIEFTAIN'S CHOICE, COCKBURN & MURRAY, KING ROBERT II, MacLEOD'S ISLE OF SKYE, MASON'S, QUEEN'S SEAL, RED ROOSTER, THE SEVEN STILLS.

RUSTY NAIL
A digestif cocktail: stir 1½ oz. Scotch and ¾ oz. Drambuie with ice cubes in a tumbler.

RYE BASE
Japanese blend with a rye component from NIKKA.

RYE WHISKEY
American whiskey variety. Now almost completely forgotten, rye was for a long time the New World's most popular whiskey. As early as the 18th century it was distilled primarily by Scottish and Irish immigrants in Pennsylvania and Maryland. In the 19th century it was felt that a particularly successful example of the type was Monongahela Whiskey, named after the valley in Pennsylvania in which it was produced. In terms of production, rye is distinguished from BOURBON solely in its raw material: more than 51 percent of the grain mixture must be rye. This gives it a particular zest and makes it seem dry, almost bitter. It was perhaps this intense flavor that cost rye its popularity once Prohibition was repealed. The ban on alcohol in the United States led to the closing of almost all the country's distilleries, and the illegally imported Canadian and Scotch whiskies changed the nation's tastes.

Rye enjoyed a small renaissance in the early 1980s thanks to the rye version of Jim Beam, but it still commands only a very marginal share of the market.

Brands: JIM BEAM RYE, OLD OVERHOLT, OLD POTRERO, PIKESVILLE SUPREME, RITTENHOUSE RYE, WILD TURKEY Rye (see also A. H. HIRSCH RESERVE).

There is no such thing as bad whiskey.
Some whiskeys just happen to be better than others.

William Faulkner

SAINSBURY'S

The British supermarket chain Sainsbury has sold its own whisk(e)y label, produced by Peter J. RUSSELL, for more than 30 years. Included in the program are 3- and 5-year-old blends, a vatted ISLAY malt, and a 12-year-old SPEYSIDE malt.

Recently Sainsbury added a malt that is simply a relabeled TYRCONNELL, from COOLEY.

SAINT BRENDAN'S SUPERIOR

Irish whiskey cream liqueur, 34 proof, introduced in 1983 by Golden Vale Group, a Dublin grocery concern. The whiskey purportedly comes from the BUSHMILLS distillery, and the brand's major market is the United States.

ST. JAMES'S

Blended Scotch, standard and 12-year-old de luxe, from BERRY BROS. & RUDD.

ST. LEGER LIGHT DRY

Blended Scotch from HILL, THOMSON & CO. (SEAGRAM), chiefly for the Canadian market.

ST. MAGDALENE

Scottish single malt (Lowlands) from UD.

A smooth malt, relatively strong for a Lowland.

Original bottling: 23 years old, 116.2 proof ("Rare Malts Selection").

GORDON & MACPHAIL
100 years of quality and excellence

CENTENARY RESERVE

SINGLE MALT SCOTCH WHISKY
1895·1995
PRODUCT OF SCOTLAND

Gordon & MacPhail: Vintages 1965, 1966, 80 proof; 15 years old (distilled 1980), 80 proof ("Centenary Reserve").

Cadenhead: The firm recently had a 10-year-old from 1982 at 124.6 proof, as well as older bottlings under the place name Linlithgow.

The distillery was established in about 1800, and in 1941 it passed to the DCL. It was closed in 1983 and converted into apartments.

SANDERSON, WM & SON

William Sanderson (1839–1908), who owned his own firm in Leith from 1863 on, was one of the great pioneers in the blending business. Among the 100 blends he produced himself (in addition to diverse liqueurs) were not only such curiosities as A.M. and P.M. (whiskies appropriate for morning or afternoon consumption), but also the famous VAT 69—a best-seller ever since its creation in 1882.

"at 69, please!"

Sanderson was one of the first to sell his blends in bottles. He was also one of the co-founders of North British and for a time the owner of the Glen Garioch distillery and the director of Royal Lochnagar. In 1937 Sanderson & Son was taken over by the DCL, and it now belongs to UD (see also The Antiquary).

SANDERSON'S GOLD

A new blended Scotch from Wm Sanderson & Son (UD), developed in 1991 especially for the West African market. Appropriately, given that tropical climate, it is rather light.

SANDY COLLINS

A collins made with Scotch.

SANDY MACDONALD

Blended Scotch from Macdonald Greenlees Ltd. (UD).

This brand has been around since the middle of the 19th century. Today it is sold mainly in Latin America.

SANDY MACNAB

Blended Scotch from Macnab Distilleries, a subsidiary of Allied Domecq.

This blend has a malt component of roughly 30 percent, the major part of which probably comes from Lochside, the distillery operated by Macnab.

SANRAKU OCEAN

Japanese producer. The firm began with the production of sake in 1937 and has been active in the whisky business only since the 1960s. Its distillery, Karuizawa, in the spa town of the same name east of Tokyo, imports its only-lightly-peated barley malt from Scotland and employs both new oak barrels and sherry casks. Sanraku has its own grain distillery and produces the following brands: Asama, Karuizawa, Ocean, Route, Status.

SAVOY

The legendary Savoy Hotel, in London, has had its own whisky (and gin) label since the 1930s. The Savoy blend is available not only in the hotel itself but also in other London establishments and in luxury lodgings and restaurants in France.

SAZERAC

U.S. spirit producer with headquarters in New Orleans. The firm was

SINCE 1850

SAZERAC

NEW ORLEANS

founded in 1850 and owns a whole series of whisk(e)y brands. The most important are doubtless those from the LEESTOWN DISTILLING COMPANY (which belongs to the Japanese concern TAKARA, SHUZO & OKURA). Sazerac's portfolio includes the following brands:

Bourbon: ANCIENT AGE, BENCHMARK, BLANTON'S, EAGLE RARE, ELMER T. LEE, HANCOCK'S RESERVE, KENTUCKY DALE, ROCK HILL FARMS.

Blends: ANCIENT AGE, BROOKSTONE, CANADIAN AGE, CARSTAIRS WHITE SEAL.

Canadians (imported): JAMES FOXE, MCCAULEY'S.

In addition the firm produces a pre-mix for the SAZERAC COCKTAIL.

SAZERAC COCKTAIL

A drink related to the OLD-FASHIONED, probably developed in New Orleans: crush a sugar cube soaked in Angostura (or Peychaud bitters), add 1½ oz. rye and ½ oz. Pernod, and top with water or soda. Originally, absinthe was used instead of Pernod, and cognac instead of whiskey—hence the cocktail's name: Sazerac-de-Forge was at one time one of the most popular cognac brands in New Orleans. It was imported by the owner of the Sazerac Coffee House there, in which this drink was supposedly first mixed around the middle of the 19th century (and which was almost certainly the parent firm of the SAZERAC concern). For a while the whiskey and cognac (or brandy) versions of the cocktail were both in vogue, and the whiskey one was then also called a Zazarac.

SCAPA

Scottish single malt (Orkney Islands) from Taylor and Ferguson, a subsidiary of ALLIED DISTILLERS (ALLIED DOMECQ).

A hearty whisky, salty and dry, with a wonderful balance of malt and peat.

Original bottling: 10 years old, 86 proof (Scapa has been marketed by the producer itself since 1995; previously it was available only from independent bottlers).

Gordon & MacPhail: 8 years old, 80 proof; vintages 1979, 1983, 1984, each 80 proof.

Cadenhead: Recently the firm had a 24-year-old from 1965 at 100.2 proof.

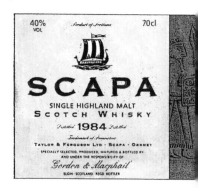

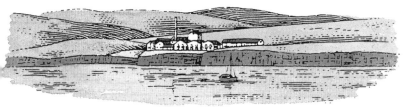

The distillery was established in 1885 and in 1954 it was acquired by HIRAM WALKER & SONS. Most of the time its whisky has been used almost exclusively in blends, such as AMBAS-SADOR. At the moment it appears that it will also be available regularly as a single—at least as long as supplies last, for the operation was closed down in 1993.

Scapa had 2 stills; its water came from the Lingro Burn and was so peaty that they didn't even dry their malt over peat; aging was done exclusively in bourbon barrels. (See LOMOND STILL.)

SCHENLEY

Canadian blend from UD.

Schenley whiskies are offered in 2 versions: as the 4-year-old Schenley Golden Wedding and as an 8- or, for export, 6-year-old Schenley OFC. The Schenley firm originally had its headquarters in the United States, where it began buying into the whiskey business even during Prohibition. In 1929 it acquired what is now known as the LEESTOWN DISTILLING COMPANY; then in 1937 it added the BERNHEIM DIS-TILLERY, with its attendant brands, as well as GEORGE DICKEL. In addition, beginning at this same time Schenley was the U.S. marketing firm for DEWAR'S whiskies. In the late 1940s the firm established a branch in Canada and brought its first Canadian whisky onto the market. In 1956 it bought the British firm Seager Evans and with it the brand LONG JOHN. In the following years various Scottish distilleries were bought by Schenley, among them LAPHROAIG and TORMORE, but in 1971 it divested itself of all its Scotch interests. In 1982 it also sold Leestown, so that when UD acquired the business in 1987 it consisted of only Bernheim, George Dickel, and Schenley Canada.

At that time Schenley Canada owned the distillery VALLEYFIELD and, in addition to Schenley, the brands GIBSON'S FINEST and ROYAL COMMAND.

Schenley
Golden
Wedding

Canadian Whisky Canadien

UNITED DISTILLERS CANADA INC.
HALIFAX, MONTRÉAL, TORONTO, WINNIPEG, EDMONTON,
VANCOUVER, CANADA

40% alc./vol. 750 mL

SCOTCH MALT WHISKY SOCIETY
An independent bottler and club founded in Edinburgh in 1983 by a group of malt whisky aficionados with the aim of preserving the traditional stature of Scotch whisky. To that end the society bottles select barrels of various malts unfiltered and at barrel strength. These are sold only to members and bear no brand names on the label. Instead, each whisky has a number, with the help of which one can learn who produced it and what its characteristics are in publications distributed to members. (See SINGLE-BARREL BOTTLINGS, INDEPENDENT BOTTLERS.)

SCOFF-LAW
A MANHATTAN variant made of Canadian, dry vermouth, lemon juice, a dash of grenadine, and a dash of orange bitters.

SCORESBY RARE
Blended Scotch produced by LONG JOHN and bottled in the United States by BARTON DISTILLING. The brand can be found all over the country.

SCOTCH ISLAND
Blended Scotch produced for the U.S. market by MAJESTIC.

Membership No. 16418

SCOTCH WHISKY

Legally, Scotch must be distilled in Scotland and aged a minimum of 3 years.

It is necessary to distinguish among malt, grain, and blended Scotch.

Malt whisky is distilled from barley malt in so-called pot stills. The result is a distillate distinguished by a more or less intense flavor of malt and smoke. Malt whisky cannot have anything added to it except water and yeast. It is aged in oak barrels, normally from 8 to 12 years, and is diluted with water to drinking strength before bottling. Malt is bottled either as a SINGLE MALT or a VATTED MALT: a single is a malt that comes from one specific distillery; a vatted is a blend of malts from various distilleries. The production of malt is time-consuming and expensive.

Grain whisky is distilled from unmalted grain, chiefly corn, that has a small amount of barley malt added. It is produced by continuous distillation in patent stills (also called Coffey stills) and is a pure, light, and almost flavorless spirit. Grain is also aged before bottling, but it is only rarely bottled as a single. It is used mainly in blended Scotch, a mixture of malt and grain whisky. Compared to malt, grain is inexpensive to produce, though it is of high quality and by no means a neutral spirit.

"FOR AULD LANG SYNE."

Blended Scotch whisky is a mixture of malt and grain. Blends are normally made up of from 15 to 50 individual whiskies, the greater number of them malts—although grains make up the majority in terms of volume. Since the latter are almost colorless, a little sugar coloring (caramel) is frequently added to achieve the typical whisky color. The art of blending consists of combining the characteristics of the individual components to achieve the desired flavor.

Although the malts are what determine the taste and character of the blend, the grains serve to reduce their intensity and unify them.

The success of Scotch whisky is largely owing to this moderating influence of the grain, which gives it a lighter body but, more importantly, makes it less expensive and therefore affordable by the masses. Roughly 95 percent of the Scotch consumed worldwide

DEWAR'S
THE WHISKY

is in the form of blended whisky. (For more on the production of Scotch see the headings BOTTLING, BLENDED SCOTCH WHISKY, BARREL, GRAIN WHISKY, MALT WHISKY, LIGHT WHISK(E)Y, PATENT STILL, POT STILL.)

History: Historically, malt is the oldest form of Scotch. The first mention of it dates from 1494, but one can assume that at that time whisky was already a common product in Scotland. In the beginning it was probably simply a by-product of agriculture, a way of using up excess grain. If it resulted in a stimulant, so much the better. The production of whisky began in the home and was in no way subject to universal regulations. The first distilleries were probably created in the 17th century. The oldest ones still in operation in Scotland were built in the 18th century.

The imposition of a tax on spirits contributed greatly to the history of Scotch. The first alcohol tax in 1644 forced many distillers to break the law, and turned whisky into POITÍN, which became, in the 18th and early 19th centuries especially, a symbol of Scottish resistance to English authority. In 1823 it became profitable to operate a distillery legally, and the number of registered operations increased exponentially.

The Industrial Revolution, and with it the modern history of whisky, began with the development of the patent still, beginning in 1830. This technique made it possible to produce light and inexpensive grain, which would hence-

BUMFOOZLE

forth be mixed with malt to make blended whisky. The first experiments in this direction were undertaken by Andrew Usher (see USHER'S GREEN STRIPE), William Sanderson (see WM SANDERSON & SON), and W. P. Lowrie (see LOWRIE'S) in the 1860s. It was as a blend that Scotch first became known outside its homeland, for south of the Lowlands the heavy malts were considered a drink for peasants. In London, civilized people drank brandy at that time—mostly cognac, preferably mixed with soda. It was not only the vine-louse plague, which devastated France's vineyards and thereby interrupted the steady supply of cognac, that allowed Scotch to find its way into better-class homes. It was even more the vision and energy of those producers who offered their blends not by the barrel, as was customary, but in labeled bottles. The notion of brand names was new at the time, and blended Scotch was one of the first products made popular in this way. The pioneers in the brand whisky business were BUCHANAN, DEWAR, HAIG, Mackie (see WHITE HORSE), and Walker (see JOHNNIE WALKER), who made fortunes in it in the late 19th century and conquered London society as whisky barons.

On the world market at that time, IRISH WHISKEY predominated, and this did not change until the 1920s. The great era for Scotch producers began with PROHIBITION in the United States. With the tacit approval (if not the full support) of the British government, they stepped forward as blockade breakers and smugglers and prepared the way for Scotch after the great drought (see CUTTY SARK, LIGHT WHISK(E)Y, STODART). By the time Prohibition was repealed, Scotch dominated the world market, and despite the decreased demand since the 1970s (in favor of clear spirits such as rum and vodka) it is still one of the best-selling spirits in the world.

SCOTIA ROYALE
Blended Scotch, 12-year-old de luxe, from A. Gillies, a firm that formerly belonged to Gibson International.

Gibson went bankrupt in 1994, and its assets, including the brand Scotia Royale, were acquired by GLEN CATRINE, which is not currently producing it. One of the base malts was GLEN SCOTIA.

SCOTS CLUB
Blended Scotch from INVERGORDON DISTILLERS (WHYTE & MACKAY, AMERICAN BRANDS).

SCOTS EARL
Blended Scotch from GLEN CATRINE Bonded Warehouse Ltd.

SCOTS GREY
Blended Scotch, premium, from INVERGORDON DISTILLERS (WHYTE & MACKAY, AMERICAN BRANDS).

HIGHLANDS

- 77 Aberfeldy
- 5 Balblair
- 70 Ben Nevis
- 74 Blair Athol
- 4 Clynelish
- 8 Dalmore
- 69 Dalwhinnie
- 81 Deanston
- 75 Edradour
- 71 Fettercairn
- 72 Glencadam
- 73 Glenesk
- 67 Glen Garioch
- 83 Glengoyne
- 6 Glenmorangie
- 26 Glen Ord
- 78 Glenturret
- 84 Loch Lomond
- 79 Lochside
- 78 Oban
- 3 Pulteney
- 25 Royal Brackla
- 68 Royal Lochnagar
- 66 Speyside
- 9 Teaninich
- 63 Tomatin
- 80 Tullibardine

INSELN

- 1 Highland Park
- 95 Isle of Jura
- 102 Lochranza
- 2 Scapa
- 7 Talisker
- 76 Tobermory

CAMPBELTOWN

- 103 Glen Scotia
- 104 Springbank

LOWLANDS

- 89 Auchentoshan
- 92 Glenkinchie
- 87 Inverleven
- 88 Littlemill

GRAIN

- 82 Cameron Bridge
- 86 Dumbarton
- 106 Girvan
- 10 Invergordon
- 91 North British
- 93 Port Dundas
- 94 Strathclyde

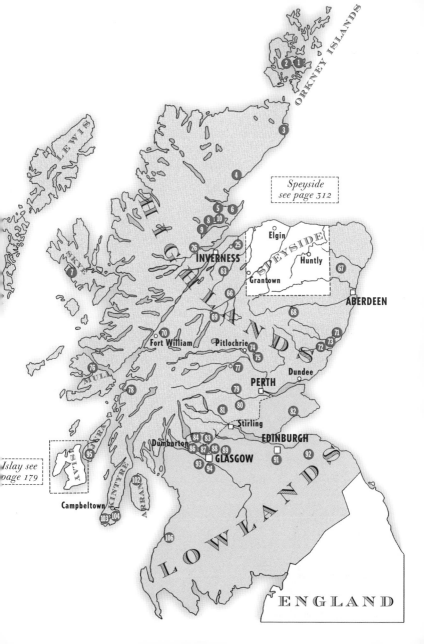

ORKNEY ISLANDS

LEWIS

SKYE

Speyside see page 312

Elgin

Huntly

Grantown

SPEYSIDE

INVERNESS

ABERDEEN

Fort William

Pitlochrie

Dundee

PERTH

Stirling

EDINBURGH

MULL

Dumbarton

GLASGOW

Islay see page 179

ISLAY

JURA

KINTYRE

ARRAN

Campbeltown

LOWLANDS

ENGLAND

HIGHLANDS

SCOTS LION
Blended Scotch from Donald Hart & Co. (see HART's).

SCOTS POET
Blended Scotch from INVERGORDON DISTILLERS (WHYTE & MACKAY, AMERICAN BRANDS).

SCOTTISH & NEWCASTLE BREWERIES
British brewing concern that once owned the distilleries GLENALLACHIE and ISLE OF JURA, as well as the blends MACKINLAY and CLUNY.

At the moment Scottish & Newcastle is represented on the whisky market only with the brand BENEAGLES.

THE SCOTTISH COLLIE
Blended Scotch from William GRANT & SONS.

SCOTTISH DANCE
Blended Scotch from H. STENHAM LTD.

Like all Stenham Scotches, available as a 3-, 5-, 8-, 10-, and 12-year old and produced primarily for the Latin American and Southeast Asian markets.

SCOTTISH ENVOY
Blended Scotch from MAYERSON & Co.

SCOTTISH ISLAND
Scottish malt whisky herb liqueur, 80 proof, from Melldalloch Liqueur Co., Argyll.

SCOTTISH LEADER
Blended Scotch from BURN STEWART DISTILLERS.

This supermarket whisky popular in Great Britain is available as a 12-, 15-, and 25-year-old blend; it is sold in 50 countries around the world, chiefly in Asia, and is Burn Stewart's best seller.

THE SCOTTISH NATIONAL TARTAN
Blended Scotch, 21 and 30 years old, 86 proof, from BENNACHIE.

A luxurious blend in luxurious packaging that came on the market in 1995 and is sold mainly in duty-free shops.

SCOTTISH QUEEN
Blended Scotch from UD.

SCOTTISH ROYAL
Blended Scotch from ANGUS DUNDEE

SEAGRAM

The Canadian Seagram Company, in Montreal, is one of the most important beverage concerns in the world. The spirit business is run by the subsidiary firm, The House of Seagram, whose Scotch interests are overseen by the CHIVAS & GLENLIVET GROUP.

Since it was established in 1928 (see CANADIAN WHISKY), Seagram has always had a sure sense of international market trends, and accordingly it owns such leading names as CHIVAS REGAL, SEAGRAM'S 7 CROWN, CROWN ROYAL, and THE GLENLIVET. Wherever a new market opened up, one could be sure that Seagram would soon be there. The firm is the only foreign producer to play a role in the whisky business in Japan (see KIRIN-SEAGRAM), and the same can be said of New Zealand (see WILSON'S) and, more recently, of the growing markets in China (see SEAGRAM'S 7 STAR) and Thailand (see MAS-

TER BLEND). It is only in India that the concern has as yet to gain a proper foothold (see also BLENDED AMERICAN WHISKEY).

Worldwide Seagram owns the following brands:

Malt: ALLT-Á-BHAINNE, BENRIACH, BRAES OF GLENLIVET, CAPERDONICH, CENTURY, GLEN GRANT, GLEN KEITH, THE GLENLIVET, LONGMORN, STRATHISLA, LAMMERLAW.

Blended Scotch: Chairman's Reserve, Chivas Regal, 100 Pipers, Passport, Royal Citation, Royal Salute, and the blends of the firm Hill, Thomson & Co.; Seagram buys the grain for its blends mainly from North British.

Liqueur: Lochan Ora.

American: Seagram's 7 Crown, Four Roses.

Canadian: Crown Royal, Seagram's Canadian Hunter, Seagram's V.O.

Japan: Crescent, Emblem, Robert Brown.

(See also Bushmills, Master Blend, Natu Nobilis, Valley 9 Gold, and Oddbins.)

THE HOUSE OF Seagram

In addition, Seagram's produces gin and vodka, owns the cognac brand Martell, among others, and the sherry house Sandeman, and is heavily engaged in the French wine and champagne business.

For years the concern has coveted the glitter of Hollywood. After its acquisition of MGM Studios in the late 1960s lost it billions, Seagram boss Edgar Bronfman, Jr., made a second attempt in 1995 with

the purchase of MCA, the parent company of Universal Studios and owner of a number of music and book publishers. Bronfman has tried his hand at songwriting and screenwriting himself.

SEAGRAM'S CANADIAN HUNTER
Canadian blend.

SEAGRAM'S 7 CROWN
Blended American; in the 1960s the best-selling spirit in the world and even now one of the top 50 brands worldwide.

SEAGRAM'S 7 STAR
Chinese whiskey from Shanghai Seagram, a joint venture of Seagram and Shanghai Distillers that has been in operation since 1988. It is impossible to discover whether the whiskey contains Scottish malts in addition to Chinese grain distillates.

SEAGRAM'S V.O.

Canadian blend; a popular everyday whisky worldwide. The brand has been on the market since 1912 and is made up of 6-year-old single whiskies.

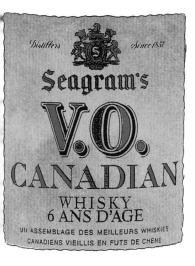

SENATOR'S CLUB

Blended American from LAIRD & Co.

SEVEN STAR

Blended American from LAIRD & Co.

THE SEVEN STILLS

Scottish vatted malt from Peter J. RUSSELL. This brand was formerly produced by the house of COCKBURN & MURRAY.

77

Blended Scotch from Douglas LAING & Co.

SHEEP DIP

Scottish vatted malt from INVERGORDON DISTILLERS (WHYTE & MACKAY, AMERICAN BRANDS).

This brand, a sister of PIG'S NOSE, has been available since 1974.

The odd name is supposed to recall the time when Scottish farmers hid their (homemade) whisky from the excise officers by putting it in barrels marked "sheep dip," an insecticide.

SHERMAN, DAVID

U.S. firm founded in 1958, with headquarters in St. Louis.

Sherman does not own any distilleries, but it does have a bottling plant and a number of brands, some very old, which it has produced by unidentified distilleries: BOURBON SUPREME, CANADIAN DELUXE, CANADIAN SPRINGS, COUNTY, DAVIESS COUNTY, EZRA BROOKS, GOVERNORS CLUB, TOWN CLUB, YELLOWSTONE.

SIGNATORY

Independent bottler founded in Edinburgh in 1988. In its first years Signatory had to content itself with whatever barrels were turned down by the old, established firms such as Wm CADENHEAD and GORDON & MACPHAIL. But it has since made a name for itself as a reliable bottler of

desirable, in some cases extremely rare, single barrels. Signatory has a second label, Dun Eideann.

SILK TASSEL See McGuinness.

SINGLE-BARREL BOTTLING
In the past few years, single-barrel bottlings have become especially popular with malt whisky lovers. Since every barrel produces a different whisky, the contents of various barrels are normally mixed so as to even out any differences. In single-barrel bottlings, however, the contents of each barrel are bottled separately, usually unfiltered and undiluted. This makes for a few hundred unique bottles, and it is altogether possible that 2 whiskies of the same brand from the same year can differ markedly from each other in color and taste—to say nothing of the differences that may show up among different years of a single brand. This not only increases their collectors' value, but also gives whisky lovers the sense that they are onto something exclusive, and to that end they will pass up even a superb ordinary bottling in favor of a malt that may be less than satisfactory.

In Scotland they don't normally bottle the best barrels as singles, as is the case with SINGLE-BARREL BOURBONS; they bottle the over-runs (see also BOTTLING, BUSH PILOT'S PRIVATE RESERVE, BARREL, INDEPENDENT BOTTLERS).

SINGLE-BARREL BOURBONS
Noting the increasing success of Scottish malt whiskies on the U.S. market, the

American whiskey industry has countered with similarly exclusive, showpiece bourbons. The LEESTOWN DISTILLING COMPANY was first off the mark with a brand called BLANTON'S, which was produced only in small quantities and bottled by hand from selected barrels. Particular emphasis was put on the fact that the whiskey was not required to reach some arbitrary age but was bottled when the stillman felt that the barrel had attained its optimum maturity. Each bottle is numbered and has the date of bottling on its label.

Blanton's was and continues to be a great success in the United States, and the same house has since brought out other single-barrel bourbons: BENCHMARK, ELMER T. LEE, HANCOCK'S RESERVE, ROCK HILL FARMS. Other producers were quick to follow this example. JIM BEAM introduced its BOOKER'S, and WILD TURKEY created the brands KENTUCKY LEGEND and KENTUCKY SPIRIT.

If the trend toward single-barrels continues, there is of course the danger that the regular bottlings will suffer, for when the best barrels are used for other purposes, the quality of the standard products is bound to decline.

In contrast to the single-barrel bottlings of malt whisky, most single-barrel bourbons are filtered and diluted to drinking strength (see also SMALL-BATCH BOURBON).

SINGLE MALT

A whisk(e)y type. A single malt is the product of a single distillery, as opposed to a VATTED MALT, which is composed of various singles (see also MALT WHISKY).

Today Scottish single malts are considered the finest whiskies in the world. This was by no means always the case, for up until the 1960s they were virtually unknown outside of Scotland and were used primarily as the base for BLENDED SCOTCH WHISKY.

The first brands to reach the international market as singles were GLENFIDDICH and GLEN GRANT.

THE SINGLETON OF AUCHROISK
Scottish single malt (Speyside, Mulben) from IDV/Grand Metropolitan.

A silky-smooth malt, tasting of the sherry cask, that was first bottled as a single in 1986. Because it was so elegant, it was then dismissed as a "designer whisky"—and there is some truth to the charge, for there is reason to believe that IDV created it especially as a malt counterpart to J & B for its yuppie clientele.

Original bottling: Singleton is bottled without age designation; the only date given is the year in which it was distilled. So far it has been issued in the vintages 1975, 1976, 1981, 1983, and 1985. As a rule they are from 10 to 12 years old and were bottled at 80 or 86 proof. A 10-year-old at 80 proof was also recently issued, and for the Japanese market there is a 12-year-old Singleton Particular.

Cadenhead: There was recently a 12-year-old from 1978, 117.4 proof, under the name Auchroisk.

The distillery Auchroisk was built in 1974, in the "Lego-block style," as the British author Gordon Brown observed. It has 8 stills and gets its water from Dorie's Well. Singleton is aged in bourbon barrels and then finished for 2 years in oloroso casks.

The J & B blends, of which this malt is one of the components, are also aged for a time in Auchroisk before bottling.

(Tel. 1542 86 03 33)

SIR MALCOLM
Blended Scotch produced for the U.S. market by SAZERAC.

SIR WALTER RALEIGH
Blended Scotch from Douglas LAING & Co.

SLAINTHEVA
Blended Scotch, 12 years old, from ALEXANDER DUNN & Co., on the market since 1959.

The customer's name is inscribed on the label at the time of purchase. In addition to the standard bottles there are the "kingnum" (1.75 liters) and a ½ oz. miniature that appears in the *Guinness Book of World Records* as the smallest whisky bottle in the world.

SMALL-BATCH BOURBON
A collective term for U.S. whiskeys that are produced in relatively small quantity. With this category the firm JIM BEAM Brands tried to horn in on the success of SINGLE-BARREL BOUR-

bons. Unlike those, small-batch bourbons are not from a single barrel but are rather a blend of especially successful ones.

Brands: BASIL HAYDEN'S, BAKER'S, KNOB CREEK (see also MAKER'S MARK).

SOMETHING SPECIAL

Blended Scotch, de luxe, 80 proof, from HILL, THOMSON & CO. (SEAGRAM).

A good, mainstream whisky that has been completely out of fashion for some time now.

SOUR MASH

Part of the fermentation process in the production of U.S. whiskey. In addition to the yeast added to the fresh mash, or grain mixture, to start fermentation, a certain amount of the leftovers from a previous distillation is mixed in as well. This so-called backset (also called "setback" or "stillage") helps to preserve the character of the whiskey, passing it on to the new batch, as it were. With its high acid content, it also serves to kill off undesired yeast bacteria, so that the fermentation process does not get out of control. (Bakers use the same principle when they work with sourdough.) The proportion of backset added to the yeast varies from one distillery to the next.

All STRAIGHT WHISKEYS are now produced by this method; in Tennessee it is even prescribed by law. Although it was not invented by James C. Crow (see OLD CROW), it was he who developed it into a predictable practice in the middle of the 19th century.

SOUTHERN COMFORT

U.S. liquor from St. Louis, Missouri, 80 proof, produced by BROWN-FORMAN.

Despite all the rumors, Southern Comfort has nothing in common with whiskey; it is made of a neutral spirit mixed with peach and citrus flavors and aged in oak barrels for roughly 9 months. This aging gives it a certain bourbonlike, vanilla flavor, and that is doubtless why many people suspect it has a whiskey base.

On the other hand, it is conceivable that whiskey was originally used as the base alcohol instead of neutral

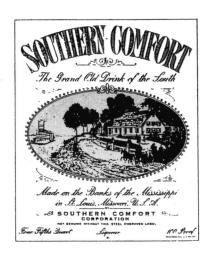

spirits. This would be in accord with the legend that Southern Comfort was first mixed by a bartender from New Orleans in around 1860 in an attempt to make a not-especially-successful whisky potable. The combination of peach flavor and whiskey is traditional in New Orleans, as we see from the SAZERAC COCKTAIL, which originated there (see also MINT JULEP).

In Germany, a Southern Comfort sour is a popular variant of the WHISKEY SOUR.

SPEAKERS
Blended Scotch from Donald Hart & Co. (see HART's).

SPECIAL
Japanese designation for whiskies with a malt component of at least 30 percent.

SPEYBURN
Scottish single malt (Speyside, Rothes) from INVER HOUSE DISTILLERS.

A sumptuous and very gentle malt.
Original bottling: 10 years old, 80 proof.

Gordon & MacPhail: Vintage 1971, 80 proof.

Cadenhead: 18 years old (distilled 1975), 92 proof; 19 years old (distilled 1975), 119.8 proof.

Speyburn was built in 1897 by John Hopkins (see GLEN GARRY), and was taken over by the DCL in 1916.

For a time the distillery was operated by John Robertson, and its malt

was mainly used in his YELLOW LABEL blend. UD, the DCL's successor firm, sold Speyside to its present owner in 1991. The distillery has 2 stills; the water comes from Granty Burn.

(Tel. 1340 83 12 13)

SPEY CAST
Blended Scotch, 12-year-old de luxe, 80 proof, from GORDON & MACPHAIL.

An old and celebrated brand named after a complicated fly-fishing technique.

SPEY ROYAL
Blended Scotch from IDV/Grand Metropolitan.

Spey Royal is strictly an export

brand, produced in Scotland but bottled in the market countries. The greater part of it goes to India; the rest to Brazil and Venezuela.

SPEYSIDE

1) Scottish whisky region. The Speyside lies in the Northeast Highlands and is considered the center of Scottish whisky production. There are more distilleries around the towns of Elgin, Rothes, Keith, and Dufftown than anywhere else in Scotland, among them such great names as GLENFARCLAS, GLENLIVET, MACALLAN, and many more.

Speyside malts are often described as elegant and complex, but in fact the whiskies produced here are so varied that there is really no uniformity to their styles.

2) Blended Scotch produced for the U.S. market by SAZERAC.

SPEYSIDE DISTILLERY

Scottish Highland malt distillery near Kingussie. It has been in operation since 1990 and belongs to the Speyside Distillery & Bonding Co., Glasgow, a firm founded in 1955 by the Christie family. At the beginning, the Christies only marketed whiskies, but later they began producing them themselves. DRUMGUISH, a malt from this distillery, appeared only recently on the market. In addition there is a Speyside Blend, labeled Rare, at 8, 12, 15, 17, and 21 years old (see also DEW OF THE WESTERN ISLES, GLENTROMIE, McGAVIN'S, MURDOCH'S PERFECTION).

SPRINGBANK

Scottish single malt (Campbeltown) from J. & A. MITCHELL.

If you are truly interested in malts you must get to know Springbank. After one tasting the London *Times* called it the *"premier grand cru classe"* of malts, and indeed it is astonishing what nobility and depth Springbank develops despite its rather light body. Connoisseurs rave about its charms even as far away as Japan, where it is the best-selling whisky of its type.

Original bottling: C.V. (without age designation), 10, 12, 15, 21, and 30 years old, all 92 proof; in addition there are a 12-year-old at 114 proof and occasional single-barrel bottlings with date—currently 1958, 1962, and 1967—each 92 proof.

SPEYSIDE DISTILLERIES

- (42) Aberlour
- (59) Allt-á-Bhainne
- (61) Ardmore
- (28) Auchroisk
- (30) Aultmore
- (52) Balvenie
- (19) Benriach
- (48) Benrinnes
- (22) Benromach
- (66) Braes of Glenlivet
- (34) Caperdonich
- (40) Cardhu
- (57) Cragganmore
- (39) Craigellachie
- (46) Dailuaine
- (23) Dallas Dhu
- (54) Dufftown
- (47) Glenallachie
- (17) Glenburgie
- (55) Glendronach
- (49) Glendullan
- (24) Glen Elgin
- (56) Glenfarclas
- (53) Glenfiddich
- (12) Glenglassaugh
- (35) Glen Grant

- (31) Glen Keith
- (64) Glenlivet
- (21) Glenlossie
- (14) Glen Moray
- (36) Glenrothes
- (37) Glen Spey
- (29) Glentauchers
- (45) Imperial
- (11) Inchgower
- (51) Kininvie
- (43) Knockando
- (27) Knockdhu
- (15) Linkwood
- (20) Longmorn
- (41) Macallan
- (13) Macduff
- (18) Mannochmore
- (16) Miltonduff
- (50) Mortlach
- (38) Speyburn
- (32) Strathisla
- (33) Strathmill
- (44) Tamdhu
- (65) Tamnavulin
- (58) Tomintoul
- (60) Tormore

Cadenhead: This firm also belongs to the Mitchell family and occasionally issues special bottlings of this malt. Recently there was a 9-year-old from 1985 at 122.4 proof, and in 1992 an 18-year-old from 1973 that had been aged in a rum cask. The latter is a pale green in color and has a most unusual taste. It is extremely drinkable and is of course a desirable collector's item.

Adelphi: 28 years old (distilled 1965), 107.6 and 109.4 proof; vintage 1964, 103 proof.

James MacArthur: 27 years old, 98.2 proof.

Signatory: 17 years old (distilled 1975), 111.6 proof.

Detail from page 301

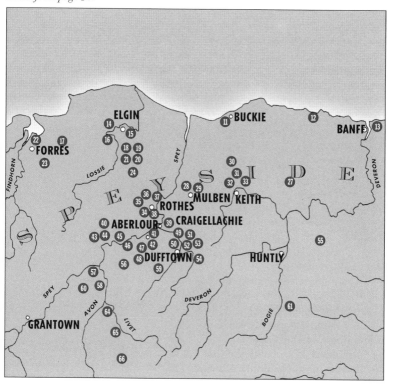

Springbank was established in 1828 and has been owned by the Mitchell family since 1837. Along with GLENFARCLAS, it is therefore one of the last independent family operations in the malt whisky industry. The owners pride themselves on accomplishing the entire business of production, from cutting the peat to the final bottling, according to traditional methods and under their own supervision. The distillery has 3 stills, and it is frequently said that Springbank products are distilled 3 times. In fact it would be more accurate to say 2½ times, for only a part of the whisky—the tail end ("feints") of the first distillation—is distilled once more; they claim this makes the end product milder.

The distillery also produces a malt called LONGROW, which is distilled twice in the normal manner.

The water for both whiskies comes from Crosshill Loch.

Springbank is probably the first distillery to use organically grown barley, and some have joked that it will soon be bottling an ecologically correct whisky. For the turn of the millennium there is to be an 8-year-old version of this malt.

(Tel. 1586 55 20 85)

S. S. PIERCE
Kentucky straight bourbon and blended American from M. S. WALKER.

SS POLITICIAN
Blended Scotch (de luxe) marketed by Douglas LAING & Co. The base for this Scotch comes from what remains of the 50,000 cases of a whisky dis-

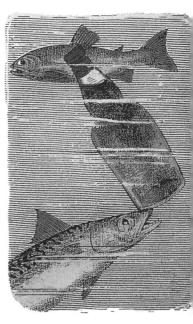

illed in 1938 that were sunk with a ship called the SS *Politician* in the Outer Hebrides in 1941. Most of it was labeled *James Martin*. This incident, especially the recovery of the whisky by the inhabitants of the nearby islands, was the inspiration behind the Scotsman Compton Mackenzie's best-selling novel *Whisky Galore*, which has been filmed a couple of times.

The wreck was raised in 1990, but instead of the expected 2,000 cases, only some 12 bottles of potable whisky were found. Even given the absurd prices that rarities of this kind might fetch at auction, it was doubtful whether the owners would ever recover their costs. It was therefore decided to stretch the find somewhat with the addition of large quantities of malt whisky. A new blend was created, and the original 12 bottles thus became 1,400. Although each clearly contained only a tiny amount of the original whisky, the strategy worked, and the new brand SS Politician was immediately sold out, even at a price of $300 a bottle.

STAG'S BREATH LIQUEUR
Scottish whisky herb liqueur, 39.6 proof, from the house of Meikle's of Scotland, Newtonmore.

Stag's Breath was introduced in 1989. Made of Speyside malts and fermented heather honey, it is lighter

and drier than most liqueurs of this kind, so that it makes a fine aperitif.

STANDARD
The lowest price category for whisk(e)y, especially Scotch and bourbon, which does not mean that these brands are necessarily inferior in quality to PREMIUM or DE LUXE whisk(e)ys.

STAR LIQUOR
U.S. trading firm established in Syosset, New York, in 1933. It markets in America the following brands: Duncan Taylor, HARTLEY PARKERS, McCOLLS.

STATUS
Japanese blend from SANRAKU OCEAN.

STENHAM, H., LTD.
Since 1953 Henry H. Stenham has been running a number of firms from London as a one-man operation. He exports whisky in bulk, mainly to Latin America and Southeast Asia, where it is then bottled under Stenham labels. But one can also find these whiskies among the lower-

priced offerings in European supermarket chains.

All Stenham whiskies are offered at various ages and in bottles of different shapes.

Of the roughly 40 brands all told, the most important are: BLACK BARREL, DIRECTOR'S SPECIAL, HIGHLANDER, HIGHLAND STAR, KING HENRY VIII, KING JOHN, QUEEN ELEANOR, QUEEN MARY I, and SCOTTISH DANCE.

THE STEWART MACDUFF
Blended Scotch from MACDUFF INTERNATIONAL.

STEWART'S CREAM OF THE BARLEY
Blended Scotch from A. Stewart & Son, a subsidiary of ALLIED DISTILLERS (ALLIED DOMECQ).

A decent, everyday blend that is equally popular in Scotland and Ireland and also sells well on the important French, Italian, and Canadian markets.

STEWART'S FINEST OLD
Blended Scotch from WHYTE & MACKAY (AMERICAN BRANDS).

Originally this brand was marketed by the firm J. & G. Stewart as a vatted malt. The Stewarts had gotten their start in Edinburgh in 1779 as wine and tea merchants, and in the following century they built up a worldwide marketing network. In 1886 the firm was taken over by a whisky blender by the name of Ebenezer Hugh, who made it even more prominent by buying, among others, the venerable brand THE ANTIQUARY. In 1917 J. & G. Stewart joined the DCL, on whose behalf it acquired the house of A. Usher (see USHER'S GREEN STRIPE) two years later.

Stewart also bought the license for the COLEBURN distillery and retained it until the distillery was finally closed down by the DCL's successor, UD. Under its new owners the firm

was forced to sell off some its brands to conform to antitrust regulations, among them Stewart's Finest Old. Stewart is now responsible only for the Usher blends.

STILL
Distilling apparatus. See LOMOND STILL, PATENT STILL, and POT STILL.

STILLBROOK
Blended American from McCORMICK.

STITZEL-WELLER
U.S. distillery in Louisville, Kentucky, owned by UD.

The UD's so-called wheat bourbons are produced in this distillery. In them wheat is substituted for rye (OLD FITZGERALD, REBEL YELL, W. L. WELLER; see also OLD RIP VAN WINKLE). The grain mixture consists of 75 percent corn, 5 percent barley malt, and 20 percent wheat.

The Stitzel brothers opened their first distillery in 1870 or 1872. The present plant was built after Prohibi-

tion, and a year later the owners merged with the Weller firm (see W. L. WELLER).

United Distillers took over the business in 1984.

STODART, JAMES & GEORGE
Scottish producers, Dumbarton, a subsidiary of HIRAM WALKER & SONS (ALLIED DOMECQ).

The Stodart brothers were important in the development of Scotch whisky in a couple of ways. As early as 1835 they started combining various malts (see VATTED MALT), and they called the resulting mixture OLD SMUGGLER, a brand still in existence today (although it is now a blend). They also were among the first producers to age their whisky in sherry casks.

The Stodart firm was bought in 1920 by James ("Jimmy") Barclay, who was already a part owner of BALLANTINE. With this purchase, Barclay (1886–1963), who had gotten his start as an errand boy in the BENRINNES distillery, set out on an astonishing career. With Ballantine's and Old Smuggler he took advantage of the opportunities created by Prohibition in

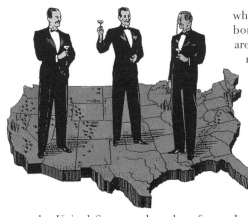

whiskey. Today, all straight bourbons, ryes, and Tennessee whiskeys are also produced by the SOUR MASH method.

A number of brands (for example, FOUR ROSES, BARTON's) are available as either straights or blends.

STRATHAVON
Scottish vatted malt from AVONSIDE Whisky Ltd., a subsidiary of GORDON & MACPHAIL.

STRATHBEG
Blended Scotch from MACDUFF INTERNATIONAL.

This brand has been on the market only since the 1980s.

STRATHCLYDE
Scottish Lowlands distillery in Glasgow, which produces grain whisky and neutral spirits for ALLIED DISTILLERS. At one time it also produced a malt called KINCLAITH.

STRATHCONAN
Scottish vatted malt from UD.

STRATHFILLAN
Blended Scotch from Forth Wines, a trading firm established in Kinross-shire in 1963. The company also puts out a blend called KING JAMES VI. Both are intended primarily for the British market.

STRATHISLA
Scottish single malt (Speyside, Keith) from SEAGRAM.

A well balanced, rather dry malt

the United States and made a fortune. (Both labels are still best-sellers in America.) At that time Barclay had his first contact with the firm of HIRAM WALKER, which was also making a huge profit during Prohibition, and in the early 1930s he sold Stodart and Ballantine's to the Canadians. At the same time, he became the director of the Scottish branch of the concern, and in that role served as head of the CHIVAS and MCCLELLAND firms and as director of a number of consortiums concerned with buying up additional businesses.

Today J. & G. Stodart runs the distilleries GLENBURGIE and GLENCRAIG for Hiram Walker and continues to produce the Old Smuggler blends.

STRAIGHT WHISKEY
In the United States, only undiluted grain distillates can be sold as straight

Original bottling: 12 years old, 86 proof.

Gordon & MacPhail: 8, 12, and 21 years old, all 80 proof; vintages 1958, 1960, 1963, 1967, 1980, all 80 proof; 1972, 124.2 proof; 1974, 115.6 proof.

Cadenhead: 14 years old (distilled 1981), 126 proof.

The distillery was established as early as 1786 and for most of its life has been called Milltown. It was given its present name under the new Seagram regime, although the whisky itself had been sold as Strathisla for some time. This was in about 1950, when James Barclay, who had become one of the most influential names in the Scotch business thanks to his early success as a spirit smuggler (see STODART), acquired the distillery at auction for the Seagram subsidiary CHIVAS. The auction had become necessary after the former owner had been jailed for non-payment of taxes and black marketeering and his firm had been dissolved.

Strathisla is now not only one of the oldest distilleries in Scotland, it is also one of the most beautiful. It has 4 stills and gets its water from a spring called Broomhill, which had been tapped back in the 13th century by Dominican monks for their beer brewing. It is said to be visited even today by so-called kelpies, water spirits in the form of horses—which naturally gives the water a special taste.

(Tel. 1542 78 30 49)

STRATHMILL
Scottish single malt (Speyside, Keith) from Justerini & Brooks (see J & B), a subsidiary of IDV/Grand Metropolitan.

A light, malty whisky that is only rarely available as a single.

Cadenhead: Most recently an 11-year-old from 1980 at 121.8 proof.

Strathmill was opened in 1891 as the Glenisla-Glenlivet Distillery. It was created from a renovated grain mill belonging to the nearby STRATHISLA distillery. It was taken over by GILBEY in 1895 and renamed. Even then the malt was used in Gilbey's GLEN SPEY blend, and today it is also one of the components of the Dunhill blends (see DUNHILL OLDMASTER).

The distillery has 4 stills, and its water comes from a spring on the property.

STRATH-ROYE
Blended Scotch from MAYERSON & CO.

SUNNY BROOK
Kentucky straight bourbon, 80 proof, from JIM BEAM Brands (AMERICAN BRANDS). Also available as a blend.

SUNTORY
The oldest and by far the largest whisky producer in Japan. With its more than 20 brands, it commands roughly 70 percent of the market.

Japan's whisky industry owes its existence solely to the pioneering spirit of Shinjiro Torii (1879–1962), a former (sweet) wine producer who opened the country's first whisky distillery, YAMAZAKI, near Kyoto in 1924. In 1929 he introduced his first brand (White Label), but it took another 8 years of experimenting before Torii managed to produce a whisky that satisfied him (it was called Kakubin). And it would be another 20 years before the Japanese market was ready for such a product. To prime the market, Torii opened so-called Tory Whisky Bars around the country—American-style taverns that served only his brands. With them he anticipated the tastes of the post-war generation of Japanese and set off a virtual whisky boom (see JAPANESE WHISKY).

Today the Suntory firm has 2 more distilleries in Hakushu, Central Honshu, which include the largest malt distillery in the world, producing 14.5 million U.S. gallons a year. By comparison, Scotland's largest distillery, TOMATIN, produces a mere 3.2 million U.S. gallons a year. In its 3 distilleries Suntory puts out a whole series of different malts, using various types of malt and yeast and different types of stills. The majority of them are incorporated into blends. The firm's warehouses can accommodate 1.6 million barrels.

Suntory is one of the 5 largest spirit concerns in the world, yet internationally it occupies only the second tier, for the group concentrates mainly on the Japanese market. It is only gradually acquiring an international cachet.

The most important step in this direction was its purchase of a share of ALLIED DOMECQ in 1988 (at that time, still called Allied-Lyons). That firm, in turn, is involved in Suntory. Since 1994 the concern has also owned the Scottish group MORRISON BOWMORE DISTILLERS and therefore owns the distilleries AUCHENTOSHAN, BOWMORE, and GLEN GARIOCH. An interest in Glenlivet was abandoned in 1977; however, until recently Suntory still had an 11 percent interest in MACALLAN (see also SWORDS).

In addition, the concern is engaged in brewing and publishing. It owns a worldwide brand in its melon-flavored liqueur Midori, an international restaurant chain, and pharmaceutical and biotechnical plants.

Its most important brands are:

Suntory Hibiki, both as a premium and a 21-year-old super premium blend.

Suntory Kakubin, the number 1 blend in Japan, on the market since 1937. In 1989 an improved version, with more and older malts, was developed.

Suntory Old, a special blend, available since 1950 and for a long time number 1. It is now number 3 in Japan.

Suntory Reserve, a special blend, introduced in 1969, currently second on the Japanese market.

Suntory Royal, a special blend, aged in bourbon barrels. This has been on the market since the 1960s and is currently fourth in Japan.

Suntory White Label, Japan's oldest blend, came out in 1929 under the name Shirofuda but soon came to be known simply as White Label.

Suntory Yamazaki, single malt, 12 years old, from the Yamazaki distillery.

SUPERIOR MOUNTAIN DEW See J. M. & Co. SUPERIOR MOUNTAIN DEW.

SUPER NIKKA
Japanese blend from NIKKA.

On the market since the 1960s and currently Nikka's major money maker.

SUPER SESSION
Japanese blend from NIKKA.

This inexpensive brand has been available since 1989.

SWEET SCIENCE
Shake vigorously 1½ oz. Scotch, ½ to ¾ oz. Drambuie, and 1½ oz. orange juice in a shaker with ice and strain into a cocktail glass.

SWN Y MOR
[Gaelic for "sound of the sea"]

Blended Welsh whisky from THE WELSH WHISKY CO., on the market since 1976. One can assume that the base malt for this blend comes from Scotland, more specifically from TOMATIN (see PRINCE OF WALES).

SWORDS
Blended Scotch from James Sword & Son Ltd., a small blending firm founded in Glasgow in 1814. The company produces mainly for export and was taken over by MORRISON BOWMORE DISTILLERS in 1983, so it now belongs to SUNTORY.

Take two ears of wet corn.
Sprinkle it with rye and malt.
Let sit for three days.
Put in still with one chicken.
Boil until done.
Drink broth and eat the chicken
Under the moon and watch it SHINE!

American folklore

TAKARA, SHUZO & OKURA

Japanese spirit concern that produces mainly *shochu* (rice schnapps) but is also involved in the whisk(e)y market. It owns TOMATIN, the largest malt distillery in Scotland, as well as the LEESTOWN DISTILLING COMPANY in Frankfort, Kentucky.

TALISKER

Scottish single malt (Isle of Skye) from UD.

One of the very great malts: masculine and full of character, a synthesis of Highland and Islay malt. To describe this whisky, people resort to astonishing comparisons such as "explodes on the palate" or "goes down like lava." Talisker has been available as a single for a long time; Robert Louis Stevenson hailed it as "a regal drink."

Original bottling: 10 years old, 91.6 proof ("Classic Malts" series); the 8-year-old bottling from the former owner, DCL, is unfortunately sold out.

Gordon & MacPhail: Vintage 1954, 80 proof; 38 years old (distilled 1955), 105.8 and 107.2 proof.

Cadenhead: 16 years old (distilled 1979), 125 proof.

The distillery was erected in 1831–32 and for a time belonged to the Kemp family, which now operates the MACALLAN distillery. In 1925 it became part of the DCL empire and with it subsequently joined UD.

The majority of the malt disappears into the JOHNNIE WALKER blends.

Talisker has 5 stills (they distilled each batch 3 times up until 1928) and draws its water from Cnoc nan Speireag. The high peat content of this hill gives the water a rusty tint.

(Tel. 1478 64 02 03)

TAMDHU

Scottish single malt (Speyside) from HIGHLAND DISTILLERIES Co.

A malty-sweet, medium-heavy whisky that can serve as a good introduction to Speyside malts.

Original bottling: Not dated, 10 and 15 years old, each 80 proof.

Gordon & MacPhail: 8 years old, 80 proof.

Cadenhead: 30 years old (distilled 1963), 96.6 proof; 29 years old (distilled 1963), 98.8 proof; 13 years old (distilled 1981, sherry cask), 119.8 proof.

Tamdhu was opened in 1897, and since 1899 it has belonged to Highland Distilleries. It is the last Speyside distillery to produce all of its own malt. Here it is produced in so-called Saladin boxes, large concrete or metal troughs in which the grain is

turned mechanically and the sprouting is regulated by the introduction of hot air. The majority of this whisky goes into the Famous Grouse blends.

Tamdhu has 6 stills and gets its water from a spring right under the distillery.

(Tel. 1340 81 02 21).

TAMNAVULIN
[Gaelic for "the mill on the hill"]

Scottish single malt (Speyside, Glenlivet) from Whyte & Mackay (American Brands).

A mild but flavorful lightweight, a good aperitif and everyday whisky.

Original bottling: 10 years old, 80 proof; 25 years old, 90 proof ("Stillman's Dram").

Cadenhead: 19 years old (distilled 1973), 92 proof.

The distillery was built in 1966 by Invergordon Distillers, and like most of the group's distilleries it was mothballed after the takeover by Whyte & Mackay.

The distillery had 6 stills and got its water from the surrounding hills. Aging took place exclusively in new American oak barrels.

(Tel. 1807 59 02 85)

William Teacher (1811–76) was one of the pioneers of blended whisky and a successful bar owner. He had 18 "dram shops" in Glasgow, small pubs in which he sold his whiskies (and in which smoking was prohibited). His descendants built the Ardmore distillery and ran the firm until it was taken over by Allied in 1976.

TEACHER'S

Blended Scotch from Wm Teacher & Sons, a subsidiary of ALLIED DISTILLERS (ALLIED DOMECQ).

One of the great old brands in the blended Scotch business. The ubiquitous standard version, Teacher's Highland Cream, has been on the market since 1884 and is still one of the most popular Scotches in the world. It is known for its high malt content of at least 45 percent—as much as 60 percent in periods of overproduction. In addition there is a 12-year-old DE LUXE called Teacher's Royal Highland. The base malts are ARDMORE and THE GLENDRONACH.

TEAL'S

Blended whisky from the Republic of South Africa, 3 years old, made from Scottish malt and local grain, on the market since 1990.

TEANINICH

Scottish single malt (Northern Highlands) from UD.

A gentle malt with a pleasant balance between smoke and sweetness.

Original bottling: 10 years old, 86 proof ("Flora & Fauna" series).

Gordon & MacPhail: Vintages 1975, 1976, both 80 proof.

Cadenhead: 11 years old (distilled 1983), 120 proof.

James MacArthur: 21 years old, 114.4 proof.

The distillery was established in 1817 and was taken over by the DCL in 1905. Its subsidiary R. H. THOMSON

& Co. operated Teaninich until it was temporarily closed in 1985 and used the whisky mainly for its own blends, such as OLD ANGUS. The malt is also one of the components of DRAMBUIE.

In 1990 the distillery was reopened. It has 10 stills, and the water comes from Dairywell Spring.

(Tel. 1349 88 24 61)

TÉ BHEAG NAN EILEAN
[Gaelic for "little lady of the islands"]

Blended Scotch, premium, from PRABAN NA LINNE.

On the market since 1976, this whisky is especially popular in France and Canada; half of it goes to Paris.

TEN HIGH
Kentucky straight bourbon, 80 proof, from BARTON DISTILLING (Canandaigua).

A sweetish, medium-heavy everyday whiskey, Barton's best-seller.

The brand is named after the poker hand, a ten-high straight.

TENNESSEE WHISKEY
A type of whiskey officially recognized—by the tax authorities, that is—since 1941.

By definition, Tennessee whiskey is distinguished from BOURBON because it is produced by the "Lincoln County process." This is a special filtration step in which the fresh whiskey flows through a layer of maple charcoal roughly 10 feet thick. The process, also referred to as "charcoal mellowing" or "leaching," gives the whiskey a special flavor and makes it unusually mild (see also FILTRATION).

THOMSON, J. G.
Scottish producers, founded in Leith in 1709, for a time associated with A. Usher (see USHER'S GREEN STRIPE) and the owner of the distilleries GLEN GARIOCH and LITTLEMILL.

In 1921 Thomson became part of the DCL, and it now belongs to the brewing concern Bass Charrington, for which it produces the brands AS WE GET IT and OLD INVERNESS.

THOMSON & CO., R. H.
Scottish blending firm, a subsidiary of UD, for which it operated the TEANINICH distillery for a time and currently produces the blends OLD ANGUS, ROBBIE BURNS, and WINDSOR CASTLE.

THREE FINGERS
An unofficial measure, indicating the height of the whisk(e)y in the glass, used mainly in the United States.

THREE SHIPS

Blended whisky from the Republic of South Africa, produced from Scottish malt and local grain. Three Ships has been available as a 3-year-old since 1977; since 1992 a 5-year-old has also been on the market.

THREE STILLS

Irish spirits from the MIDLETON distillery of IDG (PERNOD RICARD).

This inexpensive brand, marketed by the firm Fitzgerald & Co., cannot be called whiskey because of its low alcohol content of 30 percent by volume.

TIPPERARY

A variant of the MANHATTAN using 1 oz. Irish, ¾ oz. white vermouth, and ½ oz. Chartreuse Verte.

T.N.T.

A hangover drink: mix 1 oz. bourbon and ½ to ¾ oz Pernod with ice and top with soda, if desired.

TOBERMORY

Scottish distillery on the Isle of Mull owned by BURN STEWART DISTILLERS. It produces 2 single malts.

One of these, called Tobermory, is a light, flavorful 8-year-old at 80 proof. It is distilled solely from unpeated barley and was a vatted malt without age designation until 1995. Formerly there was also a blend with the same name. The second malt, distilled from peated barley, is called LEDAIG. It is bottled only in very small quantities. Currently there are 2 versions from 1974: an 18-year-old at 86 proof and a 21-year-old at 120 proof. A 1975 was also recently issued.

The distillery was founded in 1795 and was acquired by the DCL in 1916. Between extended closings the distillery was operated under the name Ledaig from 1972 to 1975. In 1990 the operation was started up again under the present name, and since 1993 it has belonged to Burn Stewart.

The distillery has 4 stills and draws its water from the Mishnish Lochs.

(Tel. 1688 30 26 45)

TOMATIN

Scottish single malt (Highlands, Inverness) from TAKARA, SHUZO & OKURA.

An aperitif malt, smooth and spicy.

Original bottling: 10 years old, 86 proof; a 5-year-old version used to be bottled for the Italian market.

Gordon & MacPhail: Vintages 1964, 1968, both 80 proof.

Cadenhead: 18 years old (distilled 1976), 115.4 proof.

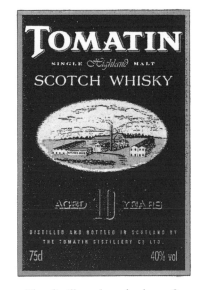

The distillery dates back to 1897. Beginning in the 1950s it was continually expanded until it had 12 stills, a huge operation by Scottish standards. Apparently the owners overreached somewhat, for in 1985 Tomatin was forced to declare bankruptcy. The distillery was taken over by the Japanese concern Takara, Shuzo & Okura, which added 11 stills. Tomatin is now the most productive malt distillery in Scotland, but the greater part of its whiskies are shipped to Japan and there diluted with domestic ones (see JAPANESE WHISKY). Tomatin is also used in the blended Scotch BIG T (see also OLD ST. ANDREWS, WELSH WHISKY).

The water comes from a brook called Alt na Frithe Burn. The large number of stills means a tremendous amount of water is required for cooling. As a means of using at least a part of this waste water, Tomatin started an eel farm. The young eels grow more than twice as fast in the warm water than they would in cold. As yet it is unclear what they are going to do with all of this fish.

(Tel. 1808 51 14 44)

TOM HANNAH
Kentucky straight bourbon produced by HEAVEN HILL DISTILLERS and bottled by CONSOLIDATED.

TOMINTOUL
Scottish single malt (Speyside, Glenlivet) from WHYTE & MACKAY (AMERICAN BRANDS).

A light, spicy malt, ideal for beginners.

Original bottling: 8 and 12 years old, 80 proof; for export, 86 proof.

Cadenhead: 11 years old (distilled 1985), 130.8 proof.

Signatory: Vintage 1971, 86 proof.

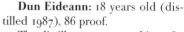

Dun Eideann: 18 years old (distilled 1987), 86 proof.

The distillery was opened in 1965, and since 1973 it has been in the hands of Whyte & Mackay, which uses the malt mainly in its own blends.

Tomintoul has 4 stills, and the water comes from a spring called Ballantruan. Aging is accomplished in new American oak barrels and in sherry casks.

(Tel. 1807 59 02 74)

TOM MOORE
Kentucky straight bourbon, 80 proof and bottled in bond (100 proof), from BARTON DISTILLING (Canandaigua).

A light and rather sweet everyday whiskey.

The man for whom this brand is named established 2 distilleries in the 19th century. One of them survives in the form of a brand name (see MATTINGLY & MOORE); the other is now called Barton and produces the brand Tom Moore. It was first introduced in 1879, and there is currently a 10-year-old version as well—Tom Moore's Kentucky Heritage—but only on the lucrative Taiwan market. In the United States there is also a light version.

TORMORE
Scottish single malt (Speyside) from ALLIED DISTILLERS (ALLIED DOMECQ).

A subtle digestif malt, smooth and round.

T

Original bottling: 10 years old, 80 and 86 proof.

Tormore was opened in 1960 by LONG JOHN, then taken over along with that firm by Allied Distillers. The malt is still one of the components of the Long John blend.

The distillery has 8 stills and draws its water from Achvochkie Burn. Most of the aging is done in bourbon barrels.

(Tel. 1807 51 02 44)

TOWN CLUB
American blend from SHERMAN.

TRAVELERS CLUB
Blended American from MAJESTIC.

TREASURY
Blended Scotch, de luxe, from HILL, THOMSON & CO. (SEAGRAM).

TRIBUTE
Blended Scotch, standard, 5 years old, and de luxe, 15 years old, from WM LUNDIE & CO.

TSURU
Japanese blend from NIKKA.

The noblest brand from the house of Nikka is presented in porcelain and glass decanters.

TULLAMORE DEW
Blended Irish whiskey, 80 proof, from CANTRELL & COCHRANE (ALLIED DISTILLERS, ALLIED DOMECQ).

A smooth, very light, and almost harmless blend with a long past and an uncertain future. The brand was first produced by the Tullamore distillery, established in 1829 in Tullamore, County Offaly. In the late 19th century it was taken over by Daniel E. Williams, who gave the whiskey its present name. (The Dew, in addition to its regular meaning, reproduces Williams's initials.) Under his ownership it became one of the most famous brands in Ireland. In the 1950s (Williams had

just introduced the liqueur IRISH MIST), the firm fell into difficulties; the distillery was closed and the brand ended up first with John Power & Son and then with the IDG. Since 1994 it has belonged to the present owners, who still have the whiskey produced by the MIDLETON distillery.

Tullamore Dew has sunk to almost total insignificance in Ireland. In Germany, to be sure, it is the best-selling Irish whiskey, and in France it also has its admirers, who pronounce the name "tout l'amour."

Cadenhead: There are currently several bottlings available: 38 years old, 137.8 proof; 41 years old (distilled 1949), 130 proof; and 42 years old, 125.2 proof.

PRODUCT OF SCOTLAND

Tullibardine

SINGLE HIGHLAND MALT SCOTCH WHISKY

A Single Malt Scotch Whisky of quality and distinction distilled and bottled by

TULLIBARDINE DISTILLERY LIMITED
BLACKFORD   PERTHSHIRE   SCOTLAND

TULLIBARDINE

Scottish single malt (Southern Highlands) from WHYTE & MACKAY (AMERICAN BRANDS).

A spicy, medium-weight malt, smooth and malty.

Original bottling: 10 years old, 80 and 86 proof; 25 years old, 90 proof ("Stillman's Dram").

Cadenhead: 27 years old (distilled 1964), 102.4 proof.

There was already a distillery of the same name on the spot where the present-day Tullibardine stands in 1800, and as early as the 15th century there had been a brewery here. The modern distillery dates from 1949. It was taken over by INVERGORDON DISTILLERS in 1953, and that firm passed into the hands of Whyte & Mackay in 1994. Tullibardine was mothballed in 1995.

The distillery had 4 stills and drew its water from Dunny Burn. Its malt aged in new American oak barrels.

(Tel. 1764 68 22 52)

TWELVE STONE FLAGONS

A firm established in Pittsburgh, Pennsylvania, in 1971, with a branch in Glasgow. Its blended Scotch Usquaebach is becoming increasingly popular, especially in the United States. In addition, Twelve Stone Flagons produces a bourbon called AMERICAN BIKER.

The history of the firm reads like a screenplay from some bottom drawer in Hollywood. Stan Stankiwicz, from Pittsburgh, a whisky-collecting wood-veneer salesman, hears of an exclusive Scotch brand that was served at President Nixon's inauguration celebrations. After years of effort he finally acquires the rights to the brand, but no one is interested. Stankiwicz sends Prince Rainier of Monaco a few bottles for his birthday, is given an audience, meets Elizabeth Taylor there, and both like his Scotch. Liz has lots of friends who also like to drink, and so forth. Happy ending.

T. W. SAMUELS

Kentucky straight bourbon, 86 proof, from HEAVEN HILL DISTILLERS.

A small brand of only local importance. Why it is part of Heaven Hill is a mystery, for Taylor W. Samuels was the founding father of MAKER'S MARK.

THE TYRCONNELL

Irish single malt from COOLEY.

A light whiskey for every occasion but one that lacks a certain degree of expressiveness. At the moment it is bottled without age designation (3 or 4 years old) at 80 proof, but there is hope that in future more mature versions will also reach the market. (The Cooley distillery has been in operation only since 1989.) Tyrconnell is distilled twice, with unpeated barley in contrast to its sister brand, CONNEMARA. The whiskey may be young, but the brand name is quite old: it was produced by the house of A. A. Watt until 1970 and was a best-seller in the United States even before Prohibition. It is named after an almost legendary racehorse that was also owned by the Watt family. The firm was revived by Cooley in the late 1980s, and its name appears on the label as the producer—doubtless so as to recall the glorious days of Irish whiskey and to lend more distinction to the brand than its taste, so far, would seem to warrant.

U

Whiskey is taken into the [congressional] committee rooms
in demijohns and carried out in demagogues.

Mark Twain

UBIQUE

Blended Scotch, 80 proof, from GOR-
DON & MACPHAIL.

UD (UNITED DISTILLERS)

British spirit concern based in London, a subsidiary of the Irish beer
giant Guinness.

Guinness's powerful entry into the
whisky business began in 1985 with
the hostile takeover of Arthur Bell &
Sons (see BELL'S), one of the most
successful whisky distillers in Scotland (with a market share in Great
Britain of 25 percent). But this by no
means slaked Guinness's thirst, and
a year later it set out to conquer the DCL. The onetime
battleship of the Scottish
whisky industry was then
only limping along and
was actually supposed to
go to the Argyll Group.
Guinness boss Ernest Saunders unleashed a dramatic
takeover battle, from which his firm
emerged victorious in April 1986 but
which saddled Saunders himself with
a 5-year prison sentence. In order to
drive up the price of Guinness stock,
he had engaged in illegal stock-market
manipulation that came to light in the
course of the Ivan Boesky scandal in
the United Sates. Guinness was un-
harmed by all of this; the concern thus
became the largest whisk(e)y producer in the world.

But not big enough, according to
its directors. It subsequently bought
up several distilleries in the United
States and Canada: the first, in 1984,
were the U.S. firm STITZEL-WELLER
and the Canadian VALLEYFIELD distillery; SCHENLEY followed in 1987; and
finally GLENMORE in 1991. The last-
named was then sold again in 1995.

Meanwhile UD has of course become involved in the new Asian markets. Since 1993 it has been part of
a joint venture with the UB Group,
the largest spirit producer in India,
and in that same year a firm was
established in China with
the charming name Riche
Monde China. The Chi-
nese venture is a joint undertaking with the French
luxury-article concern
LVMH (Louis Vuitton–
Moët-Hennessy), with which
Guinness is linked by recipro-
cal shareholdings.

UD's chief business is still Scotch
whisky. In this area the group owns—in
addition to a whole string of world
brands such as JOHNNIE WALKER, BELL'S,
DEWAR'S, and DIMPLE (Pinch)—so many
smaller labels that even the firm's resi-
dent historian occasionally has to con-
sult the archives of the Scottish Whisky
Association in answering queries.

The most important malt brand is
CARDHU. In addition there is the very

popular series "Six Classic Malts," which includes the brands CRAGGANMORE, DALWHINNIE, GLENKINCHIE, OBAN, LAGAVULIN, and TALISKER. The remaining UD malts bottled as singles comprise the "Flora & Fauna" series; they are available only in select specialty shops and at the distilleries themselves. Finally, there is the "Rare Malts Selection," small barrel-strength bottlings of especially uncommon whiskies.

At one time UD had 5 grain distilleries, but today only CAMERON BRIDGE and PORT DUNDAS are in operation. Caledonian was shut down in 1987, CAMBUS in 1993, and CARSEBRIDGE in 1983. There are still occasional single-grain bottlings from the last 2. The malt for many of the UD's distilleries is produced in GLENESK; its warehouses are in the county of Clamannanshire.

According to as-yet-unconfirmed reports, the Guinness concern is planning to take over the foodstuffs group Grand Metropolitan, along with its spirits subsidiary IDV, before the end of 1996. The suggested purchase price is said to be more than $18 billion. With that acquisition UD would finally become the world's largest spirit producer.

Malt distilleries: ABERFELDY, AULTMORE, BALMENACH, BANFF, BENRINNES, BLADNOCH, BLAIR ATHOL, CARDHU, CLYNELISH, CAOL ILA, COLEBURN, CONVALMORE, CRAGGANMORE, CRAIGELLACHIE, DAILUAINE, DALWHINNIE, DALLAS DHU, DUFFTOWN, GLENDULLAN, GLEN ELGIN, GLENESK, GLENKINCHIE, GLENLOCHY, GLENLOSSIE, GLEN ORD, GLENUGIE, GLENURY-ROYAL, INCHGOWER, LAGAVULIN, LINKWOOD, MORTLACH, NORTH PORT, OBAN, PITTYVAICH, PORT ELLEN, ROSEBANK, ROYAL BRACKLA, ROYAL LOCHNAGAR, TALISKER, TEANINICH.

Grain distilleries: CAMBUS, Cameron Bridge (see CAMERON BRIG), CARSEBRIDGE, PORT DUNDAS.

Vatted malt: GLEN LEVEN, STRATHCONAN.

Blended Scotch: ABBOT'S CHOICE, AINSLIE'S, THE ANTIQUARY, BAIRD-TAYLOR'S SELECTED, BAXTER'S BARLEY BREE, BELL'S, BENMORE, BISSET'S, BLACK & WHITE, BUCHANAN'S RESERVE,

BL, C. & J. McDonald, Chequer's, Crawford's 3 Star (export only), Dewar's, Dimple (Pinch), Gillon's, Glenfern, Glen Garry, Glen Lyon, Golden Age, Haig Gold Label (export only), Harvey's Special, Heathwood, Highland Club, Highland Dew, Highland Nectar, Huntly, John Begg Blue Cap, Johnnie Walker, King Arthur, King George IV, King of Kings, King's Legend, King William IV, Logan, Lowrie's, MacLeay Duff, McCallum's Perfection, McDonald's Special Blend, Old Angus, Old Matured, Old Parr, Peter Dawson, President, Queen Elizabeth, Queen's Choice, The Real Mackenzie, Red Devil, Reliance, Robbie Burns, Roderick Dhu, Rodger's Old Scots Brand, Royal Household, Sanderson's Gold, Sandy Macdonald, Scottish Queen, Usher's Green Stripe, Vat 69, White Horse, Windsor Castle, Yellow Label, Ye Monks.

Bourbon: I. W. Harper, James E. Pepper, Old Charter, Old Fitzgerald, Rebel Yell, W. L. Weller.

Tennessee: George Dickel.

Canadian: Gibson's Finest, MacNaughton, Royal Command, Schenley.

UNION GLEN

Blended Scotch, 3 years old, 80 proof, from Bennachie.

A new blend at the lowest price category, which the firm's prospectus describes as "a general daily tipple."

UNITED DISTILLERS See UD.

USHER'S GREEN STRIPE

Blended Scotch, 86 proof, from J. & G. Stewart, a subsidiary of UD.

Andrew Usher (1782–1856) is considered, along with W. P. Lowrie (see Lowrie's) and Charles Mackinlay (see Mackinlay's), one of the inventors of blended Scotch whisky. He started as a spirits merchant in Edinburgh in 1813, at a time when whisky was generally drunk fresh from the still. It was known that aging in barrels was beneficial, but whiskies were seldom treated in this way. Also, the creation of a *cuvée*, already central to the cognac business, was considered a waste of time in Scotland. Usher was one of first to experiment systematically with this

technique. He began by combining various malts to create VATTED MALTS and introduced his first brand, Old Vatted Glenlivet, in 1853 (Usher had sole marketing rights for Glenlivet). Soon afterward he tried mixing malt and lighter, less expensive grain whisky, a technique later refined by his sons. They did so to keep the cost down, on the one hand, but also because they recognized that the heavy and highly individual malts from the HIGHLANDS were not really suited to the industrial age. The success of their blends in metropolises like London and Manchester proved them right, and the rising demand led the Ushers to build in 1886, together with several other blending firms, the largest grain distillery in Scotland at the time: NORTH BRITISH. Around the turn of the century, Usher's was one of the very great spirit brands worldwide.

Mindful of its trendsetting qualities, the producers of Usher's Green Stripe have increasingly invested in the growing Latin American market.

USQUAEBACH
[Gaelic for "water of life"]

Blended Scotch from TWELVE STONE FLAGONS.

There is a whole series of high-class blends under this name, mainly produced for the U.S. and duty-free markets. The Pittsburgh firm Twelve Stone Flagons has them produced in Scot-

land by INVERGORDON DISTILLERS and bottles some in old-fashioned ceramic jars.

Currently the following versions are available: Ultra Premium, Reserve Super Premium, Special Premium, De Luxe 8 Years Old, Elite Silver 25 Years Old, Elite Gold 50 Years Old, Crystal Decanter, Pure Malt 15 Years Old (vatted malt).

U.S. WHISKEY
In the United States one must distinguish among BOURBON, CORN, RYE, and TENNESSEE WHISKEYS. These basic types are available as STRAIGHT, BLENDED, or LIGHT WHISKEYS (for details, see those headings).

The oldest American whiskey variety is rye, which was not supplanted by bourbon until the 20th century. Rye had come to America with the Europeans and was distilled mainly by Scottish and Irish immigrants in Pennsylvania and Maryland.

Bourbon, based mainly on corn, was first mentioned in 1821, but settlers began growing corn in the area of present-day Kentucky at the end of the 18th century, and doubtless had begun producing whiskey from it earlier. (The first distillery in the region can be dated to 1776.) Most whiskeys sold at that time were of course very different from the product now called bourbon. Since there were no regulations covering it, practically any distillate could be marketed as whiskey, and since producers generally sold their product right after distilling it, the market was flooded with colorless and immature alcohols that were subsequently colored with sherry or tea and flavored with diverse herbs. People were particularly casual about the whiskeys traded with Indians for valuable hides, pelts, and even land: this "fire water" was dyed with tobacco juice or ink and spiced with sulphur or pepper.

It was only the BOTTLED IN BOND legislation of 1897, urged by E. H. Taylor (see OLD TAYLOR) and other quality-conscious distillers, that created a government guarantee that any whiskey so labeled was undiluted, at least 4 years old, and 100 proof. (That didn't help the Indians much; they had meanwhile lost their land, and on the few reservations left to them alcohol continues to be a problem to this day.)

The story of American whiskey in the 20th century is dominated by the phenomenon of PROHIBITION (1920–33). Only a very few distilleries were able to survive by producing medicinal alcohol; most were shut down for good. But since the prohibition on alcohol didn't mean that the population was any less thirsty, people either started distilling themselves (see MOONSHINE) or smuggled alcohol in from outside the country. Canadian and Scotch were sneaked across the border in enormous quantities, helping to shape the Americans' whisk(e)y tastes to this day (see LIGHT WHISK(E)Y). The industry began to recover from this setback after World War II, but now it was bourbon that enjoyed the greatest popularity.

In the 1950s bourbon still had strong competition from Tennessee. To be sure, Tennessee whiskey differs from bourbon only in the way it is filtered, a clever marketing strategy developed by the Jack Daniel's firm (see JACK DANIEL'S OLD NO. 7) in order to present its product as something unique. Today Jack Daniel's Tennessee Sour Mash is the second-best-selling whiskey brand on the American market, surpassed only by Jim Beam bourbon.

The next-best-selling brands belong to the blended American category, a mixture of straight whiskey and neutral spirits. Here the best-known name is SEAGRAM'S 7 CROWN.

The most important producers of U.S. whiskeys are: JIM BEAM, BROWN-FORMAN, SEAGRAM, and HEAVEN HILL DISTILLERS.

V · W · Y

Freedom and Whisky gang thegither.

Robert Burns,
The Author's Earnest Cry and Prayer

VALLEYFIELD

Canadian distillery near Montreal, owned by UD.

It formerly belonged to SCHEN-LEY, but since 1984 all of the UD Canadians have been produced here.

VALLEY 9 GOLD

Korean whisky, 80 proof, from SEAGRAM.

A blend of domestic grain and imported malt whisky that was created especially for the booming South Korean market and is less expensive than the Scotch brands imported there in huge quantities.

VAT 69

Blended Scotch from Wm SANDERSON & SON (UD).

A tried and true, substantial Scotch of the old school, on the market since 1882 and a best-seller up until the 1960s. Then somehow the brand declined.

New, lighter brands pushed Vat 69 into the background. But it is worth giving this very decent whisky a second chance. Since the 1980s it has also been available in a 12-year-old de luxe version.

Almost as old as the brand itself is the joke that insists that its name is the Pope's telephone number. The story behind its name has often been told: in an early form of market research, William Sanderson, one of the grand old men of blended Scotch, had 100 different blends tasted by his circle of friends. The vat numbered 69 received the highest praise, and a new brand was born.

VATTED MALT

Scottish whisky type. A vatted malt consists of several (at least 2) SINGLE MALTS from different distilleries. A vatted malt is almost never identified as such; it usually says simply "malt" on the label, or sometimes "pure malt" or "all malt." Pure malt can also mean a single malt, as in the case of the SCAPA bottling from GORDON & MACPHAIL.

Ultimately, any malt whisky that is not expressly identified as a single is a vatted.

Vatting is the technical process by which various whiskies are mixed together in a tub or vat. Malts from a single distillery are generally mixed in this way before bottling as well, as it evens out the discrepancies among the different distillates. The composition of blends also takes place in vats, and in Ireland vatting is synonymous with blending.

Combining different single malts is older, historically, than blending (see USHER'S GREEN STRIPE), and at one time it was perfectly common to produce a mixture for home consumption oneself. The goal is to soften the often very definite characteristics of some malts or cancel them out—in addition, it is fun to put together a whisky that suits one's own palate.

Now that passionate malt drinkers increasingly tend to prefer the real thing—that is, SINGLE-BARREL BOTTLINGS—the art of vatting has been pushed somewhat to the side. Still, one must not forget that there are outstanding examples of this type, the most prominent of which are possibly the ones in the series "Pride of . . ." from Gordon & MacPhail.

VERY OLD BARTON

Kentucky straight bourbon from BARTON DISTILLING (Canandaigua).

A simple, everyday whiskey and Barton's best seller in the United

States; available in 4 versions: as a BOTTLED IN BOND (100 proof) and as a 6-year-old at 80, 86, or 90 proof.

VIRGINIA GENTLEMAN
Straight bourbon, 80 proof, from the A. Smith Bowman Distillery in Fredericksburg, Virginia.

Shortly after its introduction in 1935, Virginia Gentleman came to be a favorite especially in East Coast political and newspaper circles. It is available at the National Press Club under the name Gentlemen of the Press, and it was supposedly part of the original inventory of the SEQUOIA, the presidential yacht.

A. Smith Bowman, Sr., was in the distilling business even before Prohi-

bition, but later made his fortune manufacturing busses. He started building a distillery in Sunset Hill, Fairfax, immediately after Prohibition was repealed. The distillery has since moved, and now it produces mainly gin, vodka, and rum.

The low wines (the first distillate) are distilled elsewhere, according to the Bowman recipe, but the second distillation, aging, and bottling are still done in the Bowman distillery, the only one still producing whiskey in Virginia. The grain mixture consists of 65 percent corn, 20 percent rye, and 15 percent barley malt.

WALDORF ASTORIA EGGNOG
Shake vigorously with ice 2 egg yolks, ½ oz. sugar syrup, ¾ oz. port (tawny), 1½ oz. bourbon, 3½ oz. milk, and ½ oz. cream, and serve on ice in a tumbler. Garnish with ground nutmeg.
WALKER'S DELUXE
Kentucky straight bourbon, 80 proof, from HIRAM WALKER & SONS (ALLIED DOMECQ).

A light, everyday bourbon, which the Canadian beverage concern has distilled in Kentucky (probably by HEAVEN HILL DISTILLERS).

WALLACE

Scottish single malt liqueur, 65 proof, from BURN STEWART DISTILLERS.

Based on DEANSTON single malt, flavored with honey, French herbs, and Scottish berries, this brand came out in 1996 and already claims to be the number-1 brand in its sector, at least in Europe and Asia. It bears the name of the Scottish freedom fighter William Wallace.

WARD EIGHT

A variant of the WHISKEY SOUR: shake vigorously in a cocktail shaker 1¾ oz. bourbon, ½ oz. lemon juice, 1 bar spoon of powdered sugar, and a dash of Grenadine, and garnish with a cherry.

WELSH WHISKY

It is said that Welsh monks were already distilling a kind of whisky (*chymreig chwisgi*) on the Lleyn peninsula in the 4th century. The first commercial distillery in Wales was established in the early 18th century by the EVAN WILLIAMS family, which later found a place in the history of American whiskey. The same can be said of the ancestors of a certain JACK DANIEL, who started distilling at about the same time in Cardigan. After an extended pause, the Welsh whisky tradition was revived by the firm THE WELSH WHISKY CO. in 1974.

THE WELSH WHISKY CO.

This Welsh producer was established in Brecon in 1974 by the former Lufthansa pilot Dafydd Gittins and his wife Gillian. It belongs to the Brecon Brewery and produces a series of brands that have so far been based on Scottish malt whiskies. Since 1994, however, the Gittins have also been operating a small distillery, whose malts are to reach the market around the turn of the millennium.

Brands: MERLYN CREAM LIQUEUR, PRINCE OF WALES, SWN Y MOR. (See also WELSH WHISKY.)

WHISK(E)Y DRINKS

Unlike gin, whisk(e)y—least of all Scotch or Irish—is not an ideal spirit for mixing, but it is nevertheless the base for a few classic cocktails. The only one originally designed for whisk(e)y, aside from the MANHATTAN, is the MINT JULEP, which comes from Kentucky. One could also mention the OLD FASHIONED, but ultimately, like the majority of whisk(e)y drinks, it is also only a variant of the

Manhattan. In addition there are sours, fizzes, and digestifs. Whisk(e)y works wonderfully in hot drinks such as IRISH COFFEE and the hot toddy.

All of the whisk(e)y drinks well known today were originated in the United States, but whisk(e)y has always been consumed in diverse mixtures in Scotland and Ireland. It is also quite possible that in its earliest years it was drunk *only* in combination with other potables, chiefly herbal potions, honey, or milk—giving rise to the LIQUEURS we know today.

WHISKEY HOT TODDY

A hot WHISKEY SOUR: heat 1½ oz. bourbon, ¾ oz. lemon juice, and ½ oz. sugar syrup in a heatproof glass, fill with hot water, and garnish with a slice of lemon pricked with cloves.

WHISKEY SOUR

One of the most famous drinks that the American bar culture ever produced. It is prepared in numerous variations, but the following is standard: shake 1½ oz. bourbon, ¾ oz. lemon juice, 1 bar spoon powdered sugar, and ½ oz. sugar syrup with ice. Traditionally whiskey sours were drunk without ice from sour glasses, similar to champagne flutes; today they are generally served in a tumbler over ice. When made with Scotch, the drink is called a London Sour.

The Indian ambassador to the United States remarked in 1966: "The Americans are a funny lot. They drink whiskey to warm themselves, then they put ice in it to cool it. They add sugar to sweeten it and then lemon juice to make it sour. Then they say 'Here's to you' and down it themselves."

WHISKY MAC

A Scottish household drink in which whisky is mixed according to taste with a quantity of ginger liqueur, for example CRABBIE'S Green Ginger Cordial.

WHITE BUSH See BUSHMILLS.

WHITE HEATHER

Blended Scotch from CAMPBELL DISTILLERS (PERNOD RICARD).

A nicely balanced standard whisky, 8 years old, probably based on ABERLOUR. Its chief market is France.

WHITE HORSE

Blended Scotch from White Horse Distillers, a subsidiary of UD. An above-average standard blend with a great past. Still one of the most successful Scotch brands internationally.

The Mackie family was running the famous White Horse Inn in the center of Edinburgh as early as the 17th century. One of their descendants, James Logan Mackie, got into the whisky

346

business by buying the LAGAVULIN distillery in 1867, but it was his nephew Peter Mackie (1855–1924) who in around 1890 had the idea of producing his own blend and naming it after the inn. Restless Peter, as he was known, was considered a slightly megalomaniac eccentric, whose energy and skill rapidly made the brand a known quantity beyond the shores of Great Britain.

He later took over the distillery CRAIGELLACHIE, made a name for himself as a master marksman, author, and bellicose politician, and finally was knighted as one of the 5 "whisky barons." After his death the Mackie firm was renamed White Horse Distillers. One of its greatest coups was its introduction of the screw-top bottle for whisky in 1926. This innovation helped to double its sales in a brief 6 months. A year later the firm was taken over by the DCL, for whose successor, UD, it still operates the distilleries Lagavulin, GLEN ELGIN, and Craigellachie. These still produce the base malts for the White Horse blend, though the percentage of Lagavulin, once so obvious, has since been somewhat reduced.

WHITE HOUSE
Indian blend from Polychem.

This brand has been on the market since 1983, and it is now also exported to Eastern Europe (see MEN'S CLUB).

A blend of matured Indian malt and rare, imported, vatted Scotch Whisky.

DISTILLED, BLENDED AND BOTTLED BY
POLYCHEM LIMITED
NIRA,
MAHARASHTRA
P.O 7. J. TATA ROAD.
BOMBAY 400 020

B N
M.D
750 ml
42.8% v/v
75° PROOF
PRODUCE OF INDIA

WHITELEY, WM

Scottish blending firm established in Leith in 1922 and later known for its HOUSE OF LORDS blend.

Whitely bought the EDRADOUR distillery in 1933 and was itself bought up in 1938 by an American financier whose supposed Mafia connections are still the stuff of speculation today. The firm has belonged to CAMPBELL DISTILLERS, and thus to PERNOD RICARD, since 1982.

In addition to House of Lords, Whiteley continues to produce the brands GLENFORBES and KING'S RANSOM.

WHYTE & MACKAY

Blended Scotch from the Whyte & Mackay Group, a subsidiary of AMERICAN BRANDS.

The rather light standard version, 80 proof, is called Whyte & Mackay Special; in addition there is a 12-year-old and a luscious 21-year-old de luxe redolent of the sherry cask, the latter at 86 proof.

Whyte & Mackay's whiskies get their special smoothness from so-called double marriage. Normally, the term *marriage* refers to the period of storage in barrels between blending and bottling. Whyte & Mackay is unusual in that it places the blended malts and grains separately in barrels for a few months in sherry casks and only then mixes them together (one

could just as well call it double blending).

The founding year 1844 on the label refers to a firm in which James Whyte was involved before his partnership with Charles Mackay. The corporation that bears the present name has been in existence only since 1882. The brand itself, which achieved its first success in the United States, is almost as old. Only after World War II was it introduced in Great Britain as well. Today it is especially popular in Scotland, most notably in the hotly contested market of its hometown of Glasgow.

The base malt for Whyte & Mackay comes from the DALMORE distillery, which has belonged to the firm since 1960. The malts from Fettercairn and TOMINTOUL probably also go into the blend, for both distilleries have been operated by Whyte & Mackay since the 1970s.

Whyte & Mackay ceased to be independent in 1972, and after several changes of ownership landed in the hands of the present owner, the U.S. concern American Brands, in 1990. Under that firm's direction it attempted a hostile takeover of INVERGORDON DISTILLERS in 1991 and was ultimately successful in 1994. In the following year Whyte & Mackay made itself unpopular in Scotland with its closing of 3 of the 4 Invergordon distilleries: BRUICHLADDICH, TAMNAVULIN, and TULLIBARDINE were sacrificed for the sake of efficiency; only ISLE OF JURA is still in operation.

In 1986 Whyte & Mackay took over the blends THE CLAYMORE, JAMIE STUART, OLD MULL, and STEWART'S FINEST OLD from UD. It later acquired JOHN BARR as well. These were simply legal maneuvers to conform with antitrust laws,

for with the purchase of Arthur Bell (see BELL'S) and DCL the UD had simply become too big.

For the same reasons the British rights to the UD brands BUCHANAN, Crawford (see CRAWFORD'S 3 STAR), HAIG GOLD LABEL, and THE REAL MACKENZIE were transferred to Whyte & Mackay (See also BENEAGLES, HARROD'S.)

WILD TURKEY

U.S. whiskey brand from the Boulevard Distillery, Lawrenceburg, Kentucky, from AUSTIN NICHOLS DISTILLING COMPANY (PERNOD RICARD).

In all of its versions, Wild Turkey is a sumptuous whiskey, for which the term "classic" is almost unavoidable.

The most popular bottling is the Old No. 8 Brand, at 8 years old and 101 proof. It has everything that a bourbon could wish; one can drink it straight, but it also makes a superb whiskey sour. The lighter Brown Label, at 80 proof, is currently on the rise in the United States. In addition there are the 12-year-old Gold Label, at 101 proof, and since 1993—in limited quantity—a Rare Breed, which consists of whiskeys that are from 6 to 12 years old and bottled at barrel strength (108 proof and more). The whiskey is offered as a single barrel in 2 versions: KENTUCKY LEGEND and KENTUCKY SPIRIT. The old duty-free brand Beyond Duplication has now been sold out.

Wild Turkey Straight Rye, at 101 proof, is probably the most mature whiskey of its type; it makes it incomprehensible to the outsider why rye whiskey fell out of fashion in the United States.

A Wild Turkey blend is marketed under the NICHOLS label, and finally, the firm produces a liqueur based on citrus and honey at 60 proof.

Wild Turkey was first introduced in 1942, and it quickly became a bestseller. At that time Austin Nichols was simply a trading company that had its whiskey produced by contract. It was only in 1970 that it bought the old D. L. Moore distillery near Lawrenceburg (founded 1855). The firm was long run by the Ripys, an Irish immigrant family that was one of the major distillers in Kentucky in the 19th century and whose descendants trained the present stillmaster, Jimmy Russel.

He works with a grain mixture of 75 percent corn, 13 percent rye, and

12 percent barley malt; for the rye, it is 65 percent rye, 23 percent corn, and 12 percent barley malt: the sour mash component amounts to 33 percent.

The IDV subsidiary HEUBLEIN INC. owns 30 percent of Austin Nichols, and is responsible for marketing the brand in the United States.

Between 1971 and 1987 the firm issued elaborate ceramic decanters (mainly in the form of turkeys, of course, but also eagles, raccoons, etc.) that are still sought after today.

(Tel. 502 839-4544)

WILLIAM GRANT'S
Blended Scotch from William Grant & Sons.

A whole series of blends is marketed under this name: the standard version is called Family Reserve (formerly Standfast) and is one of the best-selling Scotches in the world. In addition there are an 8-year-old Centenary, a 12-year-old De Luxe, a 12-year-old Old Gold, a Superior Strength at 100 proof, an 18-year-old Classic, and a 21-year-old De Luxe in a decanter (see also GRANT'S ROYAL). The decision to issue a blend was more or less forced on the Grants. In 1898 the trading and blending firm Pattison's, the chief customer for the malts from the Grant distilleries GLENFIDDICH and THE BALVENIE, went bankrupt. So as not to have its own whiskies simply lying around, Grant therefore decided to process them further itself. After a few false starts it succeeded, and the Standfast blend, especially, became a best-selling export. The base malts for the William Grant blends are certainly Glenfiddich and The Balvenie, and probably also KININVIE, which likewise belongs to the family.

WILLIAM LAWSON'S
Blended Scotch from William Lawson (Bacardi).

This typical LIGHT WHISKY was formerly called simply Lawson's—the Christian name was added to avoid confusion with PETER DAWSON. The base malt is GLEN DEVERON.

WILLIAM LOW'S FINEST
Blended Scotch that is produced by Peter J. RUSSELL for the supermarket chain William Low and sold exclusively in its stores in Scotland and Northern England. The firm goes back to a partnership established in 1868, which at the turn of the century had a number of grocery stores throughout Scotland.

WILLIAM MAXWELL
Blended Scotch from Peter J. RUSSELL.

WILLIAM PENN
Blended American from LAIRD & CO.

WILSON
Blended American from HEAVEN HILL DISTILLERS.

WILSON'S
New Zealand blended whisky, 75 proof, from Wilson Distillers (SEAGRAM).

The Wilson firm, which had formerly produced malt extract, began making whisky in 1968 in Dunedin, South Island, New Zealand. Its first whisky came on the market in 1974. It was taken over by Seagram in 1981, and today this brand is the best-selling whisky in New Zealand. In addition, the distillery produces a malt called LAMMERLAW.

WINDSOR
Canadian blends from the Alberta Distillery, property of JIM BEAM BRANDS (AMERICAN BRANDS).

The Windsor whiskies are pure, dry, and especially successful in the United States. Windsor De Luxe is a rather small brand, but Windsor Supreme is one of the best-selling Canadians worldwide.

WINDSOR CASTLE
Blended Scotch from R. H. THOMSON & CO. (UD).

WISER'S
Canadian blend from CORBY, a HIRAM WALKER & SONS subsidiary (ALLIED DOMECQ).

Corby markets its most mature products under this label. There are a 6-year-old Wiser's Special Blend, a 10-year-old Wiser's Deluxe, and a Wiser's Oldest, which at 18 years old is probably the oldest Canadian on the market.

WISER'S
DE LUXE
Canadian Whisky Canadien

W. L. WELLER
Kentucky straight bourbon from the STITZEL-WELLER distillery owned by UD.

Not inelegant whiskeys that are very smooth despite their high alcohol content.

The Special Reserve is 90 proof; the 10-year-old Centennial, 100 proof;

and the 7-year-old Old Weller The Original, 107 proof.

William LaRue Weller began trading in whiskey in 1849, and although he never owned a distillery himself, he soon became one of the most influential men in the bourbon business.

His descendants merged with the Stitzel distillery in 1903 and marketed their products (see OLD RIP VAN WINKLE). The Stitzel-Weller distillery emerged from this union in 1936 and was taken over in 1984 by UD. The Weller whiskeys are still produced there.

Like all Stitzel-Weller products, this brand is distilled with wheat instead of rye, which makes it taste somewhat milder.

WOODFORD RESERVE
Kentucky straight bourbon from BROWN-FORMAN.

This brand-new brand is currently being bottled from selected barrels at the EARLY TIMES DISTILLERY in Shively, Kentucky. Soon, however, the whiskey is to come from the Labrot & Graham distillery near Versailles, in Woodford County, Kentucky, which was reopened in October 1996.

This distillery was already in operation in 1812 and later became famous as the Old Oscar Pepper Distillery (see JAMES E. PEPPER, OLD CROW, OLD TAYLOR). In 1878 it was taken over by James Graham and Leopold Labrot, whose names it still carries. Brown-Forman bought the distillery in 1994 (it had owned it once before, from 1941 to 1972) and restored it with great care. Today Labrot & Graham is the only distillery in the United States that still—or again—uses POT STILLS, and bourbon lovers around the world are now eagerly awaiting the first samples of this whiskey. It will not be available for a few years yet, but then we will be able to get a sense of what bourbon must have tasted like before Prohibition.

W. W. BEAM
Kentucky straight bourbon from HEAVEN HILL DISTILLERS.

YAMAZAKI See SUNTORY.

YELLOW LABEL
Blended Scotch from John Robertson & Son, a subsidiary of UD.

The firm Robertson & Son, founded in Dundee in 1827, once owned the distilleries COLEBURN and SPEYBURN. Robertson operated the latter as the licensee until 1991.

YELLOWSTONE
Kentucky straight bourbon, 90 proof, from SHERMAN.

A medium-heavy everyday bourbon with a great past. Created at the end of the 19th century by one of the Dants (see J. W. DANT), and named after the recently opened national park, the brand was immediately a success, and in the 1960s it was the best-selling brand in Kentucky. The name was acquired by GLENMORE DISTILLING in 1944, and in 1991 it was purchased by UD, which surrendered it two years later to Sherman.

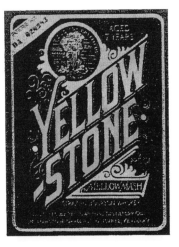

YE MONKS
Blended Scotch, standard, from Donald Fisher, a subsidiary of UD.

This brand, registered since 1898, was formerly a de luxe called Ye Whisky of the Monks. It is presented in handmade ceramic jars and destined mainly for the Latin American market.

Donald Fisher, who started in Edinburgh as a producer and trader in 1836, is considered one of the pioneers of the modern whisky business for two reasons. First, he recognized early on the importance of the age of individual whiskies for the quality of a blend. Long before minimum aging of 3 years was required by law, he therefore began building up supplies of old whiskies, which increased his costs, to be sure, but also caused his sales to soar. Second, Fisher was one of the first to age his whiskies exclusively in sherry casks (see BARREL). The Fisher firm was taken over by the DCL in 1936, and later ended up at UD.

YOUNG'S SPECIAL BLEND
Blended American from KASSER LAIRD.

THE
WHISK(E)YS
OF THE WORLD

THE WHISK(E)YS

AUSTRALIA
Bond 7
Corio
Four Seasons

BRAZIL
Drury's
Gregson's
Old Eight

CANADA
Adams
Alberta
Autumn Gold
Black Velvet
Breton's Hand & Seal
Bush Pilot's
Calgary Trail
Canada House
Canadian Club
Canadian Deluxe
Canadian Gold
Canadian Host
Canadian Hunter
Canadian Lake
Canadian Leaf
Canadian LTD
Canadian Mist
Canadian Peak
Canadian Reserve
Canadian Springs
Canadian Supreme
Crown Royal
Gibson's Finest
Grande Canadian
Harwood
Heaven Hill
James Foxe
Laird's Premium
Lord Calvert

McCalls
McCauley's
McCormick
McGuinness
McMasters
MacNaughton
Meaghers 1878
Mount Royal Light
Northern Light
OFC
Order of Merit
Phillips
Royal Canadian
Royal Command
Royal Lord Canadian
Royal Majestic
Royal Reserve
Schenley
Seagram's V.O.
Silk Tassel
Windsor
Wiser's

CHINA
Seagram's 7 Star

CZECH REPUBLIC
King Barley

ENGLAND
Red Rose

GERMANY
Edel Falcke
Der Falckner
Piraten Whisky
Racke Rauchzart

INDIA
Bagpiper
Gilbey's

Jagatjit
McDowell's
Men's Club
Peter Scot
Red Knight
Royal Secret
White House

IRELAND
Malt
Bushmills
Coleraine
Connemara
Sainsbury's
Tyrconnell

Pot Still
Green Spot
Old Comber
Redbreast

Blend
Avoca
Black Bush
Buena Vista
Bushmills
Coleraine
Crested Ten
Dunphys
Erin's Isle
Great Count O'Blather
Hewitts
Inishowen
Jameson
Kilbeggan
Locke's
Midleton
Millars
Old Dublin
Paddy
Power's
Tullamore Dew

Whiskey-like Spirits
Bunratty
Celtic Crossing
Millars
Three Stills

ISLE OF MAN
Glen Kella

JAPAN
Malt
All Malt
Karuizawa
Nikka Hokkaido
Pure Malt
Suntory Yamazaki

Blend
Asama
The Blend
Corn Base
Crescent
Emblem
From the Barrel
Gold & Gold
Grand Age
Hi
Ocean
Robert Brown
Route
Rye Base
Status
Suntory Hibiki
Suntory Kakubin
Suntory Old
Suntory Reserve
Suntory Royal
Suntory White Label
Super Nikka
Super Session
Tsuru

KOREA
Valley 9 Gold

NEW ZEALAND
Lammerlaw
Wilson's

SCOTLAND
Malt
CAMPBELTOWN
Burnside
Glen Scotia
Longrow
Springbank

HIGHLANDS
Aberfeldy
Balblair
Banff
Ben Nevis
Blair Athol
Brora
Clynelish
Dalmore
Dalwhinnie
Deanston
Edradour
Glen Albyn
Glencadam
Glenesk
Glen Garioch
Glengoyne
Glenlochy
Glen Mhor
Glenmorangie
Glen Ord
Glenturret
Glenugie
Glenury-Royal
Inchmurrin
Lochside

North Port
Oban
Old Fettercairn
Old Pulteney
Old Rhosdhu
Royal Brackla
Royal Lochnagar
Teaninich
Tomatin
Tullibardine

ISLANDS
Highland Park (Orkney)
Isle of Jura (Jura)
Ledaig (Mull)
Lochranza (Arran)
Scapa (Orkney)
Talisker (Skye)
Tobermory (Mull)

ISLAY
Ardbeg
Bowmore
Bruichladdich
Bunnahabhain
Caol Ila
Lagavulin
Laphroaig
Port Ellen

LOWLANDS
Auchentoshan
Bladnoch
Glen Flagler
Glenkinchie
Inverleven
Killyloch
Kinclaith
Ladyburn
Littlemill
Lomond
Rosebank

St. Magdalene

SPEYSIDE
Aberlour
Allt-á-Bhainne
An Cnoc
Ardmore
Aultmore
Balmenach
Balvenie
Benriach
Benrinnes
Benromach
Braes of Glenlivet
Caperdonich
Cardhu
Coleburn
Convalmore
Cragganmore
Craigellachie
Dailuaine
Dallas Dhu
Dufftown
Glenallachie
Glenburgie
Glencraig
Glen Deveron
Glendronach
Glendullan
Glen Elgin
Glenfarclas
Glenfiddich
Glenglassaugh
Glen Grant
Glen Keith
Glenlivet
Glenlossie
Glen Moray
Glenrothes
Glen Spey
Glentauchers

Imperial
Inchgower
The Inverarity Single Malt
Knockando
Linkwood
Longmorn
Macallan
Macduff
Mannochmore
Millburn
Miltonduff
Mortlach
Mosstowie
Pittyvaich
Singleton of Auchroisk
Speyburn
Strathisla
Strathmill
Tamdhu
Tamnavulin
Tomintoul
Tormore

Grain
Black Barrel
Ben Nevis
Cambus
Cameron Brig
Carsebridge
Girvan
Invergordon
Lochside
North British

Vatted
Aberfoyle
Alexander Dunn
Angus Dundee
Auchterar
Bennachie
Berry's All Malt

Blairmhor
Burberry
Century
Chieftain's Choice
Cockburn's
Diner's
Eileandour
Fine Fare
Fortnum & Mason
Gamefair
Glen Baren
Glen Blair
Glen Carren
Glencoe
Glen Corie
Glen Dew
Glen Drumm
Glen Drummond
Glenfairn
Glen Flagler
Glenforres
Glengalwan
Glen Kella
Glenleven
Glenmorriston
Glenmoy
Glentromie
Grierson's No. 1
Highland Cattle
Highlander
Highland Fusilier
Johnnie Walker Pure Malt
Loch Kindie
Lombard's
MacPhail's
Mar Lodge
Moidart
Old Elgin
Old Montrose
Poit Dhubh

Pride of Islay
Pride of Orkney
Pride of Strathspey
Pride of the Lowlands
Royal Culross
Sainsbury's
The Seven Stills
Sheep Dip
Strathavon
Strathconan
Tobermory
Usquaebach

Blend

Abbot's Choice
Age of Sail
Ainslie's
Albion's Finest Old
Alexander Dunn
Allan's
Ambassador
Ancient Privilege
Angel's Share
The Antiquary
Argyll
Auld Sandy
Avonside
Award
Bailie Nicol Jarvie
Baird Taylor's Selected
Baker Street
Ballantine's
Barrister
Barrister's
Baxter's Barley Bree
Bell's
Ben Aigen
Ben Alder
Beneagles
Benmore
Ben Roland

Big T
Bisset's
Black & White
Black Bottle
Black Prince
Black Rooster
Black Shield
Black Stag
Black Watch
Blue Hanger
Boswell's Reserve
Bristol Vat
Brodie's Supreme
Buchanan's
Bucktrout's
Bulloch Lade (BL)
Burberry
Burn Stewart
Cairnbaan
Cairndew Mist
Campbeltown Loch
C. & J. McDonald
Castle Pride
Catto's
Chairman's
Chairman's Reserve
Chequer's
Chivas Regal
Choicest Liqueur
Clan Ardoch
Clan Ben
Clan Campbell
Clan MacGregor
Clan Munro
Clan Murdock
Clan Roy
Clansman
The Claymore
Club
Cluny

Cockburn & Murray
Consulate
Corney & Barrow
Crabbie's
Crawford's 3 Star
Cumbrae Castle
Custodian
Cutty Sark
Dalmeny
Defender
Derby Special
Dewar's
Dew of Ben Nevis
Dew of the Western Isles
Dimple (Pinch)
Diner's
Diplomatic Privilege
Director's Special
Doctor's Special
The Dominie
Dons Dram
Double Q
Drake's
Dream of Barley
Duart Castle
Duggan's Dew
Duncan Taylor
The Dundee
Dunheath
Dunhill
Eaglesome's
Eaton's Special
El Vino
The Famous Grouse
Findlater's Finest
Fine Fare
Fine Old Special
Forfars
Fortnum & Mason
Firth House

Fraser's Supreme
Gairloch
Gale's
Gillon's
Glen Calder
Glen Catrine
Glen Clova
Glen Darroch
Glen Dowan
Glen Drostan
Glenfern
Glenfoyle
Glen Garry
Glen Ghoil
Glen Kella
Glen Kindie
Glen Lyon
Glen Niven
Glenrob
Glen Rosa
Glen Salen
Glenside
Glen Stuart
Glen Urquhart
Glorious 12th
Gold Blend
Golden Age
Golden Cap
Golden Piper
Gold King
Gold Label
Grand Macnish
Grant's Royal
Great Mac
Great Macaulay
Green Highlander
Haig
Hamashkeh
Hankey Bannister
Harrod's

Hartley Parkers
Hart's
Harvey's Special
Heatherdale
Heathwood
Hedges & Butler
Hielanman
High Commissioner
Highland Abbey
Highland Bird
Highland Blend
Highland Clan
Highland Club
Highland Dew
Highlander
Highland Gathering
Highland Legend
Highland Mist
Highland Nectar
Highland Pearl
Highland Queen
Highland Reserve
Highland Rose
Highland Stag
Highland Star
Highland Woodcock
House of Campbell
House of Lords
House of Peers
House of Stuart
Howard Maclaren
Hudson Bay
Huntly
Hynard's Finest
Immortal Memory
Imperial Gold Medal
The Inverarity Blend
Inver House Green Plaid
Inverness Cream
Island Prince

Islay Legend
Islay Mist
The Jacobite
James Gordon's
James Martin's
Jamie Stuart
J & B
J. M. & Co. Superior
    Mountain Dew
Jock
Jock Scott
John Barr
John Begg Blue Cap
John Dory
John Handy
John Player Special
Johnnie Walker
Kelt
King Arthur
King Charles
King Edward I
King George IV
King Henry VIII
King James VI
King John
King of Kings
King of Scots
King Robert II
King's Crown
King's Pride
King's Ransom
King's Whisky
King William IV
Lang's
Langside
Lauder's
Legacy
Lismore
Loch Ranza
Logan

Lombard's
Long John
Lowrie's
MacAndrew's
MacArthur's
McCalls
McCallum's Perfection
McColls
McDonald's Special Blend
McDowall
McGavins
McGibbon's
Mackinlay's
MacLeod's Isle of Skye
McMasters
Mac Na Mara
Major Gunn's
Majority
Malcolm Stuart
Mason's
Milner's Brown Label
Milord's
The Monarch
Monster's Choice
Moorland
Muirhead's Blue Seal
Murdoch's Perfection
The Murrayfield
Northern Scot
Old Angus
Old Argyll
Old Court
Old Curlers
Old Decanter
Old Fox
Old Glasgow
Old Glomore
Old Highland Blend
Old Inverness
Old Keg

Old Matured
Old Montrose
Oldmoor
Old Mull
Old Orkney
Old Parr
Old Royal
Old Smuggler
Old Spencer
Old St. Andrews
100 Pipers
OV 8
Parker's
Passport
Peter Dawson
Pig's Nose
Pinwinnie Royal
Pipe Major
Piper's Clan
Pot Lid
Premier
President
Prestige d'Ecosse
Putachieside
Queen Anne
Queen Eleanor
Queen Elizabeth
Queen Mary I
Queen's Choice
Queen's Seal
The Real Mackay
The Real Mackenzie
Red Hackle
Red Rooster
Reliance
Robbie Burns
Rob Roy
Roderick Dhu
Rodger's Old Scots Brand
The Royal and Ancient

Royal Citation
Royal Findhorn
Royal Game
Royal Heritage
Royal Household
Royal Salute
Sainsbury's
Sanderson's Gold
Sandy Macdonald
Sandy Macnab
Savoy
Scoresby Rare
Scotch Island
Scotia Royale
Scots Club
Scots Earl
Scots Grey
Scots Lion
Scots Poet
The Scottish Collie
Scottish Dance
Scottish Envoy
Scottish Leader
The Scottish National
   Tartan
Scottish Queen
Scottish Royal
77
Sir Malcolm
Sir Walter Raleigh
Something Special
Speakers
Spey Cast
Spey Royal
Speyside
SS Politician
The Stewart Macduff
Stewart's Cream of the
   Barley
Stewart's Finest Old

St. James's
St. Leger
Strathbeg
Strathfillan
Strath-Roye
Swords
Teacher's
Té Bheag nan Eilean
Treasury
Tribute
Ubique
Union Glen
Usher's Green Stripe
Usquaebach
Vat 69
White Heather
White Horse
Whyte & Mackay
William Grant's
William Lawson's
William Low's Finest
William Maxwell
Windsor Castle
Yellow Label
Ye Monks

SLOVENIA

Jack & Jill

SOUTH AFRICA

Teal's
Three Ships

SPAIN

DYC

THAILAND

Master Blend

TURKEY

Ankara

U.S.A.

Bourbon
American Biker
Ancient Age
A. H. Hirsch
Baker's
Barclay's
Basil Hayden's
Bellow's
Benchmark
B. J. Holladay
Blanton's
Booker's
Bourbon Deluxe
Bourbon Supreme
Bourbontown Club
Bulleit
Cabin Still
Charred Keg
Classic Club
Clementine's
Colonel Lee
Country Club
David Nicholson 1843
Dowling
Eagle Rare
Early Times
Echo Spring
Elijah Craig
Elmer T. Lee
Evan Williams
Ezra Brooks
Four Roses
Hancock's Reserve
Heaven Hill
Henry McKenna
I. W. Harper
Jacob's Well
James E. Pepper

Jim Beam
Jim Grant
Johnny Drum
J. T. S. Brown
J. W. Dant
Kennedy's
Kentucky Dale
Kentucky Gentleman
Kentucky Legend
Kentucky Spirit
Kentucky Tavern
Kentucky Vintage
Knob Creek
McCalls
McCormick
Maker's Mark
Mattingly & Moore
Medley's
Mohawk
Newport
Noah's Mill
Old Bardstown
Old Charter
Old Crow
Old Distiller
Old 1889
Old Ezra
Old Fitzgerald
Old Forester
Old Grand-Dad
Old Kentucky Rifle
Old Rip Van Winkle
Old Setter
Old Taylor
Old Weller
Old Williamsburg
Pennypacker
Phillips
Private Stock
Pure Kentucky

Rebel Yell
R. J. Hodges
Rock Hill Farms
Rowan's Creek
S. S. Pierce
Sunny Brook
Ten High
Tom Hannah
Tom Moore
T. W. Samuels
Very Old Barton
Virginia Gentleman
Walker's De Luxe
Wild Turkey
W. L. Weller
Woodford Reserve
W. W. Beam
Yellowstone

Tennessee
Gentleman Jack
George Dickel
Jack Daniel's
Lem Motlow's

Rye
Jim Beam
Old Overholt
Old Potrero
Pikesville
Rittenhouse
Wild Turkey

Corn
Cabin Hollow
Corn Crib

Georgia Moon
Golden Grain
J. W. Corn
McCormick
Mellow Corn
Old Dispensary
Platte Valley

Blended & Light Whiskeys
Ancient Age
Banker's Club
Barton's
Beam's 8 Star
Bellow's
Bourbon Deluxe
Britannia
Broker's Reserve
Brookstone
Caldwell's
Calvert
Canadian Age
Carstairs White Seal
Club 400
Corby's
County
Daviess County
Duggan's
Early Times
Five Star
Fleischmann's Preferred
Four Roses
Governors Club
Hill & Hill
Imperial
John Finch

J. T. S. Brown
Kasser's 51
Kennedy's
Kentucky Gentleman
Kentucky Tavern
Kessler
Lord Baltimore
McCormick
Monogram
Nichols
Old Thompson
Paramount
Paul Jones
Philadelphia
Phillips
P.M.
Press Club
Seagram's 7 Crown
Senator's Club
Seven Star
S. S. Pierce
Stillbrook
Sunny Brook
Town Club
Traveler's Club
William Penn
Wilson
Young's Special Blend

WALES
Prince of Wales
Swn y Mor

WHISK(E)Y LIQUEURS

IRELAND
Bailey's
Carolans
Dubliner
Emmets
Irish Mist
Meadow Cream
Millwood Whiskey Cream
O'Darby
Saint Brendan's Superior

SCOTLAND
Amber Glow
Can-Y-Delin
Columba Cream
Drambuie
Drumgray
Dunkeld Atholl Brose

Glayva
Glen Mist
Glenturret Malt Liqueur
Heather Cream
Lochan Ora
Òran Mór
Red Devil
Scottish Island
Stag's Breath Liqueur
Wallace

U.S.A.
American Cream
Rock & Rye
(Southern Comfort,
    Southern Mist)
Wild Turkey

WALES
Merlyn

WHISK(E)Y COCKTAILS

Affinity
Blackthorn
Blood & Sand
Bobby Burns
Boston Sour
Bourbon Highball
Brooklyn
Brown Fox
Captain Collins
Colonel Collins
Florian
Frisco Sour
Godfather
Golden Nail
Hair of the Dog

Horse's Neck
Hot Buttered Whisky
Hot Whiskey
Irish Coffee
Manhattan
Mike Collins
Millionaire
Mint Julep
Morning Glory Fizz
New Yorker
New York Flip
Old Fashioned
Palmer
Rattlesnake
Rob Roy

Rory O'Moore
Rusty Nail
Sandy Collins
Sazerac
Scoff-Law
Sweet Science
Tipperary
T.N.T.
Waldorf Astoria Eggnog
Ward Eight
Whiskey Hot Toddy
Whiskey Sour
Whisky Mac

FIRMS

Adelphi Distillery Ltd.
Ainslie & Heilbron
Alexander Dunn & Co.
Allied Distillers/Allied
    Domecq
American Brands
Austin Nichols
Avery's of Bristol
Barton Distilling
Berry Bros. & Rudd
Black Prince
Brown, W. & Sons
Brown-Forman
Buchanan, James & Co.
Bulloch Lade & Co.
Burn Stewart
Cadenhead, Wm
Campbell Distillers
Cantrell & Cochrane
The Castle Collection
Chivas & Glenlivet Group
Cockburn & Campbell
Cockburn & Murray
Cockburn's of Leith
Consolidated
Cooley
Corby
Corney & Barrow
CWS
(DCL)
Dewar
Eldridge, Pope & Co.
Glen Catrine
Glenhaven
Gordon & MacPhail
Grant, William & Son

Haig, John & Co.
Hall & Bramley
Hallgarten Liqueurs
Heaven Hill Distillers
Heublein
Highland Distilleries Co.
Hill, Thomson & Co.
Hiram Walker & Sons
IDG
IDV/Grand Metropolitan
Inverarity
Invergordon Distillers
Inver House Distillers
Isle of Arran Distillers
Kasser Laird
Kentucky Bourbon
    Distillers
Khoday
Kinross Whisky Co.
Kirin-Seagram
Laing, Douglas & Co.
Laird & Co.
Lawson, Wm
Leestown Distilling
    Company
Lundie, Wm & Co.
MacArthur, James & Co.
McClelland, T. & A.
McCormack
Macdonald Greenlees
Macdonald Martin
    Distillers
Macduff International
McEwan, John & Co.
Majestic
Marie Brizard

Mayerson & Co.
Meldrum House
Milroy's
Mitchell, J. A.
Montebello
Montrose Whisky
Morrison Bowmore
    Distillers
M. S. Walker
Nikka
Pernod Ricard
Praban na Linne
Racke
Red Lion Blending
Robertson & Baxter
Russell, Peter J.
Sanderson, Wm & Son
Sazerac
Schenley
Scotch Malt Whisky Society
Scottish & Newcastle
Seagram
Sherman, David
Signatory
Speyside Distillery
Star Liquor
Stenham, H. Ltd.
Stodart, J. & G.
Suntory
Takara, Shuzo & Okura
Thomson, J. G.
Twelve Stone Flagons
UD (United Distillers)
The Welsh Whisky Co.
Whitley, Wm
Whyte & Mackay

BIBLIOGRAPHY

Brown, Gordon. *Classic Spirits of the World*. London: Prion, 1995.

Craig, H. Charles. *The Scotch Whisky Industry Record*. Dumbarton: Index Publishing, 1994.

Darwen, James. *Das Buch vom Whisky*. Munich: Heyne, 1993.

Getz, Oscar. *Whiskey: An American Pictorial History*. New York: David McKay Company, 1978.

Hills, Philipp. *Scots on Scotch*. Edinburgh and London: Mainstream, 1991.

Jackson, Michael. *Michael Jackson's Malt Whisky Companion*. London: Dorling Kindersly, 1989.

——. *The World Guide to Whisky*. London: Dorling Kindersly, 1987.

Lamond, John, and Robin Tucek. *The Malt File*. Edinburgh: Canongate, 1995.

Lockhart, R. Bruce. *Scotch: The Whisky of Scotland in Fact and Story*. Glasgow: Neil Wilson, 1951.

MacLean, Charles. *The Mitchell Beazley Pocket Whisky Book*. London: Mitchell Beazley, 1993.

Malt Advocate. Emmaus, Penn.: The Malt Society.

Milroy, Wallace. *The Malt Whisky Almanac*. Glasgow: Neil Wilson, 1995.

Morrice, Philip. *The Schweppes Guide to Scotch*. Sherborne, Dorset: Alphabooks, 1983.

Moss, Michael S., and John R. Hume. *The Making of Scotch Whisky: A History of the Scotch Whisky Distilling Industry*. Edinburgh: James & James, 1981.

Murray, Jim. *Jim Murray's Irish Whiskey Almanac*. Glasgow: Neil Wilson, 1994.

Regan, Gary, and Mardee H. Regan. *The Book of Bourbon and Other Fine American Whiskeys*. Vermont: Chapters, 1995.

Schobert, Walter. *Malt Whisky Guide. Führer zu den quellen*. Weil der Stadt: Hädecke, 1994.

Waymack, Mark H., and James F. Harris. *The Book of Classic American Whiskeys*. Chicago: Open Court, 1995.

ACKNOWLEDGMENTS

THIS BOOK WOULD NOT HAVE BEEN POSSIBLE WITHOUT CHARLES SCHUMANN, Claudia Eilers, Julie, Ron, and Tim Atkin, and Günter Mattei. I'd also like to thank Becky (exit 48, Kentucky 127), Robert Denton, Peter Dunne (Mitchell & Son), Campbell Evans (SWA), David Hines (Cooley), Doug McIvor (Milroy's), Chris Morris (UD), Jimmy Russel (Wild Turkey), Max L. Shapira (Heaven Hill), Julian P. Van Winkle, as well as Dr. Johannes W. Raum, Karl Rudolf, John Gerhardt, Günter Schöneis, Otto Steudel, Alexander Grabenhorst, K. D. Salewski, Slavica, Erik Schmitz, Peter Schreiber, Markus & Philipp, and all the others who helped me.

WHISK(E)Y